ULTIMATE FANTASTIC FOUR

DEVILS

writer: **Mike Carey**

Annual #2
pencils: **Stuart Immonen**
inks: **Wade von Grawbadger**
colors: **Paul Mounts**
art and color (Mole Man sequences): **Frazer Irving**
letters: **Virtual Calligraphy's Randy Gentile**
cover: **Stuart Immonen & Richard Isanove**

"Devils"
art: **Scott Kolins, Mark Brooks & Jaime Mendoza**
colors: **Wil Quintana & SotoColor's A. Crossley**
letters: **Virtual Calligraphy's Randy Gentile, Cory Petit & Rus Wooton**
covers: **Salvador Larroca & Paco Roca**

associate editor: **John Barber**
editor: **Ralph Macchio**

collection editor: **Jennifer Grünwald**
assistant editors: **Cory Levine & Michael Short**
associate editor: **Mark D. Beazley**
senior editor, special projects: **Jeff Youngquist**
senior vice president of sales: **David Gabriel**
production: **Jerron Quality Color & Jerry Kalinowski**
vice president of creative: **Tom Marvelli**

editor in chief: **Joe Quesada**
publisher: **Dan Buckley**

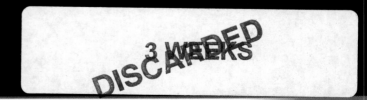

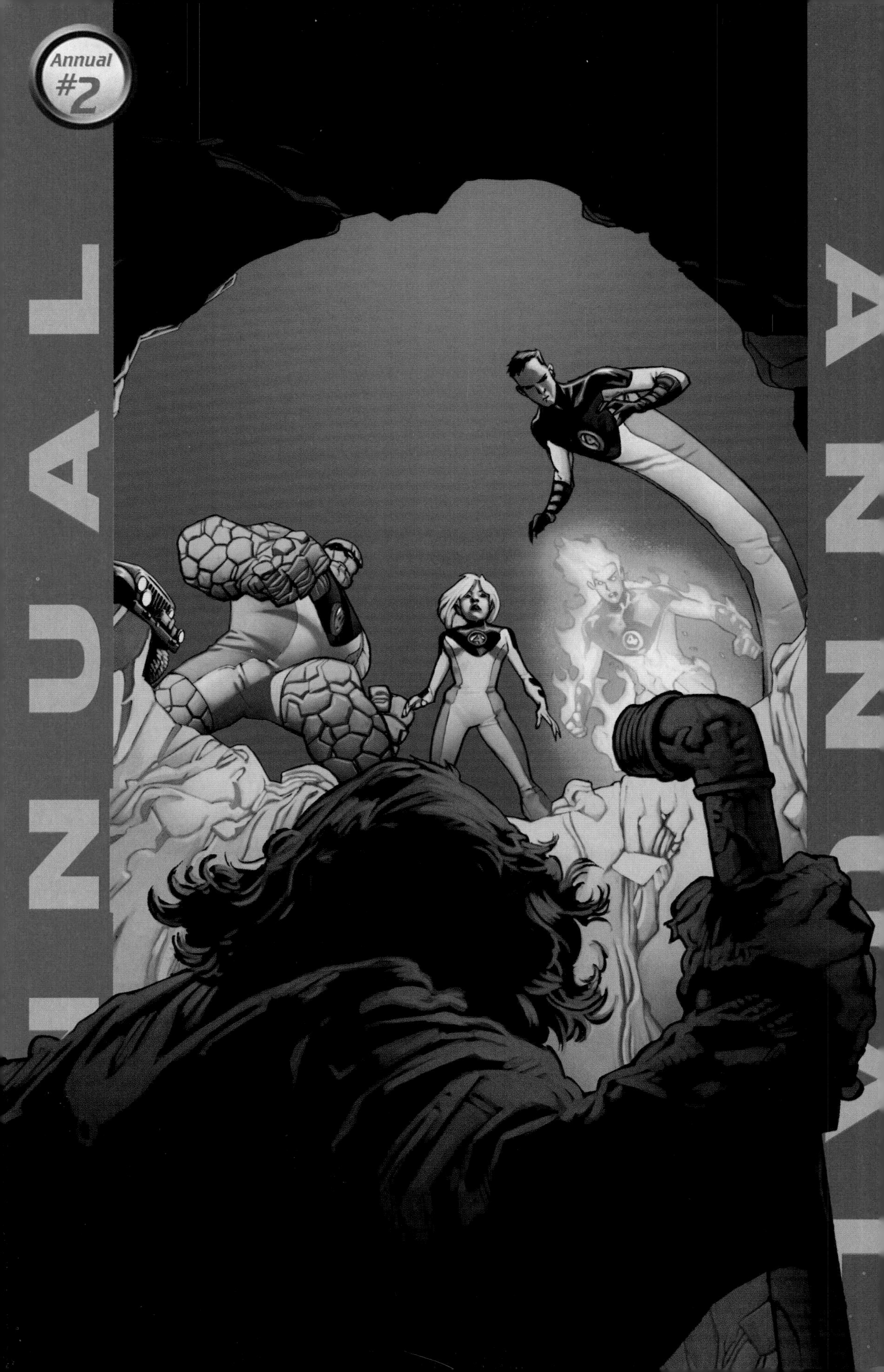
Annual
#2
ANNUAL
ANNUAL

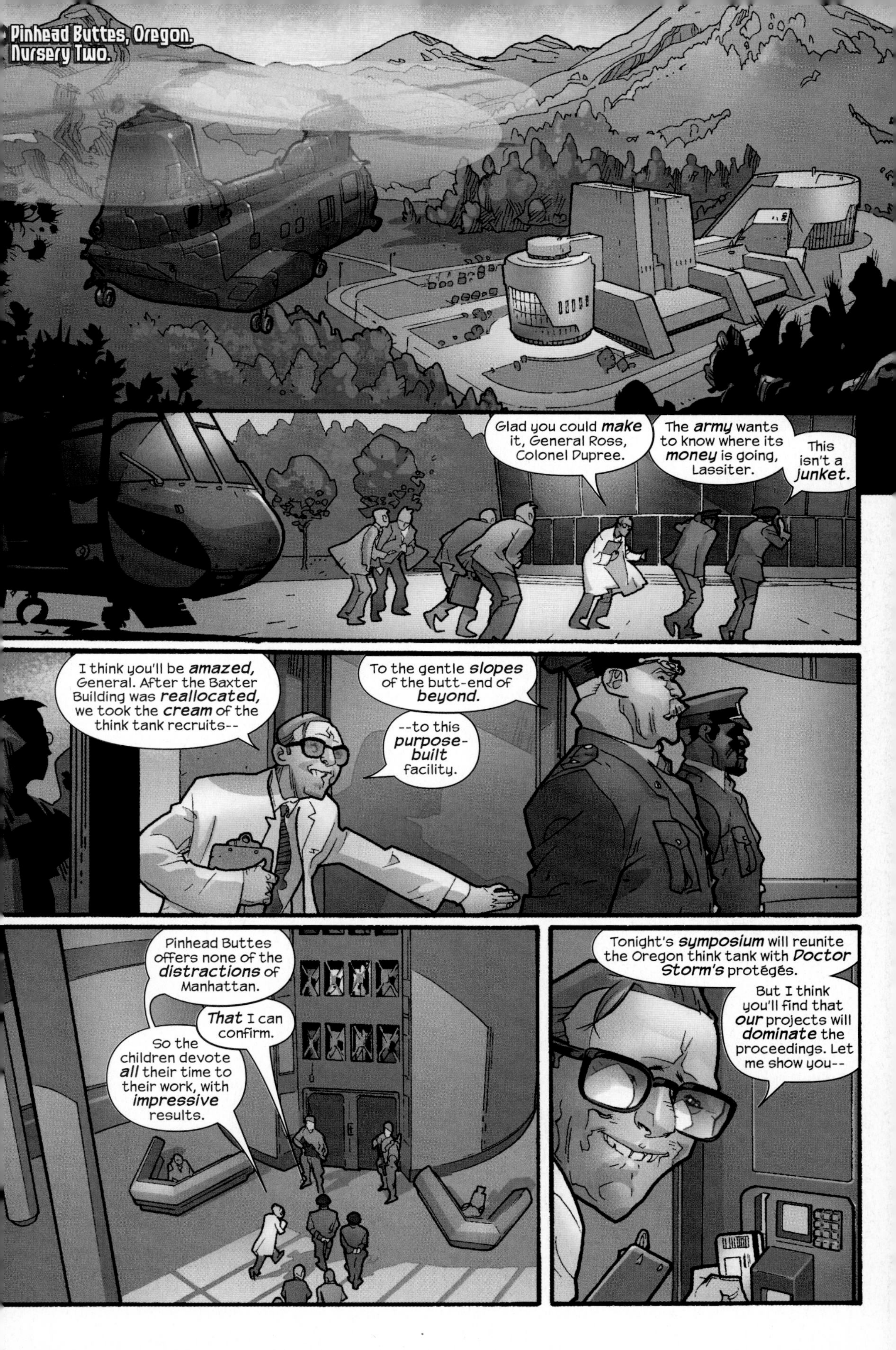
Pinhead Buttes, Oregon. Nursery Two.
Glad you could make it, General Ross, Colonel Dupree.
The army wants to know where its money is going, Lassiter.
This isn't a junket.
I think you'll be amazed, General. After the Baxter Building was reallocated, we took the cream of the think tank recruits--
To the gentle slopes of the butt-end of beyond.
--to this purpose-built facility.
Pinhead Buttes offers none of the distractions of Manhattan.
That I can confirm.
So the children devote all their time to their work, with impressive results.
Tonight's symposium will reunite the Oregon think tank with Doctor Storm's protégés.
But I think you'll find that our projects will dominate the proceedings. Let me show you--

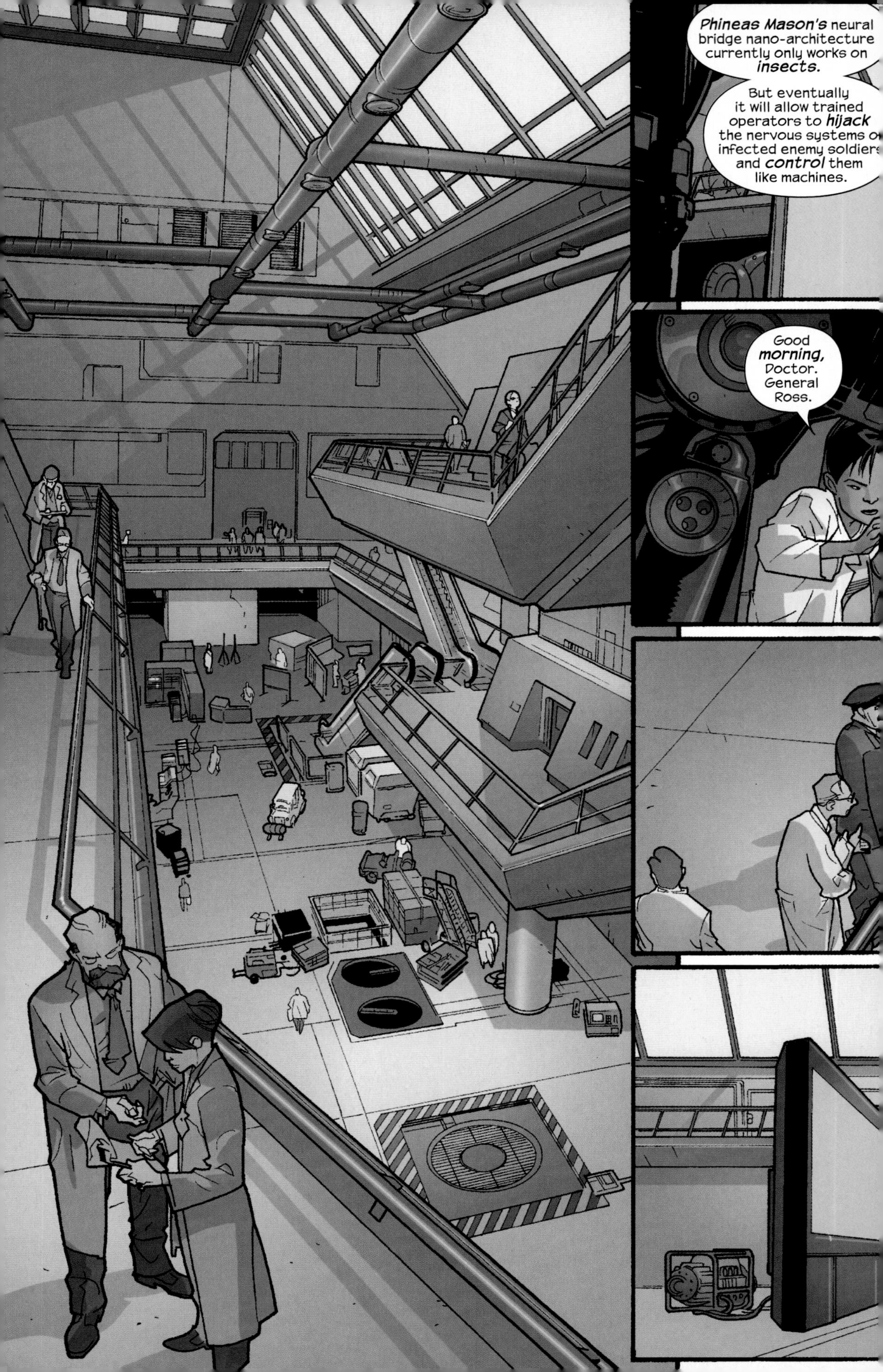

Phineas Mason's neural bridge nano-architecture currently only works on insects.
But eventually it will allow trained operators to hijack the nervous systems o infected enemy soldiers and control them like machines.
Good morning, Doctor. General Ross.

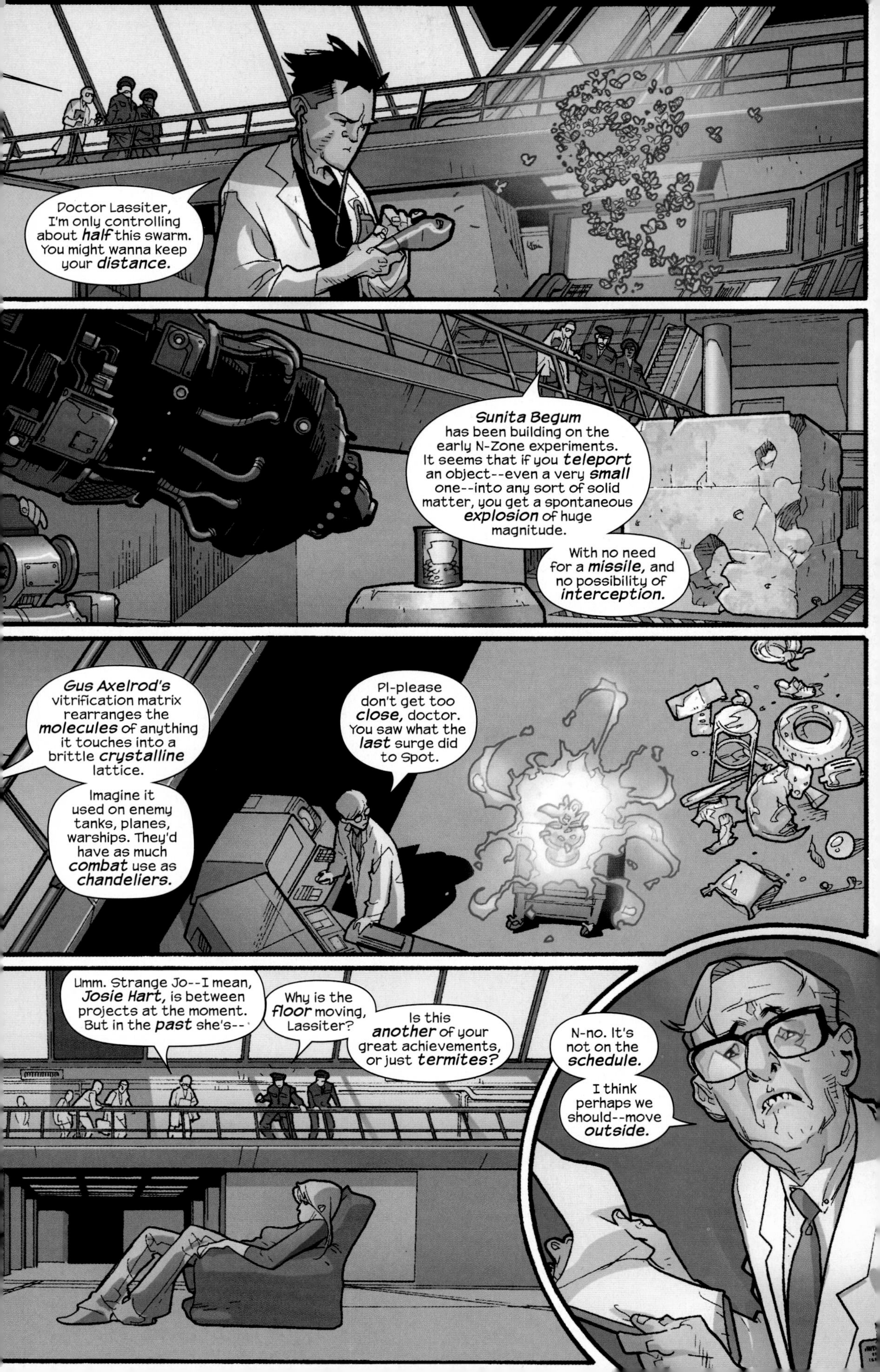
Doctor Lassiter, I'm only controlling about half this swarm. You might wanna keep your distance.
Sunita Begum has been building on the early N-Zone experiments. It seems that if you teleport an object--even a very small one--into any sort of solid matter, you get a spontaneous explosion of huge magnitude.
With no need for a missile, and no possibility of interception.
Gus Axelrod's vitrification matrix rearranges the molecules of anything it touches into a brittle crystalline lattice.
Imagine it used on enemy tanks, planes, warships. They'd have as much combat use as chandeliers.
Pl-please don't get too close, doctor. You saw what the last surge did to Spot.
Umm. Strange Jo--I mean, Josie Hart, is between projects at the moment. But in the past she's--
Why is the floor moving, Lassiter?
Is this another of your great achievements, or just termites?
N-no. It's not on the schedule.
I think perhaps we should--move outside.

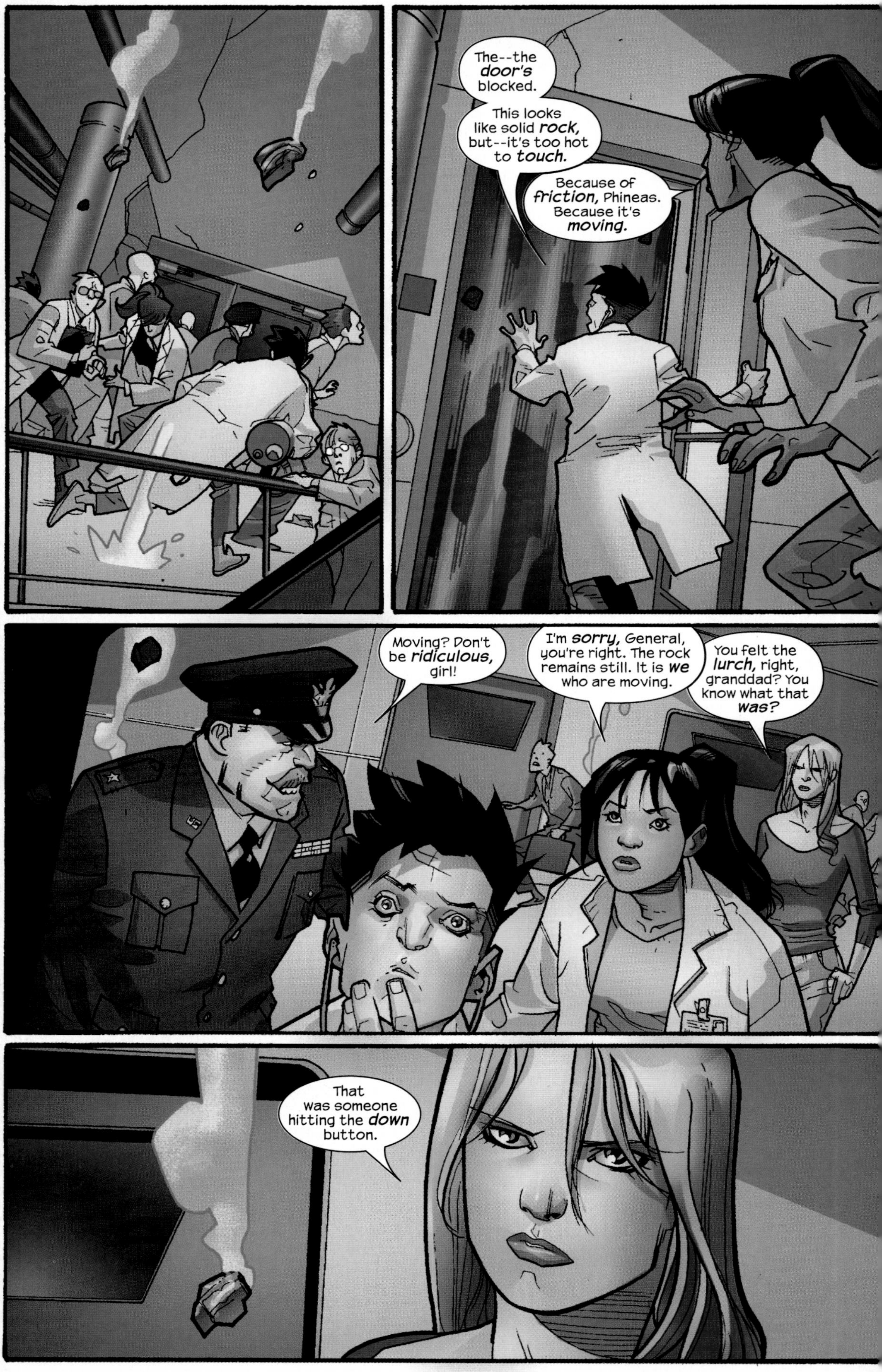

The--the *door's* blocked.
This looks like solid *rock,* but--it's too hot to *touch.*
Because of *friction,* Phineas. Because it's *moving.*
Moving? Don't be *ridiculous,* girl!
I'm *sorry,* General, you're right. The rock remains still. It is *we* who are moving.
You felt the *lurch,* right, granddad? You know what that *was?*
That was someone hitting the *down* button.

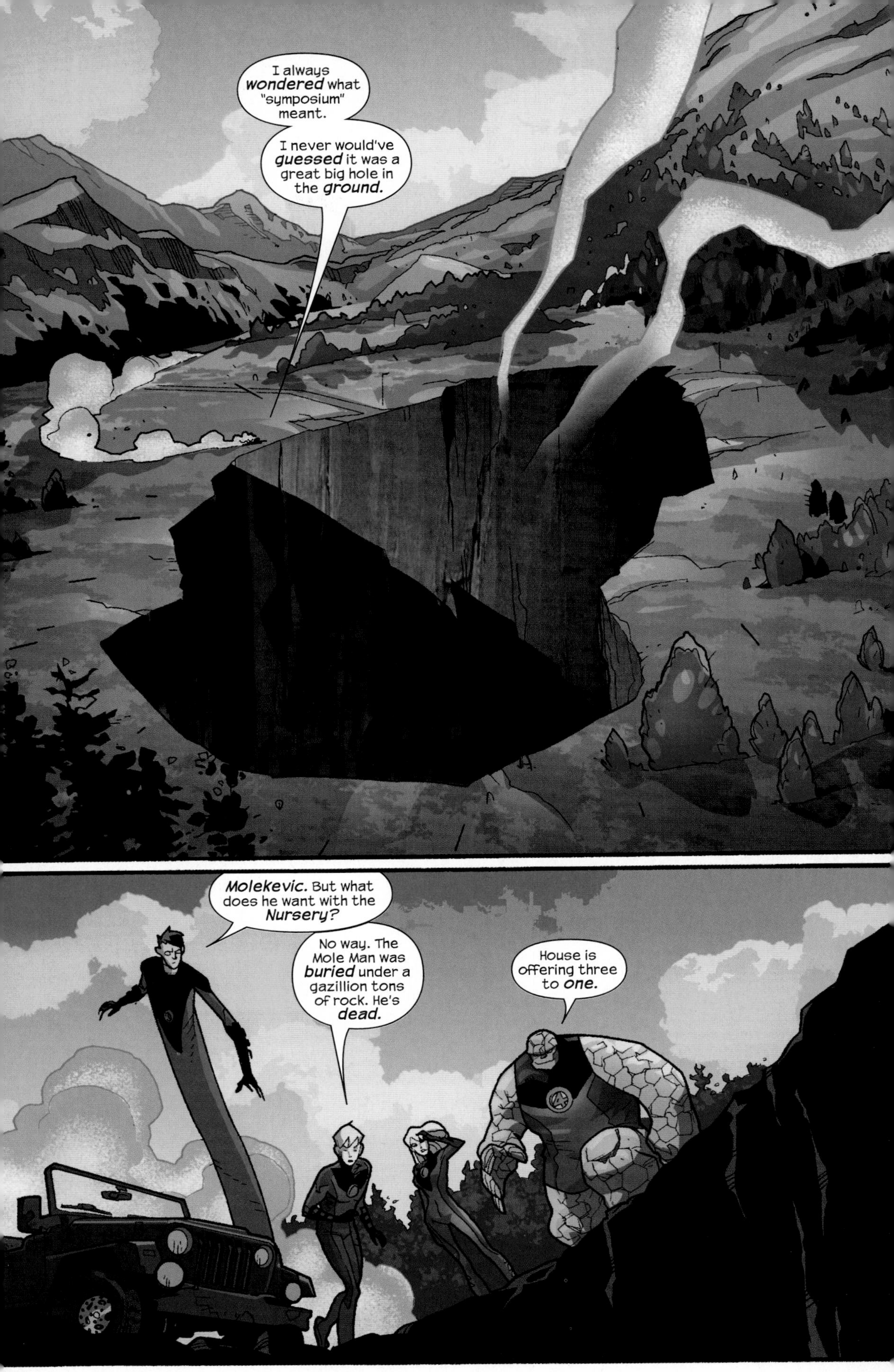
I always wondered what "symposium" meant.
I never would've guessed it was a great big hole in the ground.
Molekevic. But what does he want with the Nursery?
No way. The Mole Man was buried under a gazillion tons of rock. He's dead.
House is offering three to one.

PREVIOUSLY IN ULTIMATE FANTASTIC FOUR:

Reed Richards, handpicked to join the Baxter Building think tank of young geniuses, spent his youth developing a teleport system that transported solid matter into a parallel universe. Its first full-scale test was witnessed by Reed, fellow think tank members Sue Storm and her brother Johnny, as well as Reed's childhood friend Ben Grimm.

There was an accident. The quartet's genetic structures were scrambled and recombined in a fantastically strange way. Reed's body stretches and flows like water. Ben looks like a thing carved from desert rock. Sue can become invisible. Johnny generates flame.

Dr. Arthur Molekevic was a teacher at the think tank. Called "Mole Man" by the students, he was fired five years before the fantastic four came into being. When the young heroes made their debut, they discovered Molekevic had created a monster army underground, and was lashing out against the surface world. The team stopped Mole Man, and believed he was crushed to death in a cave-in.

Months later, after the quartet went public and became celebrity super heroes, the rest of the think tank was moved out of the Baxter Building, for their own protection...a decision which has just proved ironic...

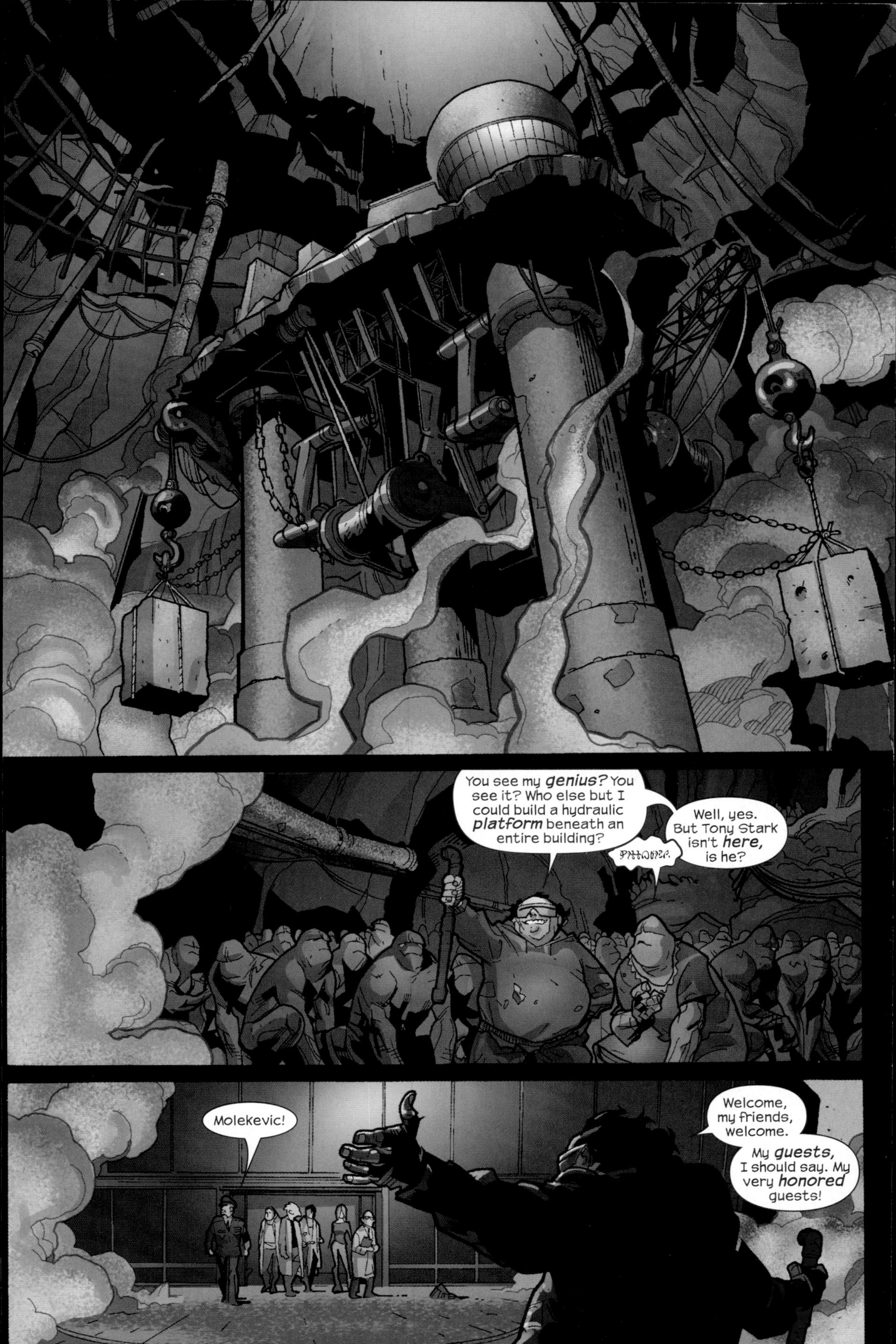
You see my *genius?* You see it? Who else but I could build a hydraulic *platform* beneath an entire building?
Well, yes. But Tony Stark isn't *here,* is he?
Molekevic!
Welcome, my friends, welcome.
My *guests,* I should say. My very *honored* guests!

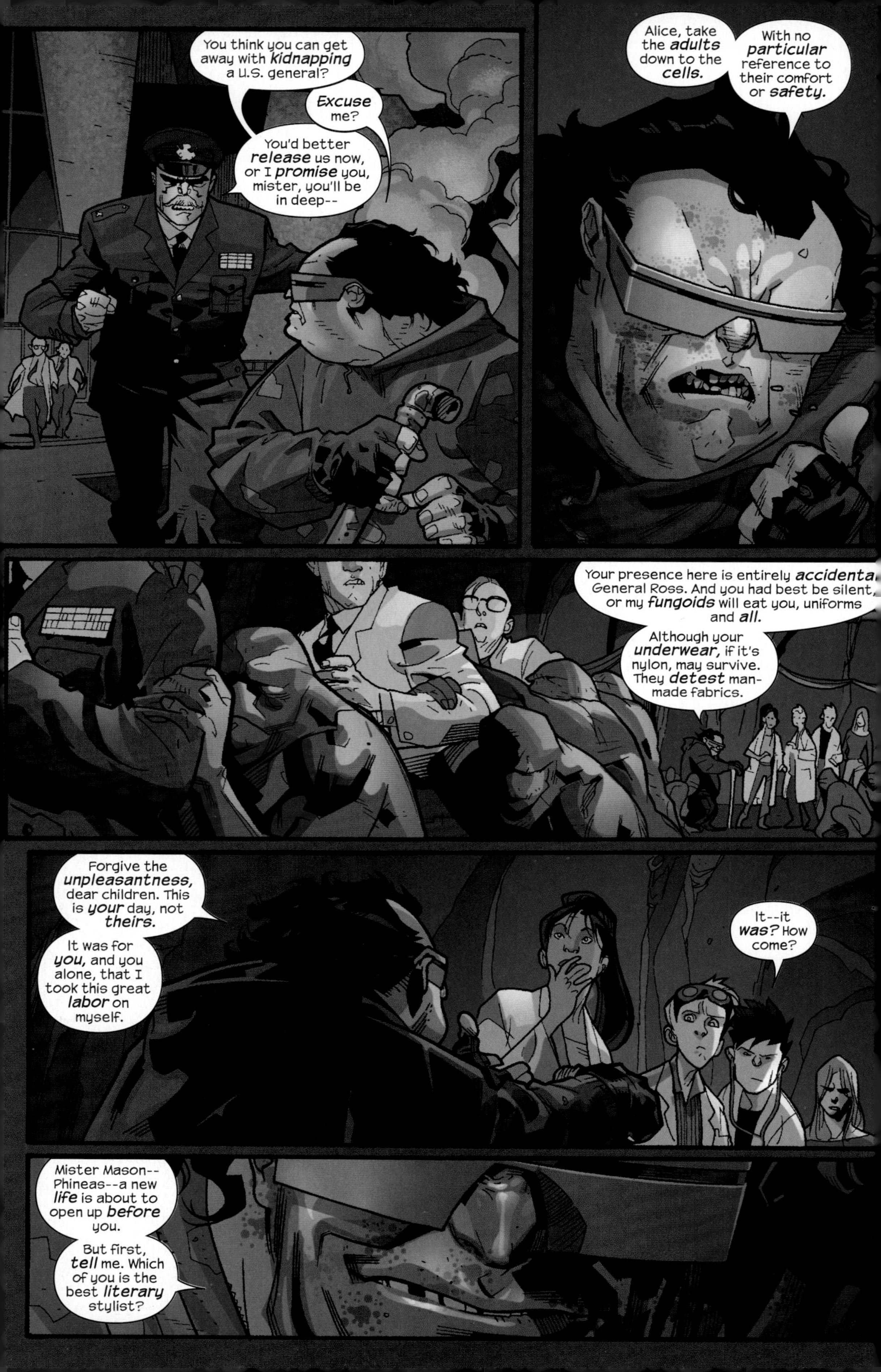

You think you can get away with kidnapping a U.S. general?
Excuse me?
You'd better release us now, or I promise you, mister, you'll be in deep--
Alice, take the adults down to the cells.
With no particular reference to their comfort or safety.
Your presence here is entirely accidenta General Ross. And you had best be silent, or my fungoids will eat you, uniforms and all.
Although your underwear, if it's nylon, may survive. They detest man-made fabrics.
Forgive the unpleasantness, dear children. This is your day, not theirs.
It was for you, and you alone, that I took this great labor on myself.
It--it was? How come?
Mister Mason--Phineas--a new life is about to open up before you.
But first, tell me. Which of you is the best literary stylist?

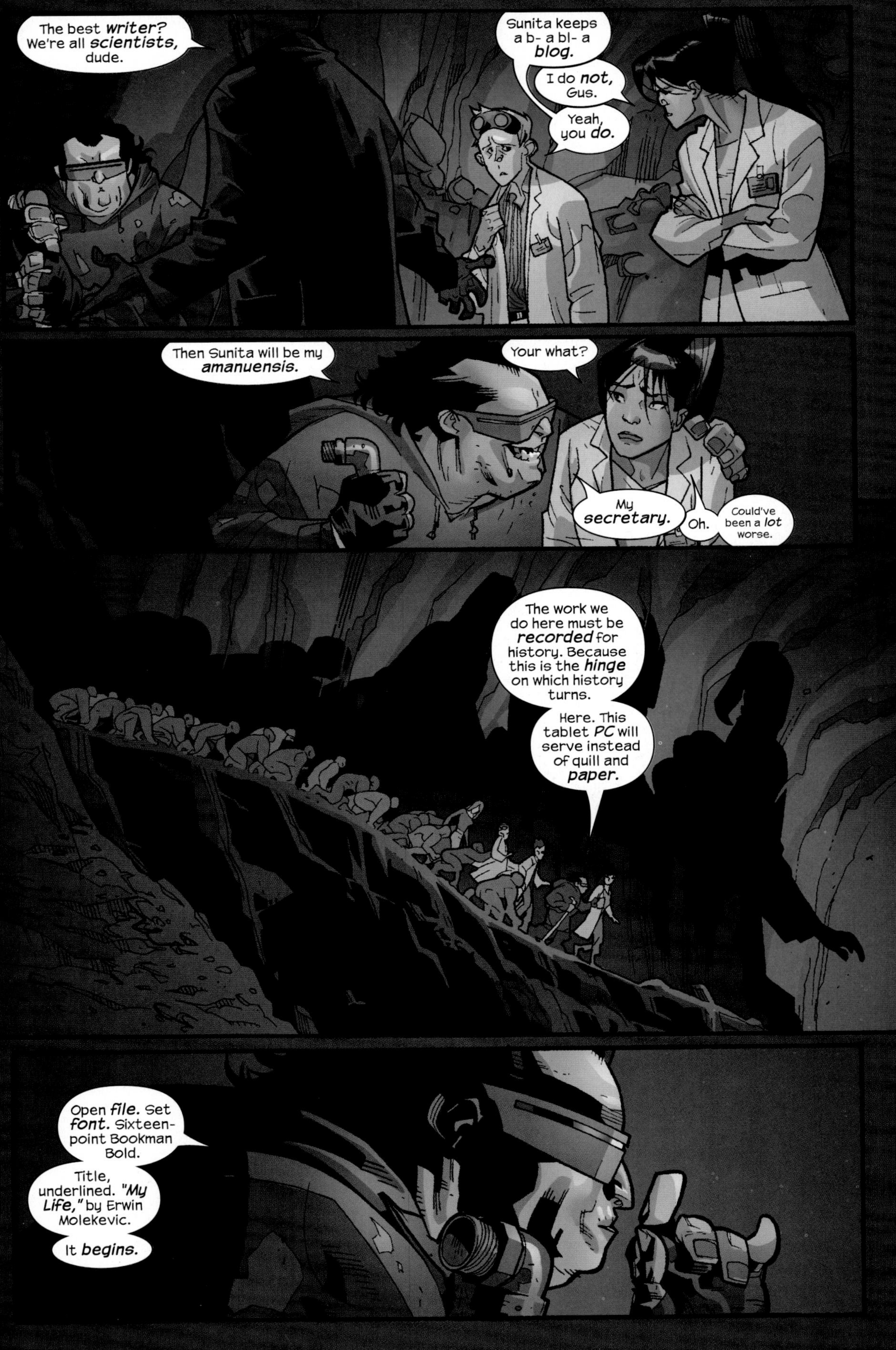
The best writer? We're all scientists, dude.
Sunita keeps a b- a bl- a blog.
I do not, Gus.
Yeah, you do.
Then Sunita will be my amanuensis.
Your what?
My secretary.
Oh.
Could've been a lot worse.
The work we do here must be recorded for history. Because this is the hinge on which history turns.
Here. This tablet PC will serve instead of quill and paper.
Open file. Set font. Sixteen-point Bookman Bold.
Title, underlined. "My Life," by Erwin Molekevic.
It begins.

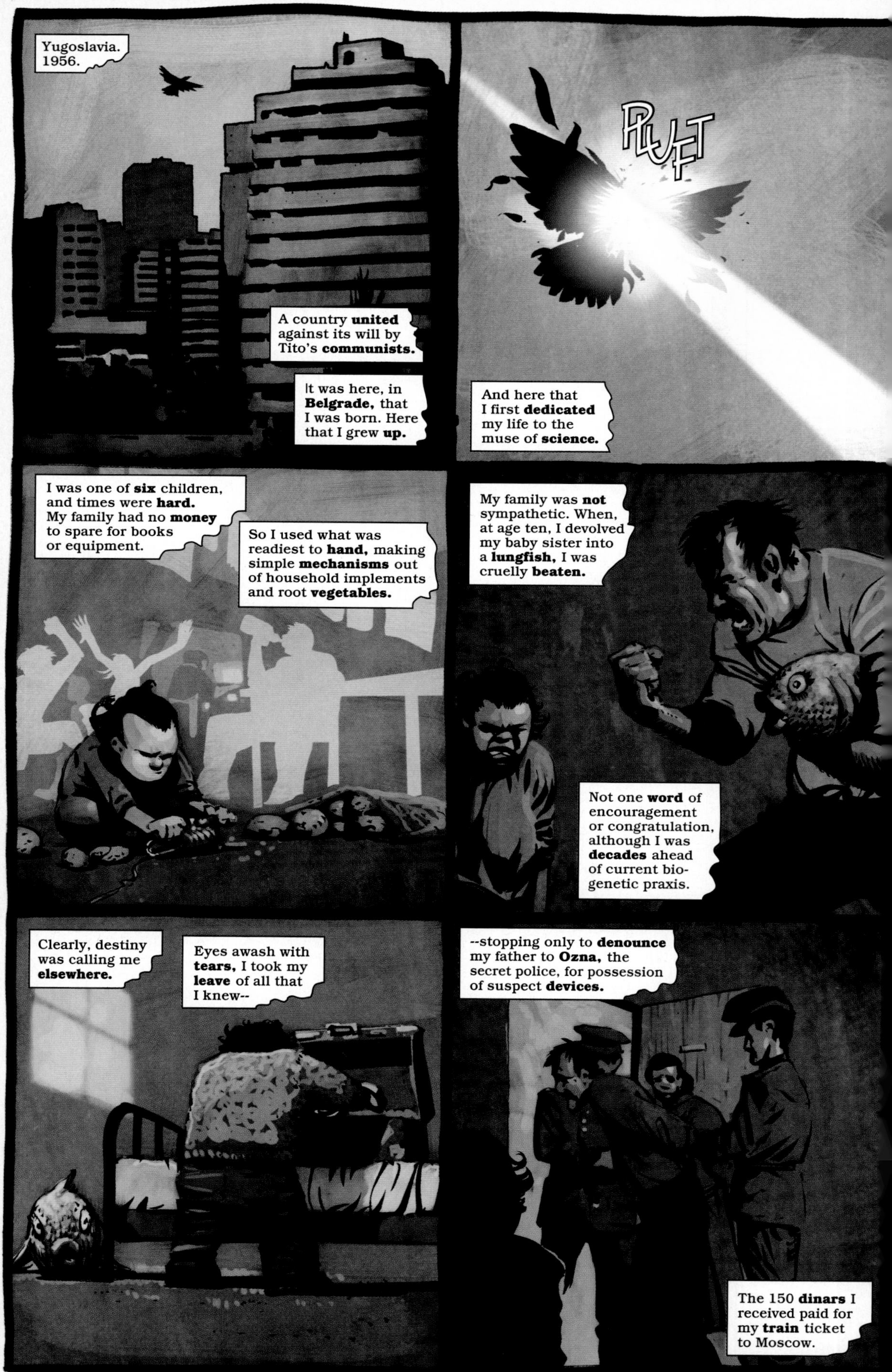
Yugoslavia. 1956.
A country **united** against its will by Tito's **communists.**
It was here, in **Belgrade,** that I was born. Here that I grew **up.**
PLUFT
And here that I first **dedicated** my life to the muse of **science.**
I was one of **six** children, and times were **hard.** My family had no **money** to spare for books or equipment.
So I used what was readiest to **hand,** making simple **mechanisms** out of household implements and root **vegetables.**
My family was **not** sympathetic. When, at age ten, I devolved my baby sister into a **lungfish,** I was cruelly **beaten.**
Not one **word** of encouragement or congratulation, although I was **decades** ahead of current bio-genetic praxis.
Clearly, destiny was calling me **elsewhere.**
Eyes awash with **tears,** I took my **leave** of all that I knew--
--stopping only to **denounce** my father to **Ozna,** the secret police, for possession of suspect **devices.**
The 150 **dinars** I received paid for my **train** ticket to Moscow.

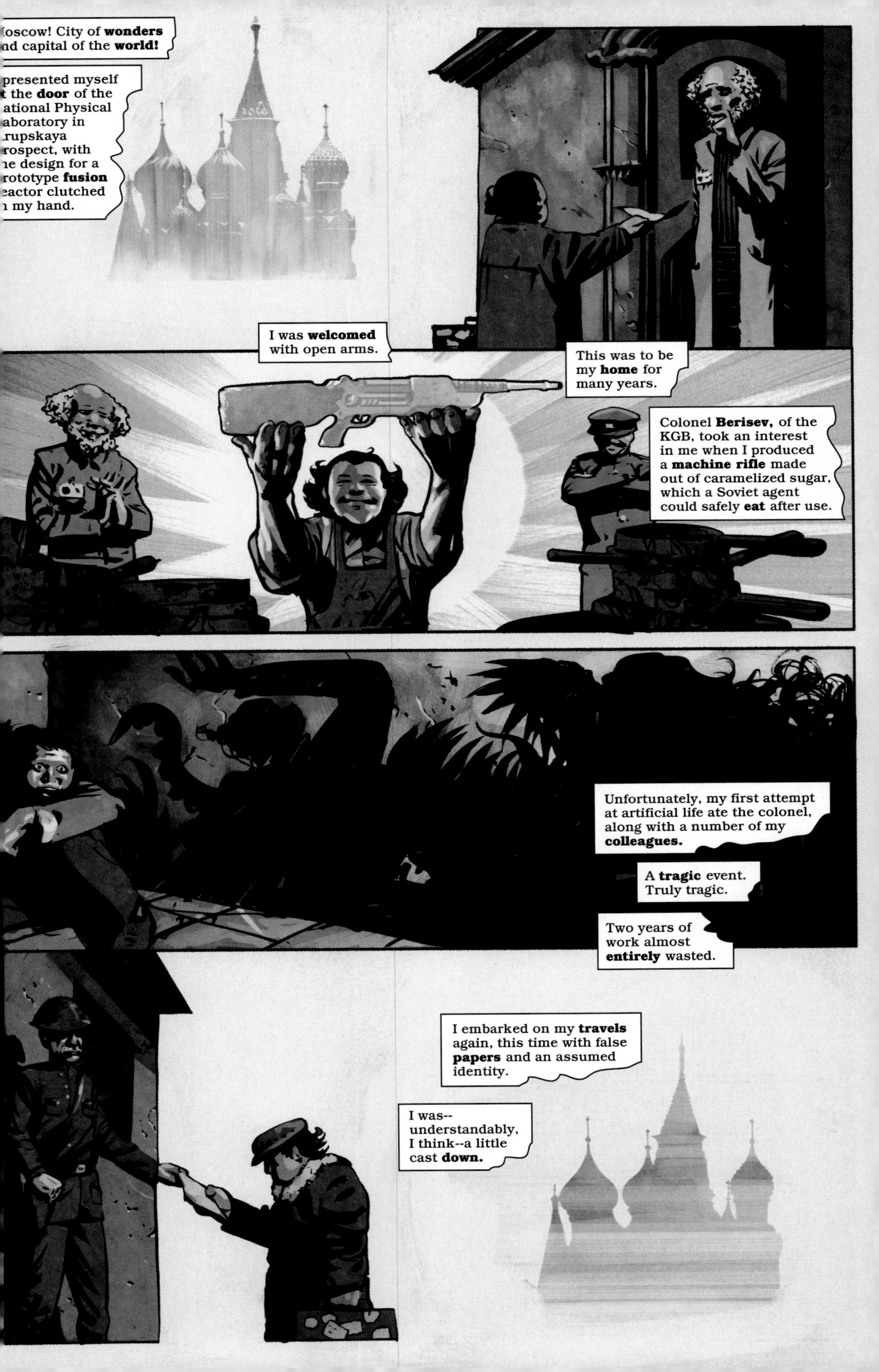

loscow! City of wonders
nd capital of the world!
presented myself
t the door of the
ational Physical
aboratory in
rupskaya
rospect, with
ne design for a
rototype fusion
eactor clutched
n my hand.
I was welcomed with open arms.
This was to be my home for many years.
Colonel Berisev, of the KGB, took an interest in me when I produced a machine rifle made out of caramelized sugar, which a Soviet agent could safely eat after use.
Unfortunately, my first attempt at artificial life ate the colonel, along with a number of my colleagues.
A tragic event. Truly tragic.
Two years of work almost entirely wasted.
I embarked on my travels again, this time with false papers and an assumed identity.
I was--understandably, I think--a little cast down.

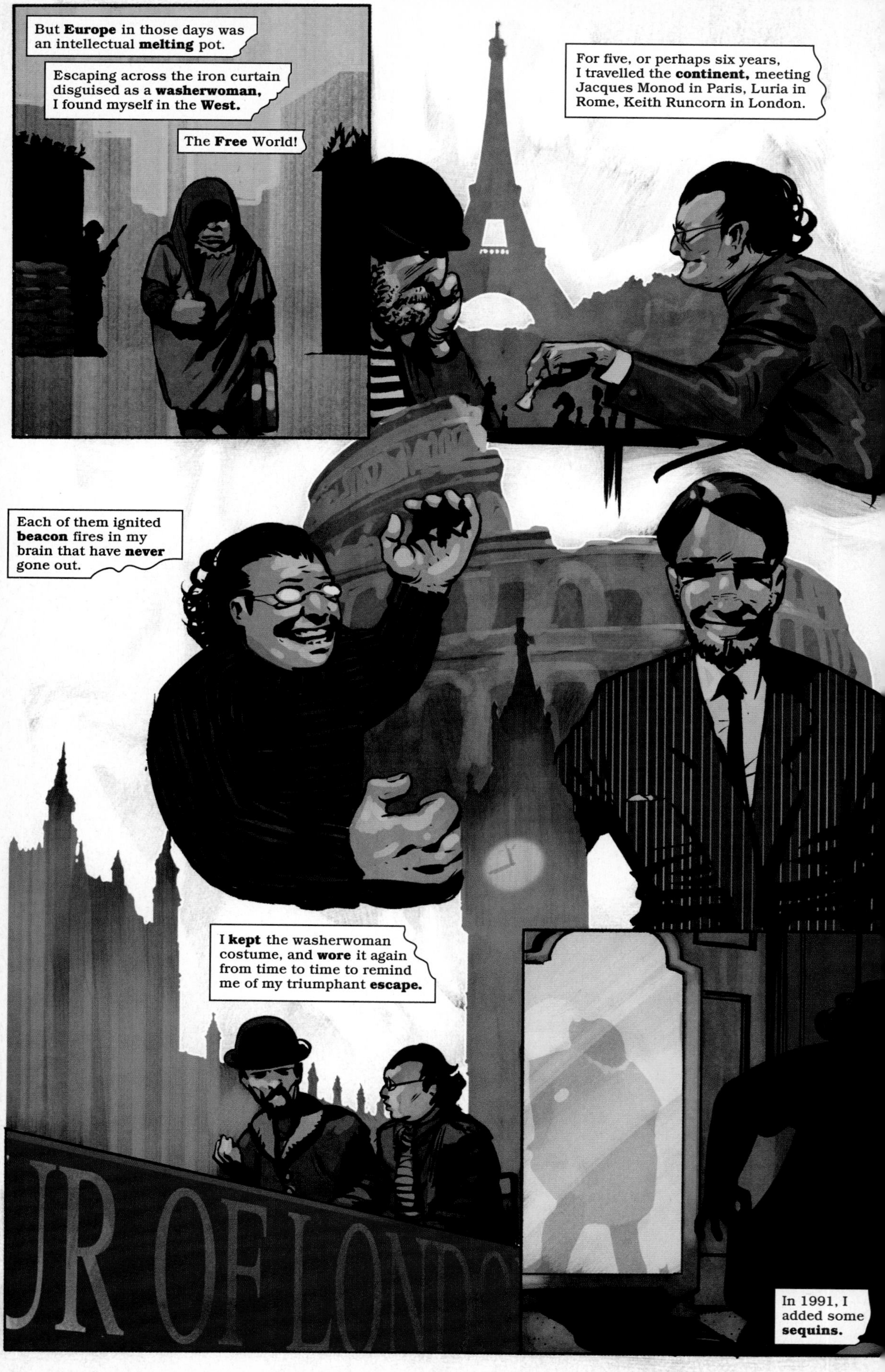

But Europe in those days was an intellectual melting pot.
Escaping across the iron curtain disguised as a washerwoman, I found myself in the West.
The Free World!
For five, or perhaps six years, I travelled the continent, meeting Jacques Monod in Paris, Luria in Rome, Keith Runcorn in London.
Each of them ignited beacon fires in my brain that have never gone out.
I kept the washerwoman costume, and wore it again from time to time to remind me of my triumphant escape.
UR OF LONDO
In 1991, I added some sequins.

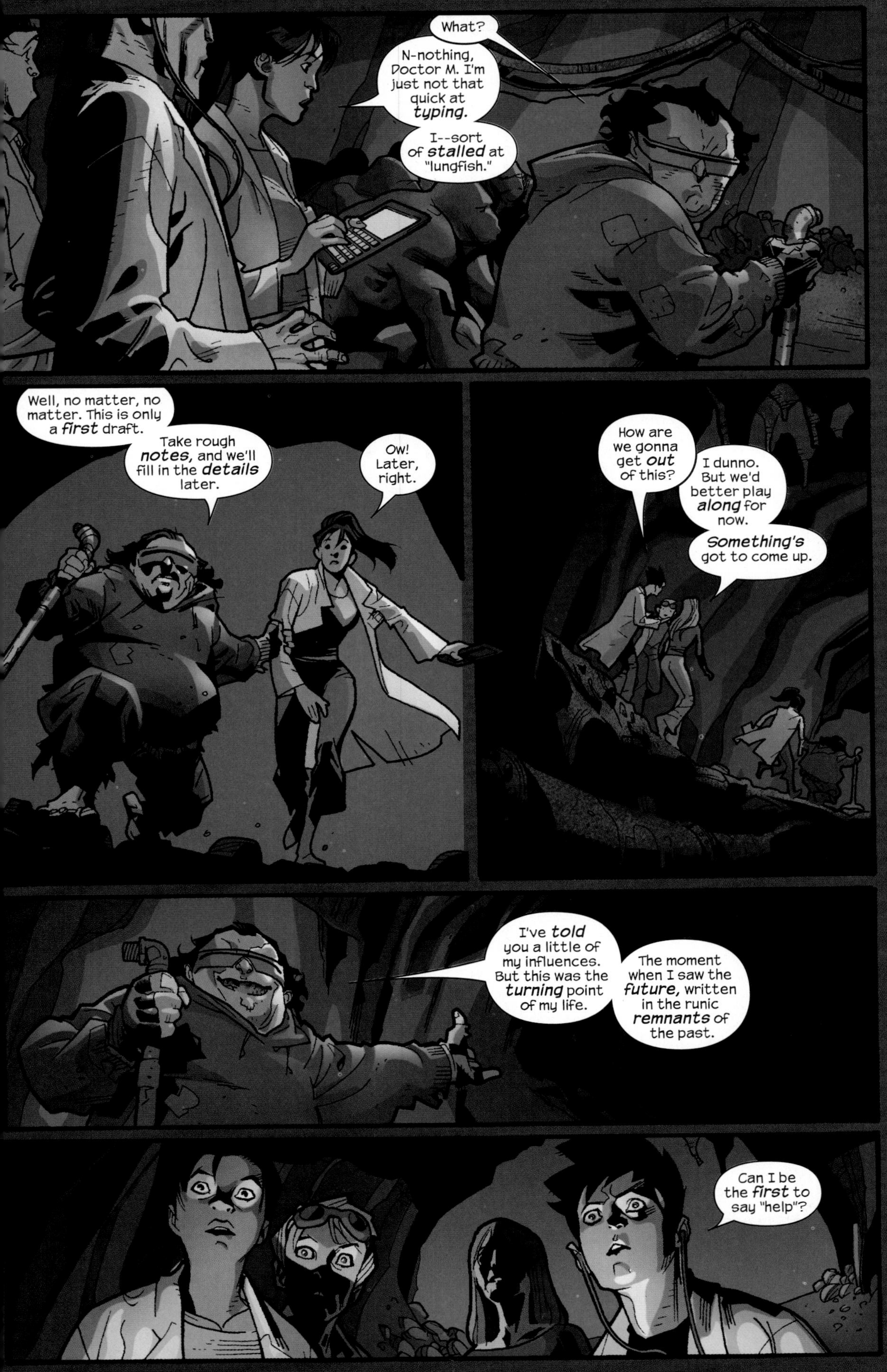
What?
N-nothing, Doctor M. I'm just not that quick at *typing.*
I--sort of *stalled* at "lungfish."
Well, no matter, no matter. This is only a *first* draft.
Take rough *notes,* and we'll fill in the *details* later.
Ow! Later, right.
How are we gonna get *out* of this?
I dunno. But we'd better play *along* for now.
Something's got to come up.
I've *told* you a little of my influences. But this was the *turning* point of my life.
The moment when I saw the *future,* written in the runic *remnants* of the past.
Can I be the *first* to say "help"?

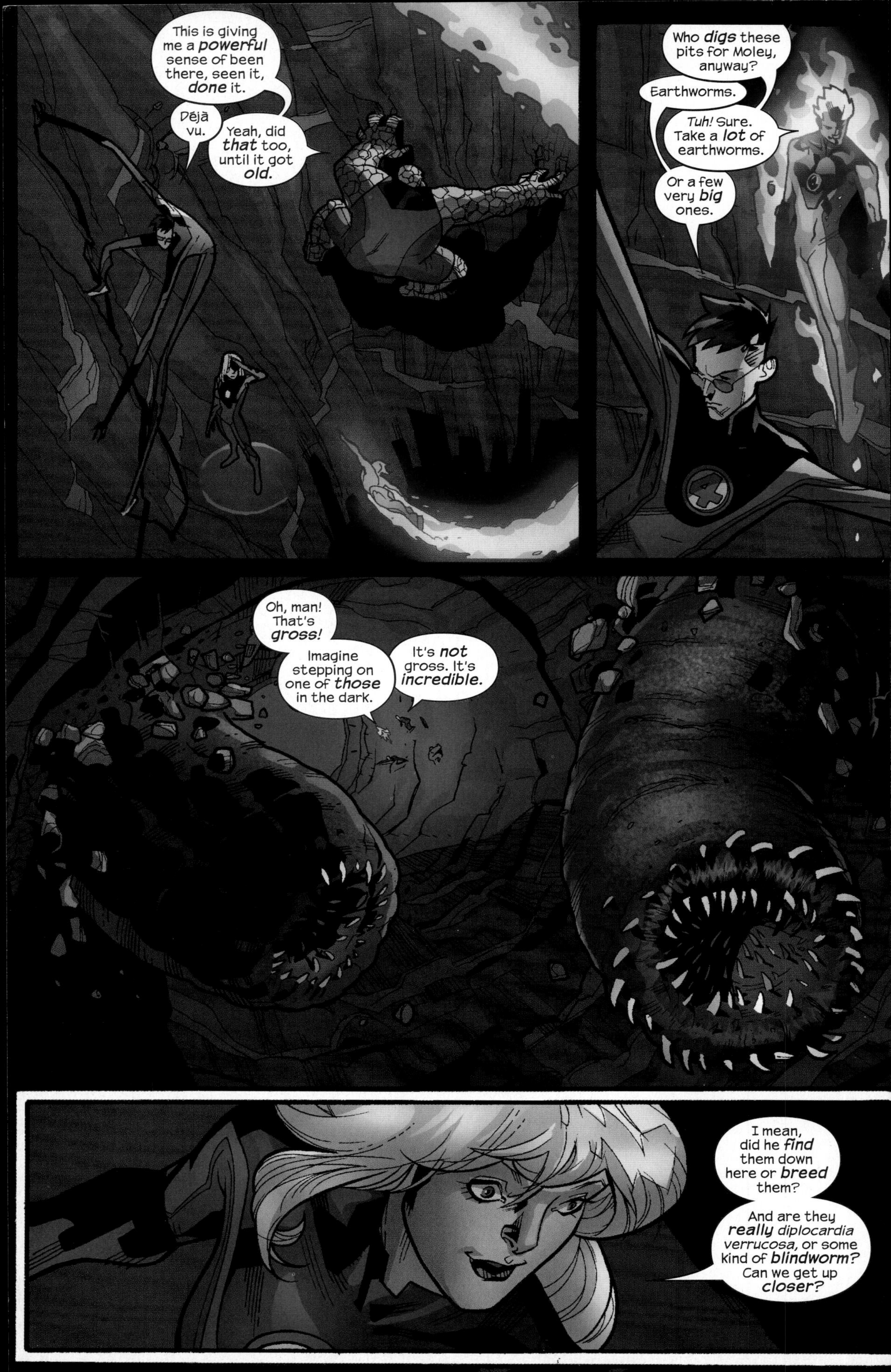

This is giving me a *powerful* sense of been there, seen it, *done* it.
Déjà vu.
Yeah, did *that* too, until it got *old.*
Who *digs* these pits for Moley, anyway?
Earthworms.
Tuh! Sure. Take a *lot* of earthworms.
Or a few very *big* ones.
Oh, man! That's *gross!*
Imagine stepping on one of *those* in the dark.
It's *not* gross. It's *incredible.*
I mean, did he *find* them down here or *breed* them?
And are they *really* *diplocardia verrucosa*, or some kind of *blindworm*? Can we get up *closer?*

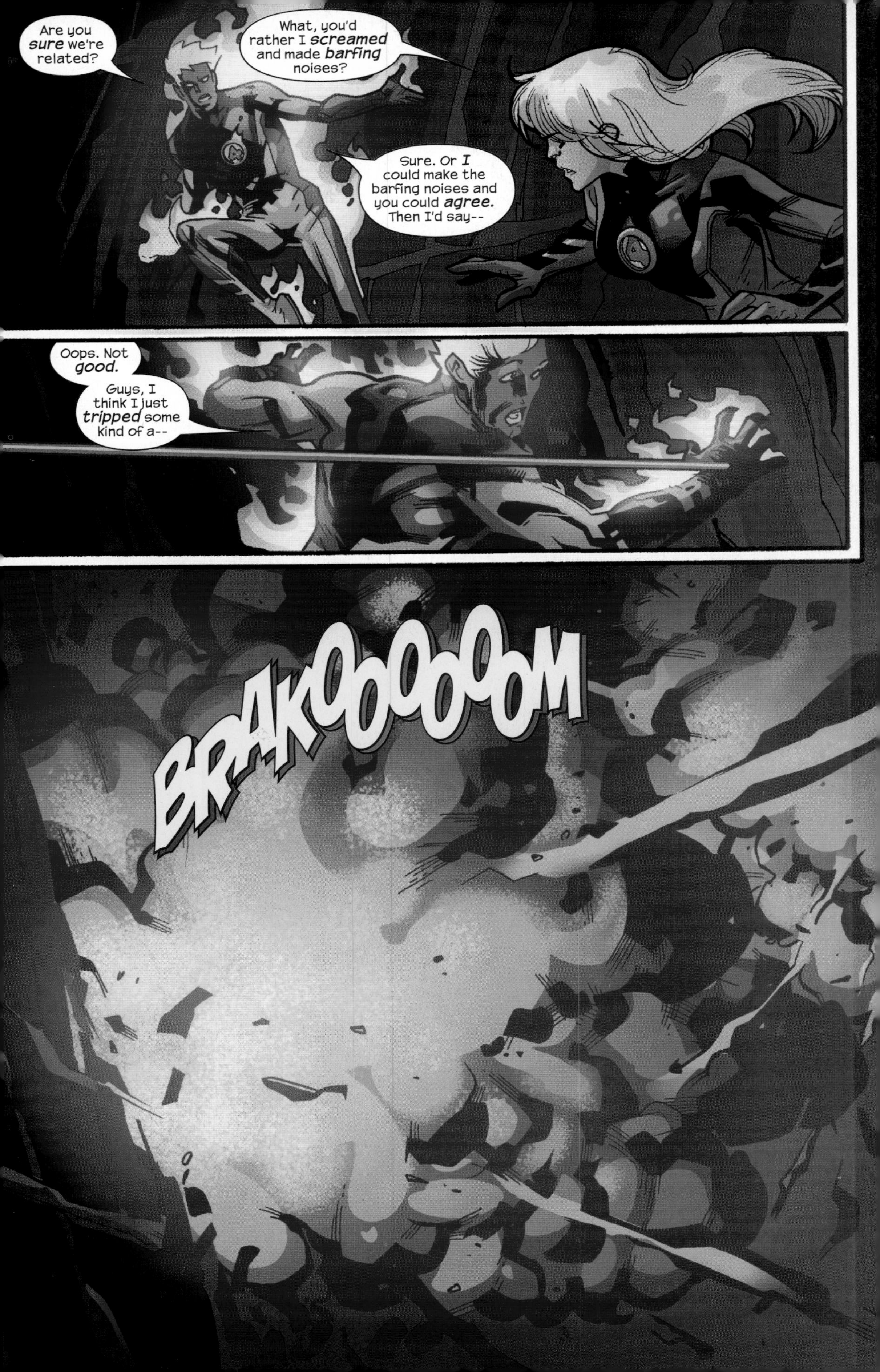
Are you *sure* we're related?
What, you'd rather I *screamed* and made *barfing* noises?
Sure. Or *I* could make the barfing noises and you could *agree.* Then I'd say--
Oops. Not *good.*
Guys, I think I just *tripped* some kind of a--
BRAKOOOOOOM

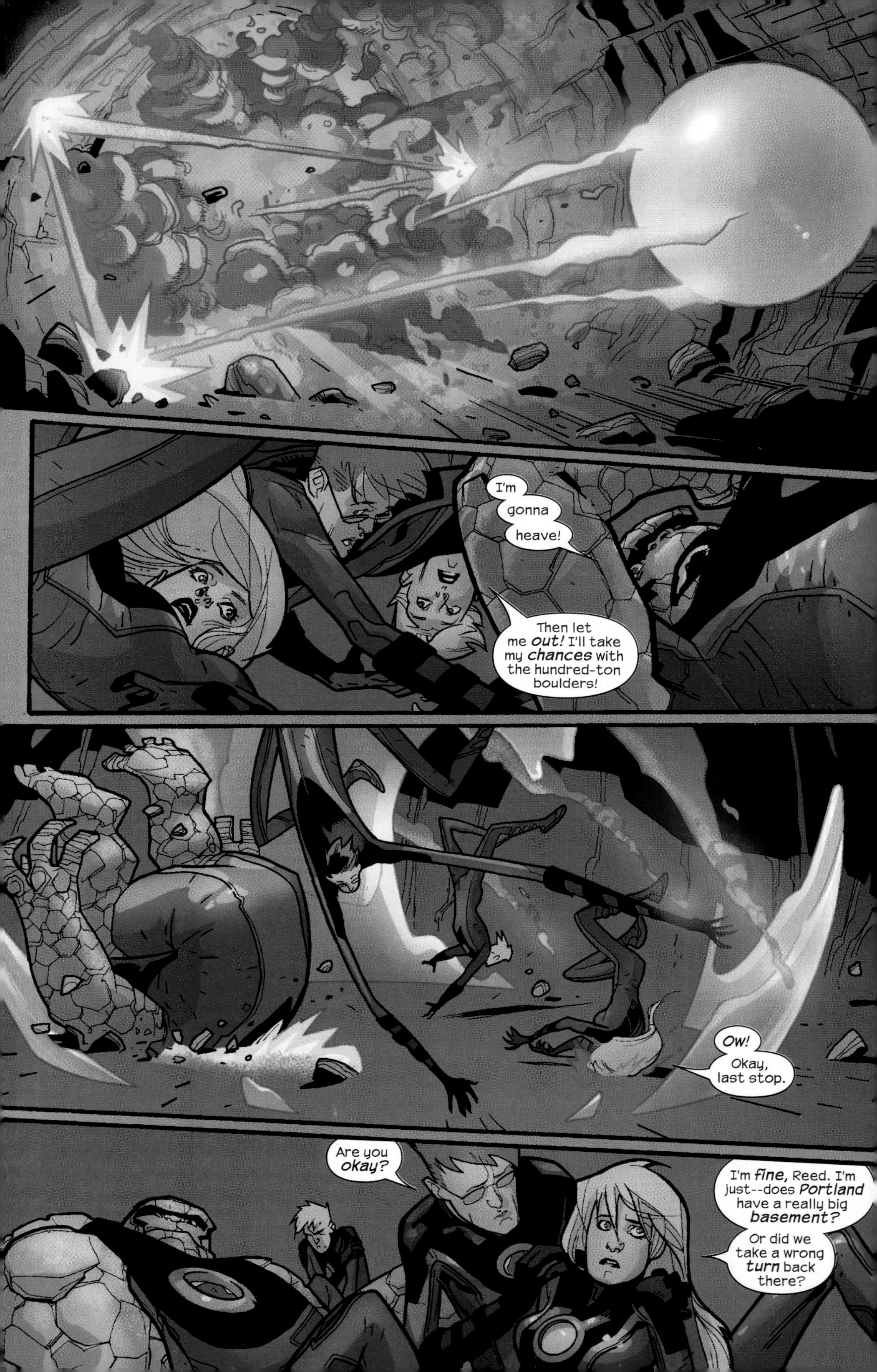
I'm gonna heave!
Then let me out! I'll take my chances with the hundred-ton boulders!
Ow!
Okay, last stop.
Are you okay?
I'm fine, Reed. I'm just--does Portland have a really big basement?
Or did we take a wrong turn back there?

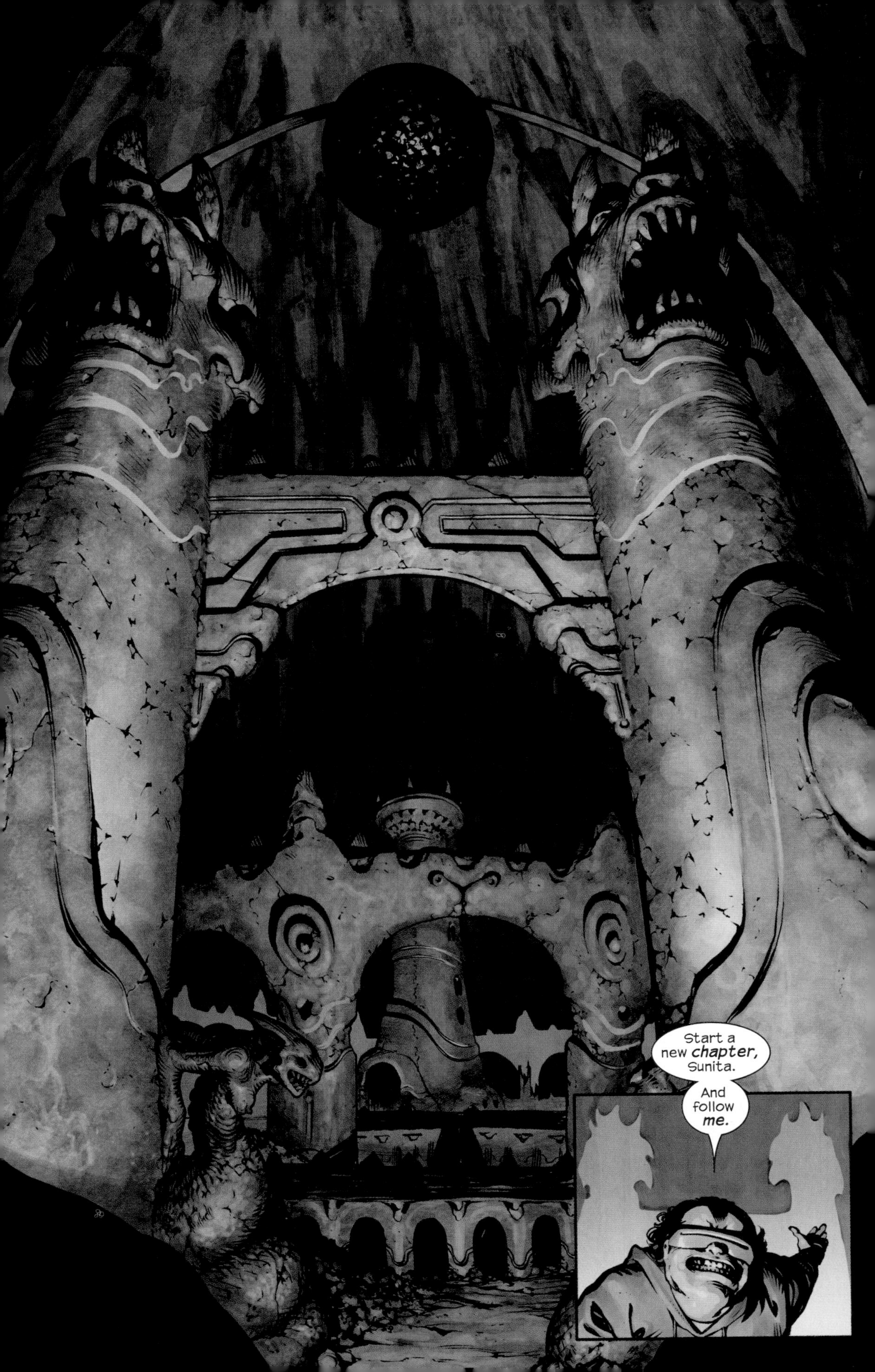
Start a new *chapter,* Sunita.
And follow *me.*

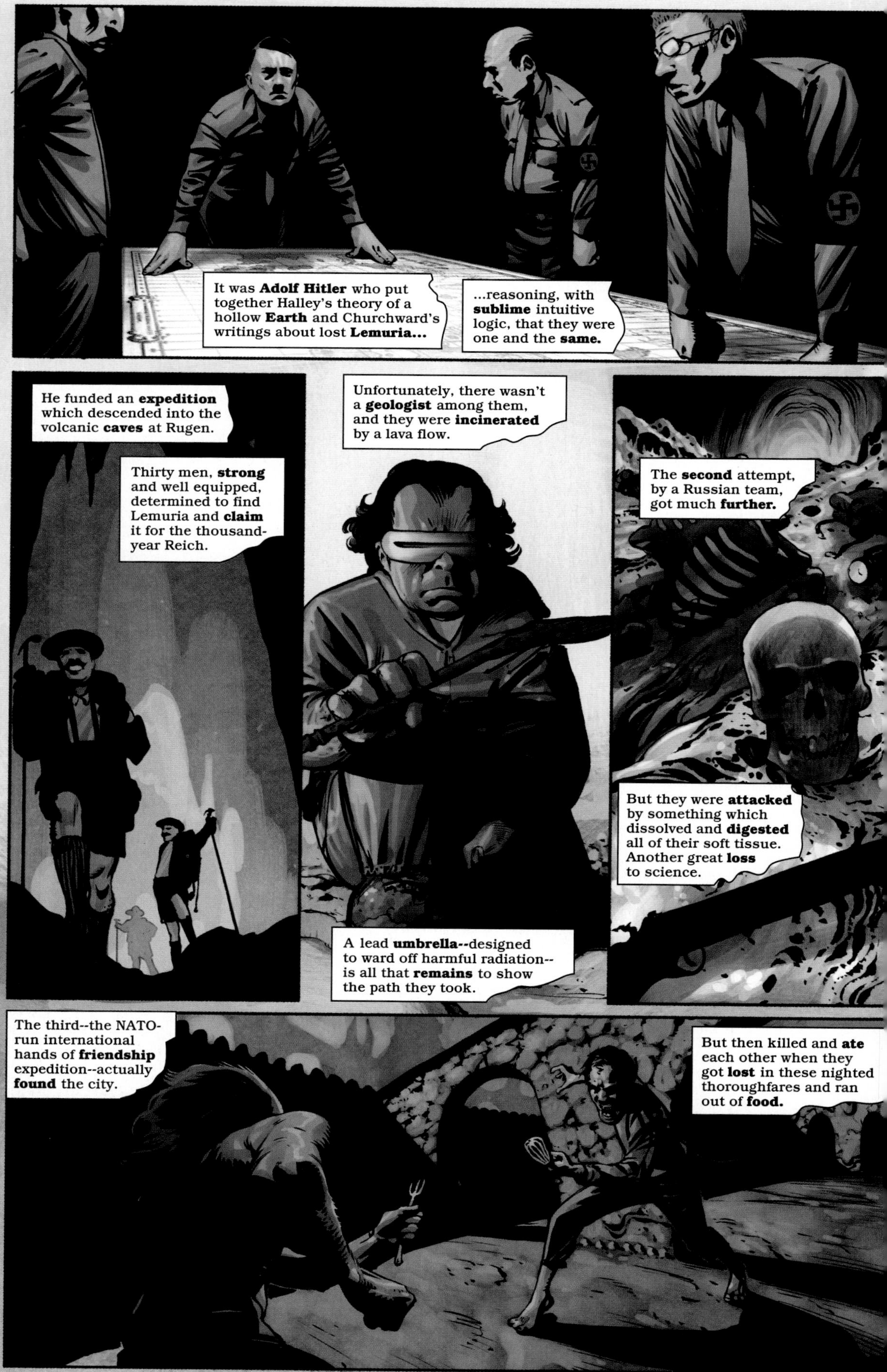
It was Adolf Hitler who put together Halley's theory of a hollow Earth and Churchward's writings about lost Lemuria...
...reasoning, with sublime intuitive logic, that they were one and the same.
He funded an expedition which descended into the volcanic caves at Rugen.
Thirty men, strong and well equipped, determined to find Lemuria and claim it for the thousand-year Reich.
Unfortunately, there wasn't a geologist among them, and they were incinerated by a lava flow.
A lead umbrella--designed to ward off harmful radiation--is all that remains to show the path they took.
The second attempt, by a Russian team, got much further.
But they were attacked by something which dissolved and digested all of their soft tissue. Another great loss to science.
The third--the NATO-run international hands of friendship expedition--actually found the city.
But then killed and ate each other when they got lost in these nighted thoroughfares and ran out of food.

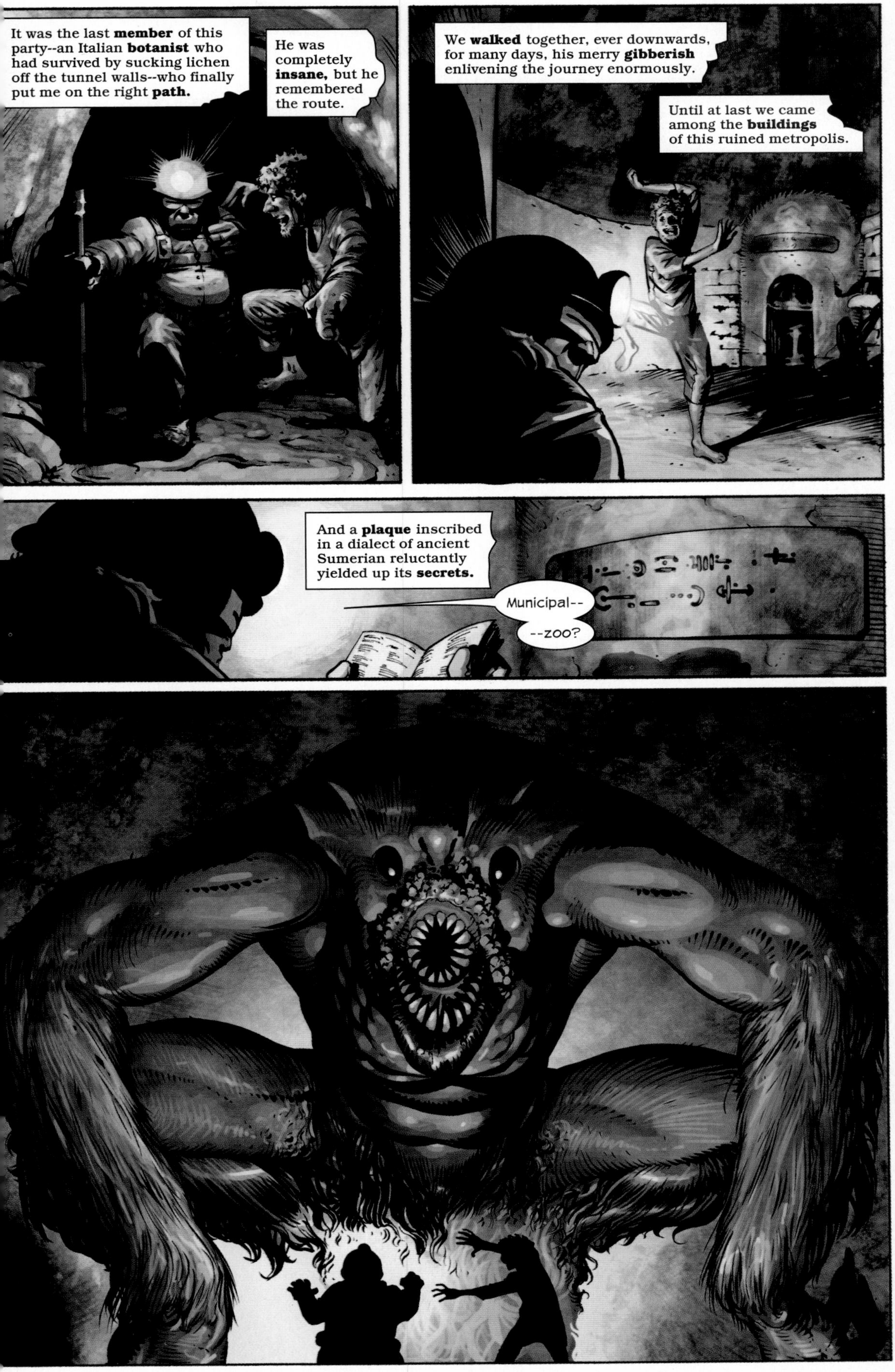
It was the last **member** of this party--an Italian **botanist** who had survived by sucking lichen off the tunnel walls--who finally put me on the right **path.**
He was completely **insane,** but he remembered the route.
We **walked** together, ever downwards, for many days, his merry **gibberish** enlivening the journey enormously.
Until at last we came among the **buildings** of this ruined metropolis.
And a **plaque** inscribed in a dialect of ancient Sumerian reluctantly yielded up its **secrets.**
Municipal--
--zoo?

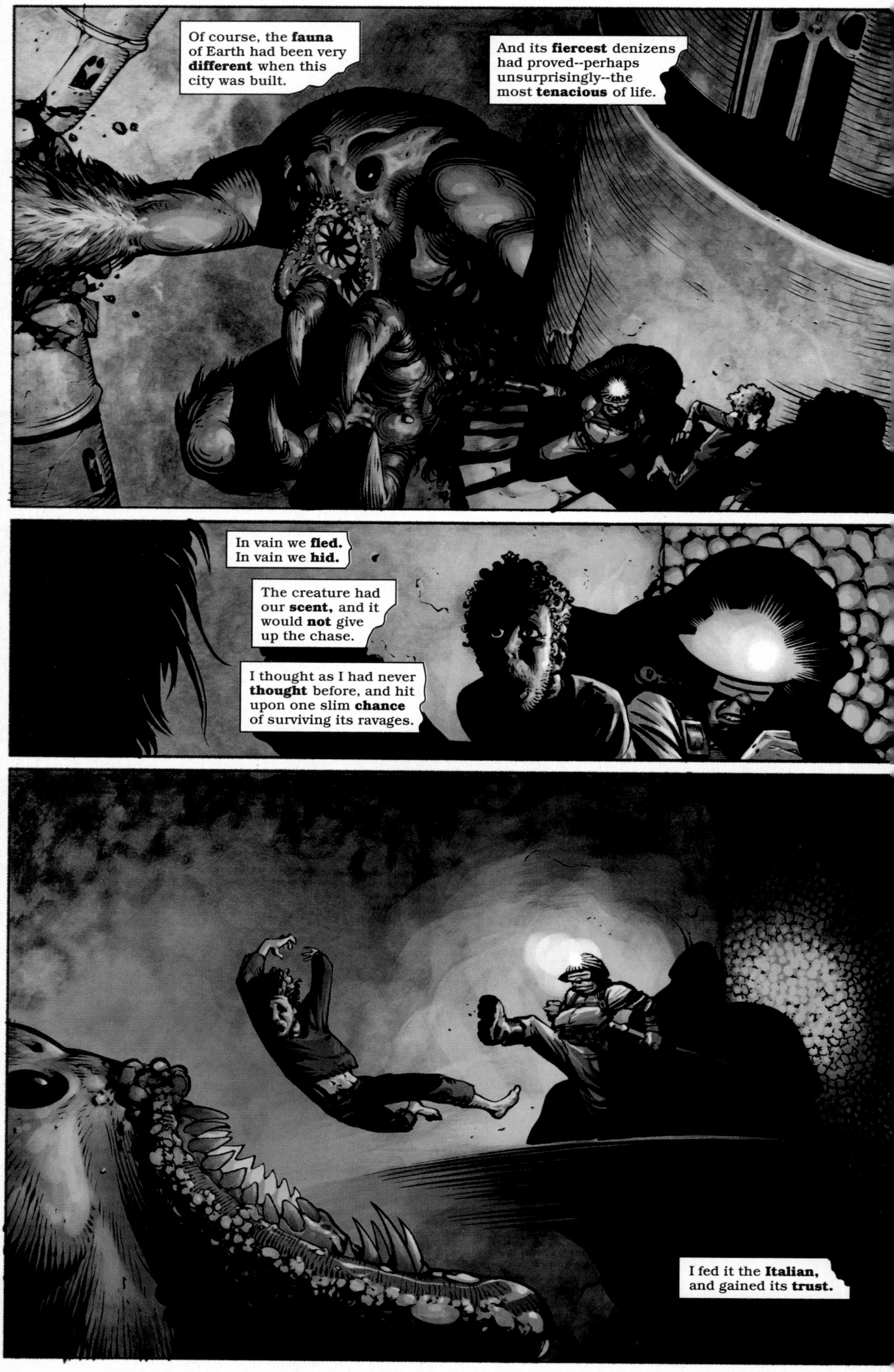
Of course, the fauna of Earth had been very different when this city was built.
And its fiercest denizens had proved--perhaps unsurprisingly--the most tenacious of life.
In vain we fled. In vain we hid.
The creature had our scent, and it would not give up the chase.
I thought as I had never thought before, and hit upon one slim chance of surviving its ravages.
I fed it the Italian, and gained its trust.

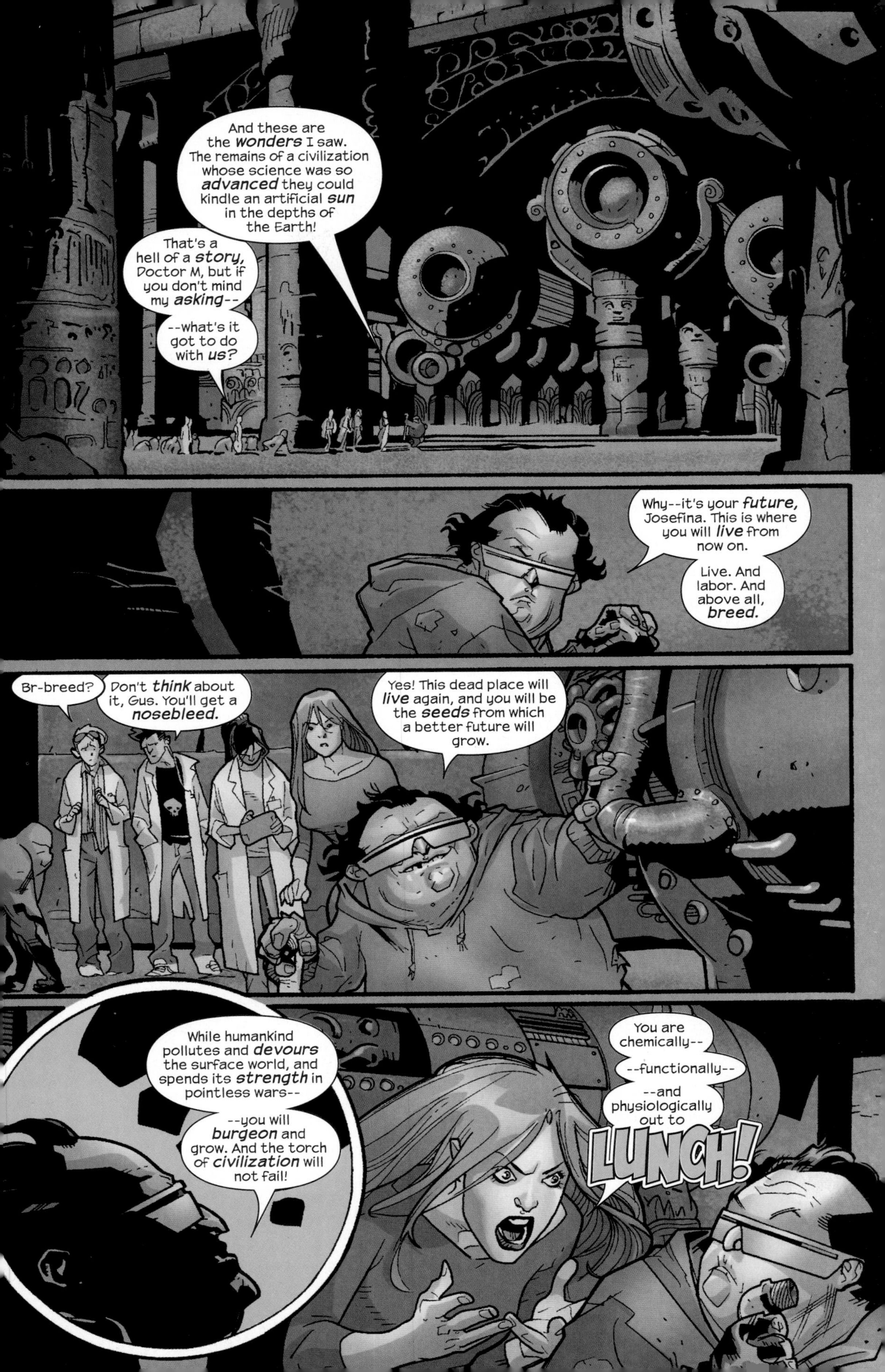
And these are the wonders I saw. The remains of a civilization whose science was so advanced they could kindle an artificial sun in the depths of the Earth!
That's a hell of a story, Doctor M, but if you don't mind my asking--
--what's it got to do with us?
Why--it's your future, Josefina. This is where you will live from now on.
Live. And labor. And above all, breed.
Br-breed?
Don't think about it, Gus. You'll get a nosebleed.
Yes! This dead place will live again, and you will be the seeds from which a better future will grow.
While humankind pollutes and devours the surface world, and spends its strength in pointless wars--
--you will burgeon and grow. And the torch of civilization will not fail!
You are chemically--
--functionally--
--and physiologically out to
LUNCH!

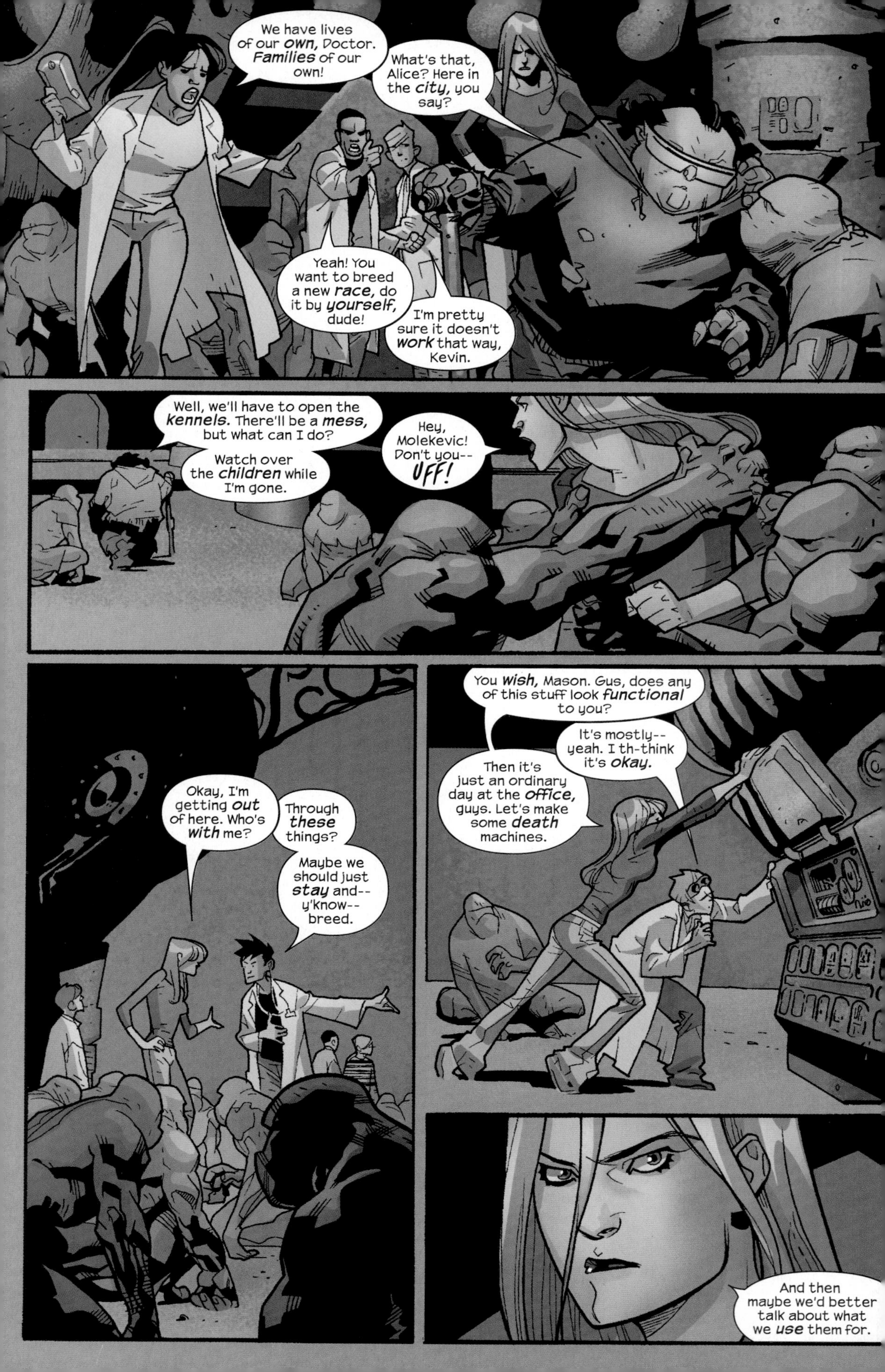
We have lives of our own, Doctor. Families of our own!
What's that, Alice? Here in the city, you say?
Yeah! You want to breed a new race, do it by yourself, dude!
I'm pretty sure it doesn't work that way, Kevin.
Well, we'll have to open the kennels. There'll be a mess, but what can I do?
Watch over the children while I'm gone.
Hey, Molekevic! Don't you--
UFF!
Okay, I'm getting out of here. Who's with me?
Through these things?
Maybe we should just stay and-- y'know-- breed.
You wish, Mason. Gus, does any of this stuff look functional to you?
It's mostly-- yeah. I th-think it's okay.
Then it's just an ordinary day at the office, guys. Let's make some death machines.
And then maybe we'd better talk about what we use them for.

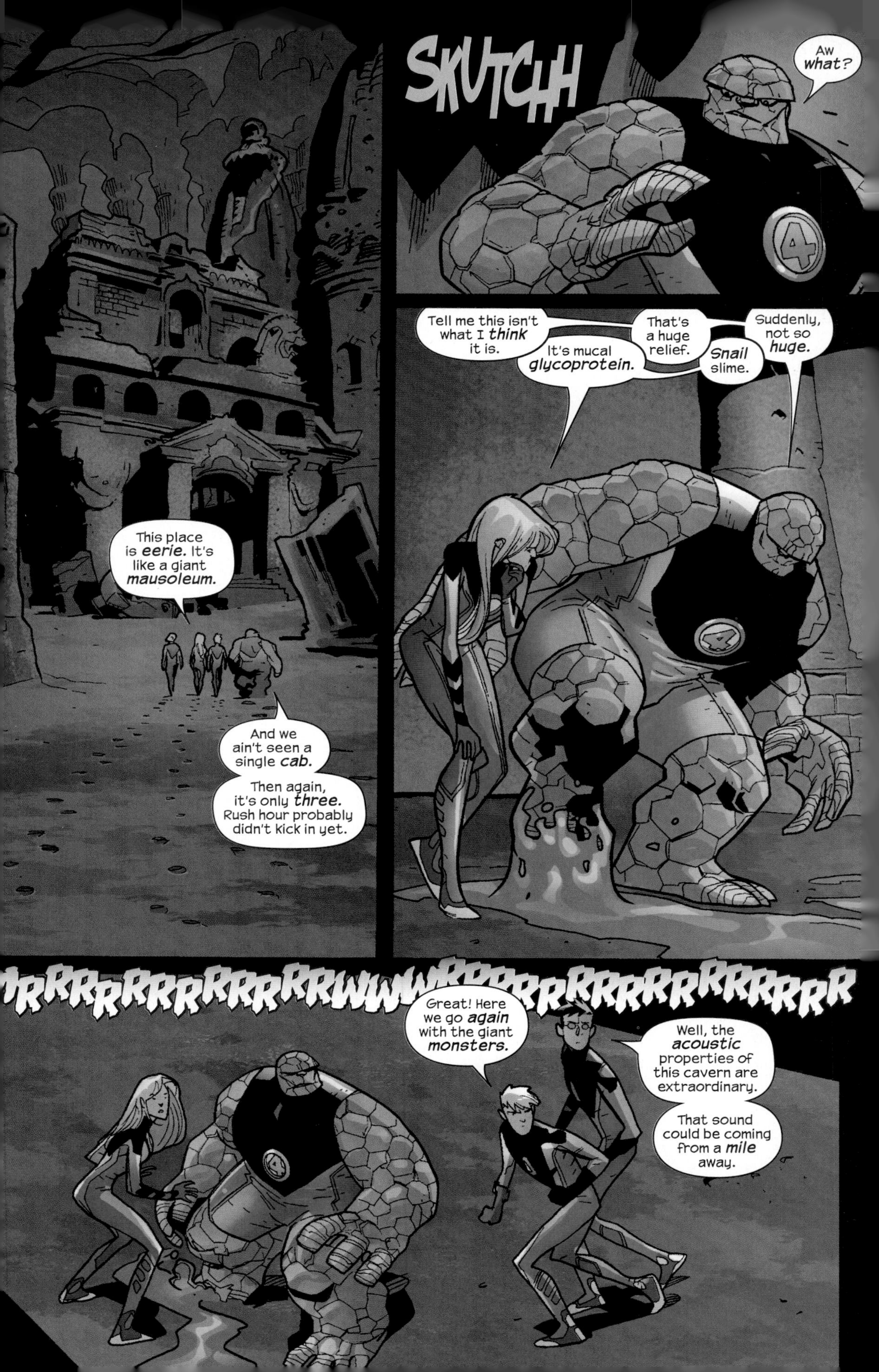
This place is *eerie.* It's like a giant *mausoleum.*
And we ain't seen a single *cab.*
Then again, it's only *three.* Rush hour probably didn't kick in yet.
SKUTCHH
Aw *what?*
Tell me this isn't what I *think* it is.
It's mucal *glycoprotein.*
That's a huge relief.
Snail slime.
Suddenly, not so *huge.*
RRRRRRRRRRRRWWWRRRRRRRRRRRRRRRRRR
Great! Here we go *again* with the giant *monsters.*
Well, the *acoustic* properties of this cavern are extraordinary.
That sound could be coming from a *mile* away.

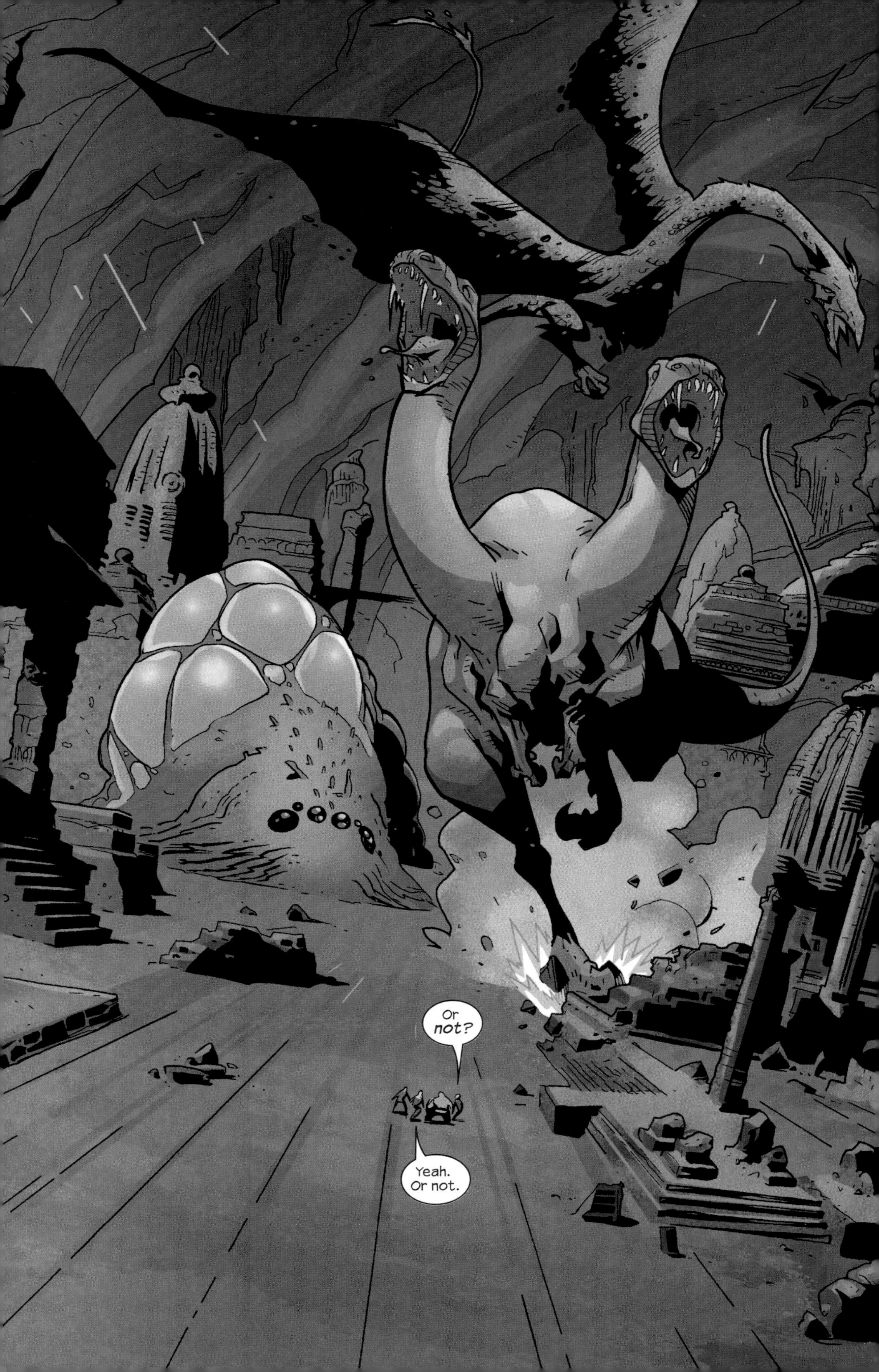
Or not?
Yeah. Or not.

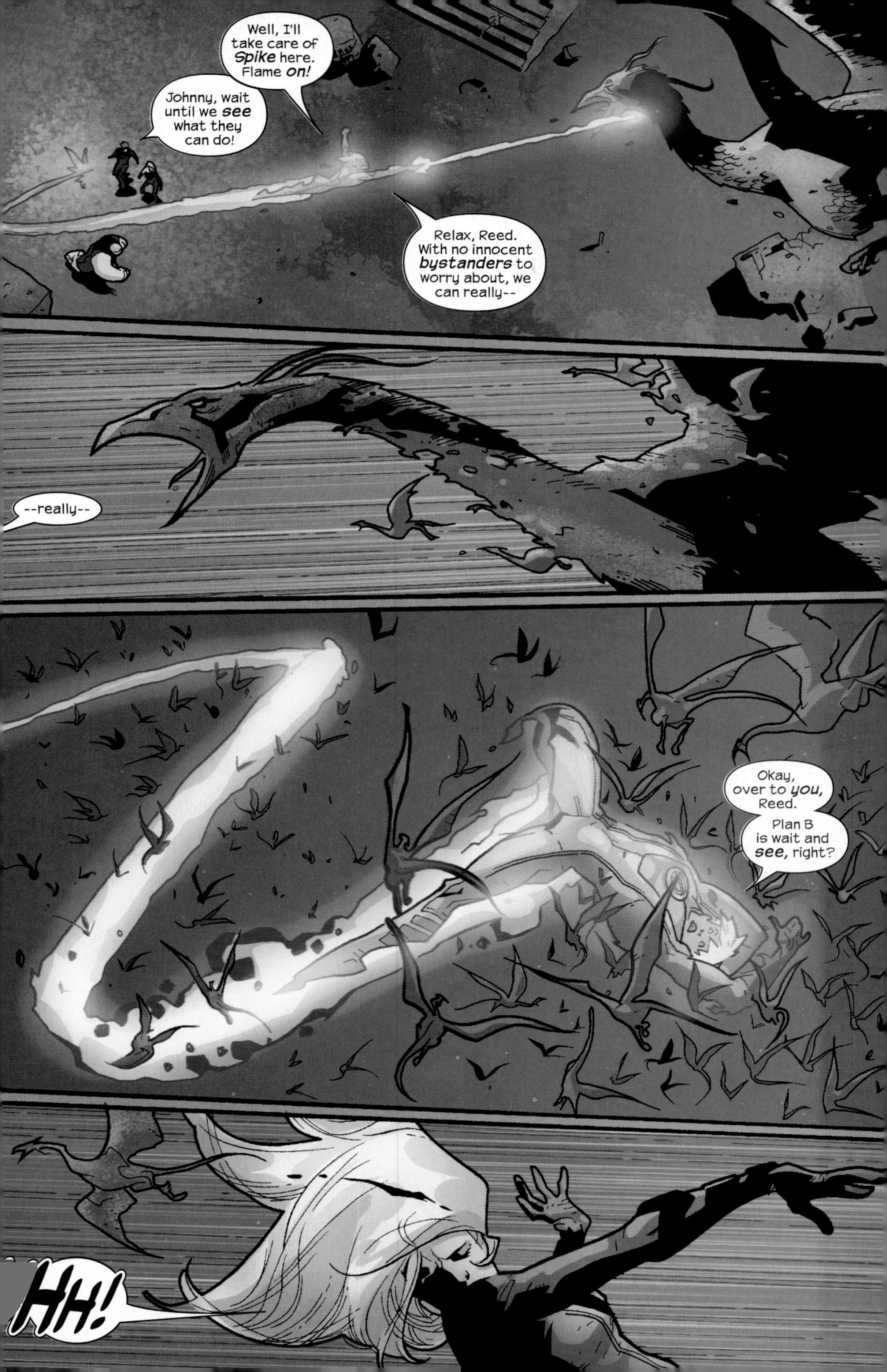
Well, I'll take care of *Spike* here. Flame *on!*
Johnny, wait until we *see* what they can do!
Relax, Reed. With no innocent *bystanders* to worry about, we can really--
--really--
Okay, over to *you,* Reed.
Plan B is wait and *see,* right?
HH!

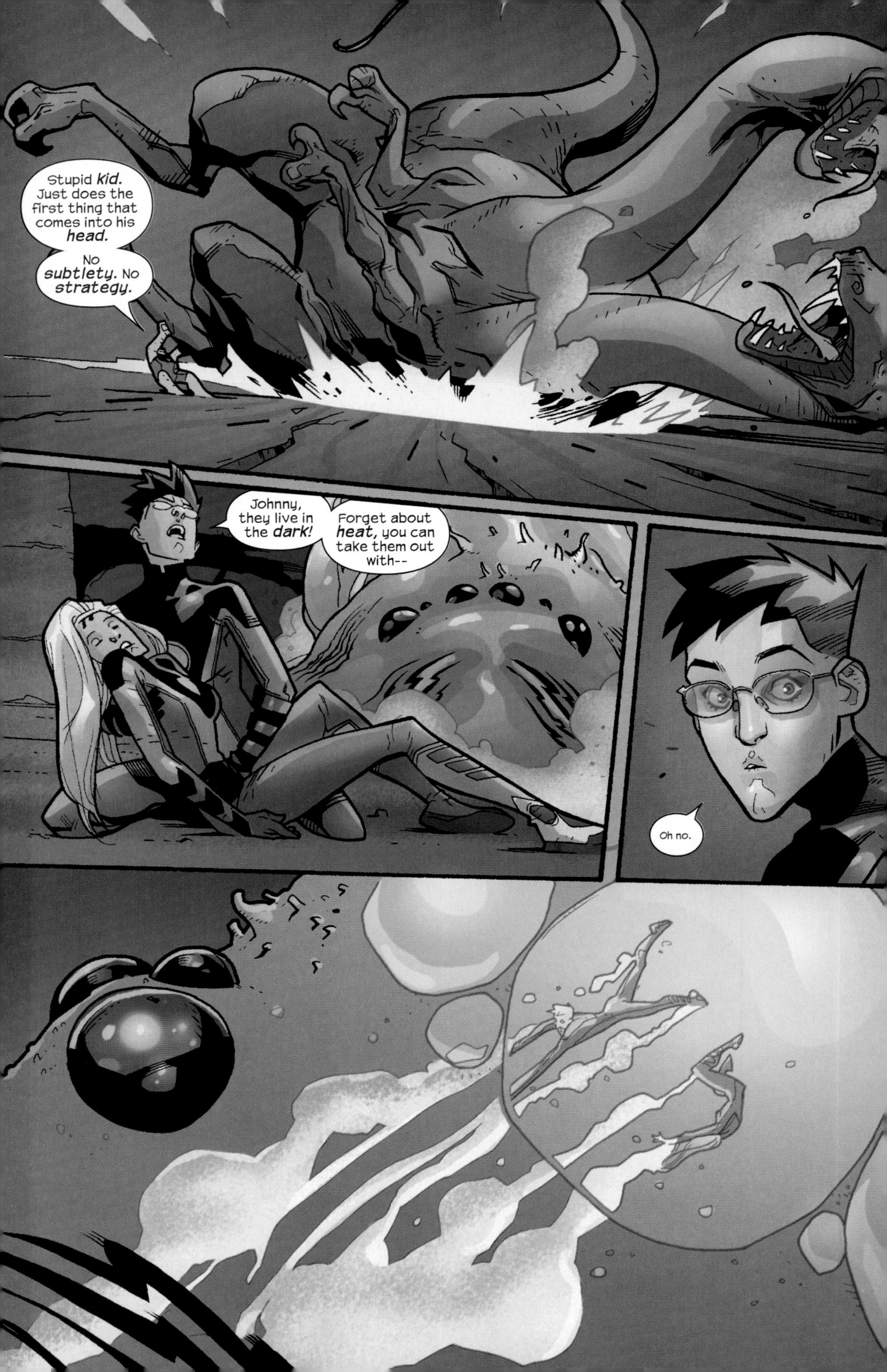

Stupid *kid.* Just does the first thing that comes into his *head.*
No *subtlety.* No *strategy.*
Johnny, they live in the *dark!*
Forget about *heat,* you can take them out with--
Oh no.

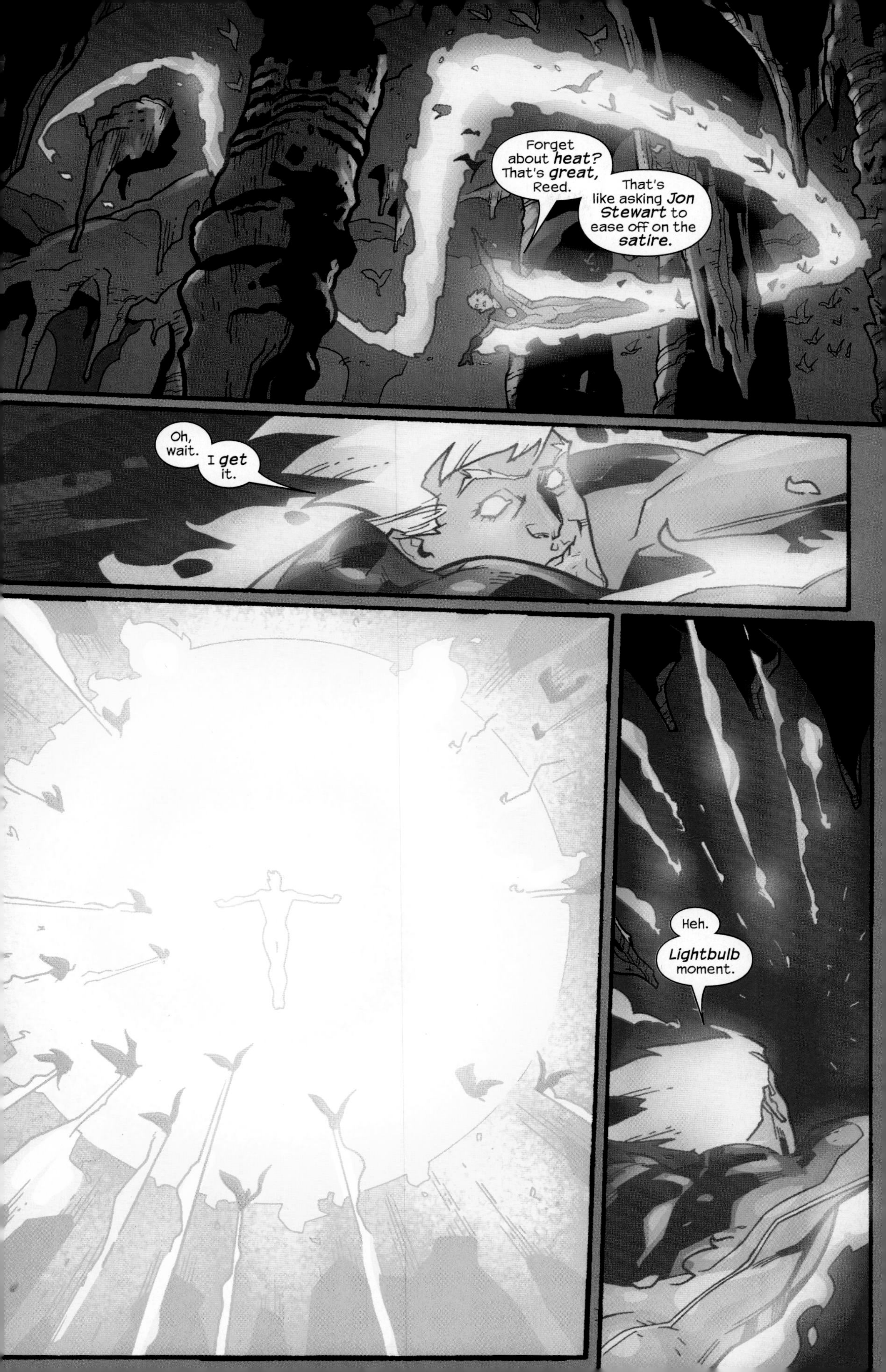

Forget about heat? That's great, Reed.
That's like asking Jon Stewart to ease off on the satire.
Oh, wait.
I get it.
Heh.
Lightbulb moment.

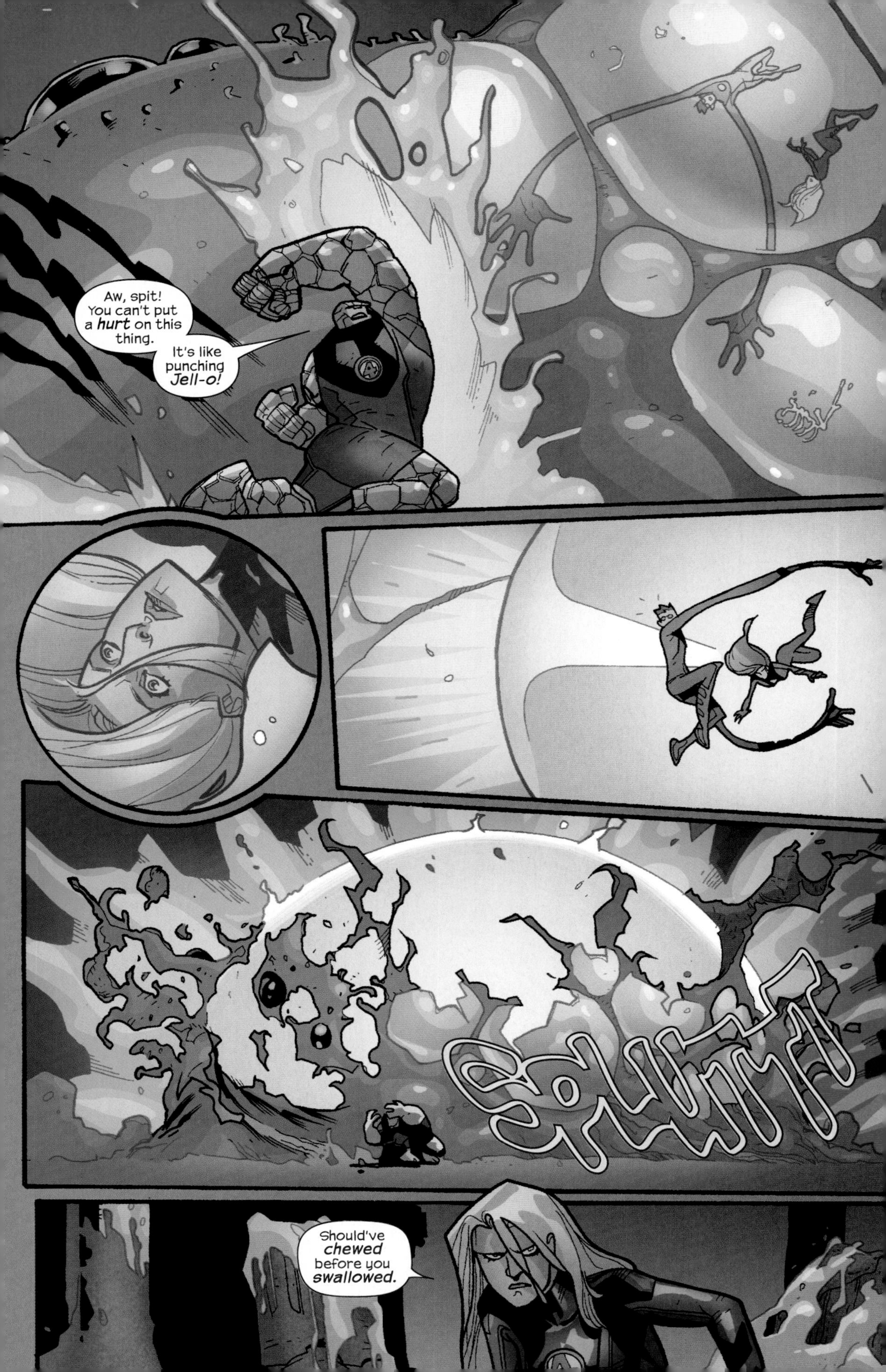
Aw, spit! You can't put a *hurt* on this thing.
It's like punching *Jell-o!*
SQUUNCH
Should've *chewed* before you *swallowed.*

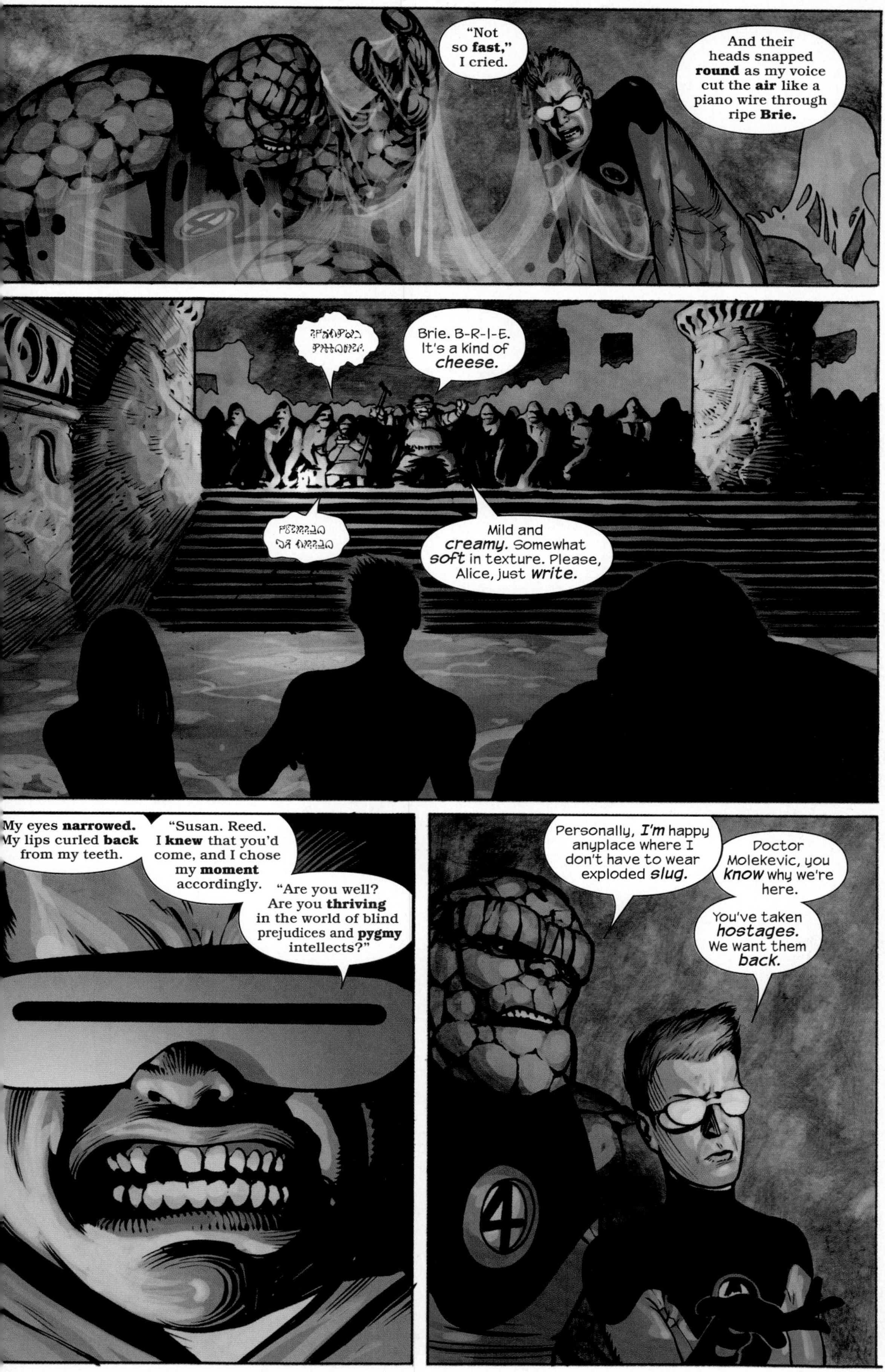
"Not so **fast,**" I cried.
And their heads snapped **round** as my voice cut the **air** like a piano wire through ripe **Brie.**
Brie. B-R-I-E. It's a kind of *cheese.*
Mild and *creamy.* Somewhat *soft* in texture. Please, Alice, just *write.*
My eyes **narrowed.** My lips curled **back** from my teeth.
"Susan. Reed. I **knew** that you'd come, and I chose my **moment** accordingly.
"Are you well? Are you **thriving** in the world of blind prejudices and **pygmy** intellects?"
Personally, *I'm* happy anyplace where I don't have to wear exploded *slug.*
Doctor Molekevic, you *know* why we're here.
You've taken *hostages.* We want them *back.*

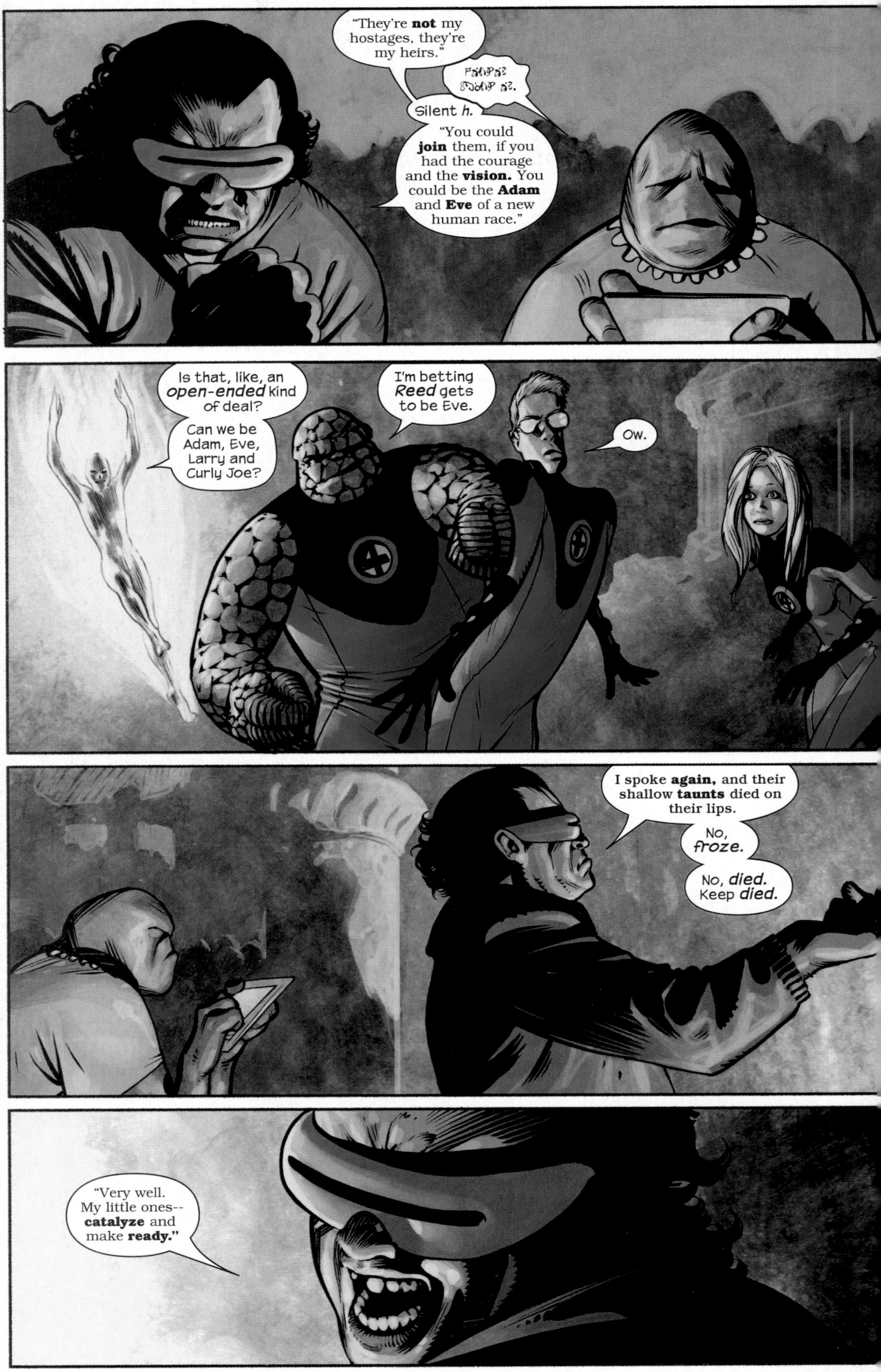
"They're **not** my hostages, they're my heirs."
Silent *h.*
"You could **join** them, if you had the courage and the **vision.** You could be the **Adam** and **Eve** of a new human race."
Is that, like, an *open-ended* kind of deal?
Can we be Adam, Eve, Larry and Curly Joe?
I'm betting *Reed* gets to be Eve.
Ow.
I spoke **again,** and their shallow **taunts** died on their lips.
No, *froze.*
No, *died.* Keep *died.*
"Very well. My little ones-- **catalyze** and make **ready.**"

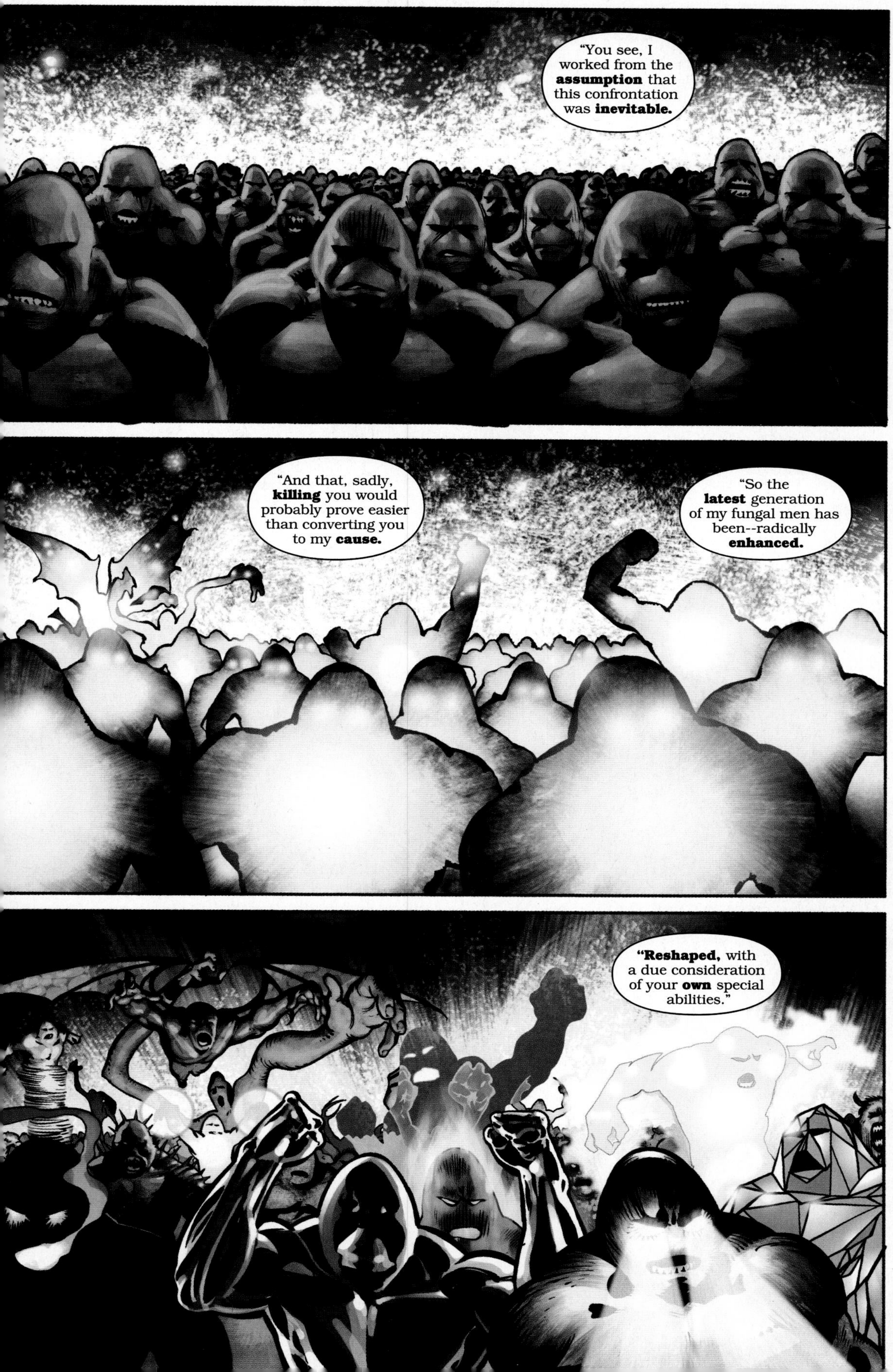
"You see, I worked from the **assumption** that this confrontation was **inevitable.**
"And that, sadly, **killing** you would probably prove easier than converting you to my **cause.**
"So the **latest** generation of my fungal men has been--radically **enhanced.**
"**Reshaped,** with a due consideration of your **own** special abilities."

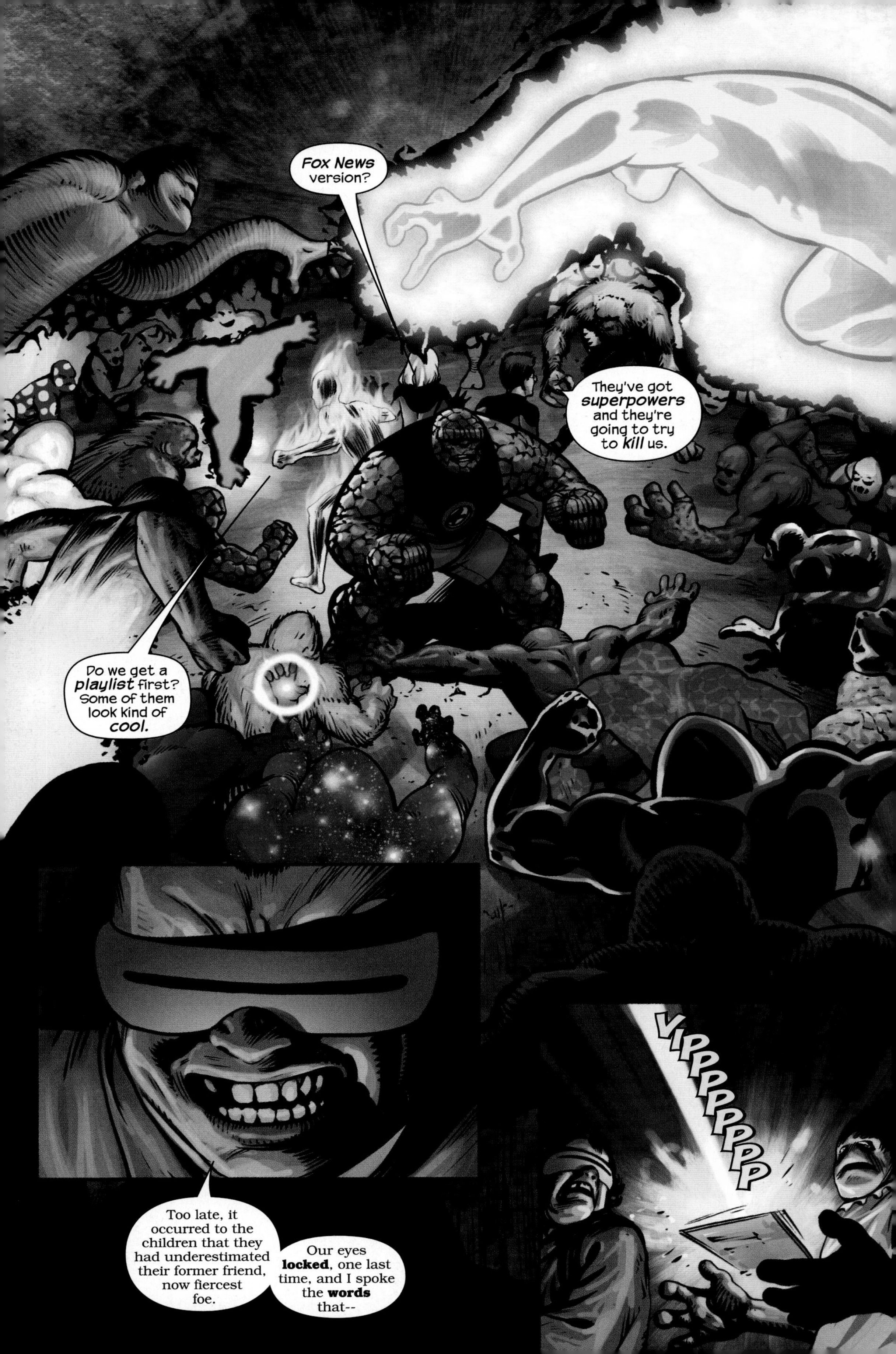
Fox News version?
They've got superpowers and they're going to try to kill us.
Do we get a playlist first? Some of them look kind of cool.
Too late, it occurred to the children that they had underestimated their former friend, now fiercest foe.
Our eyes locked, one last time, and I spoke the words that--
VIPPPPPP

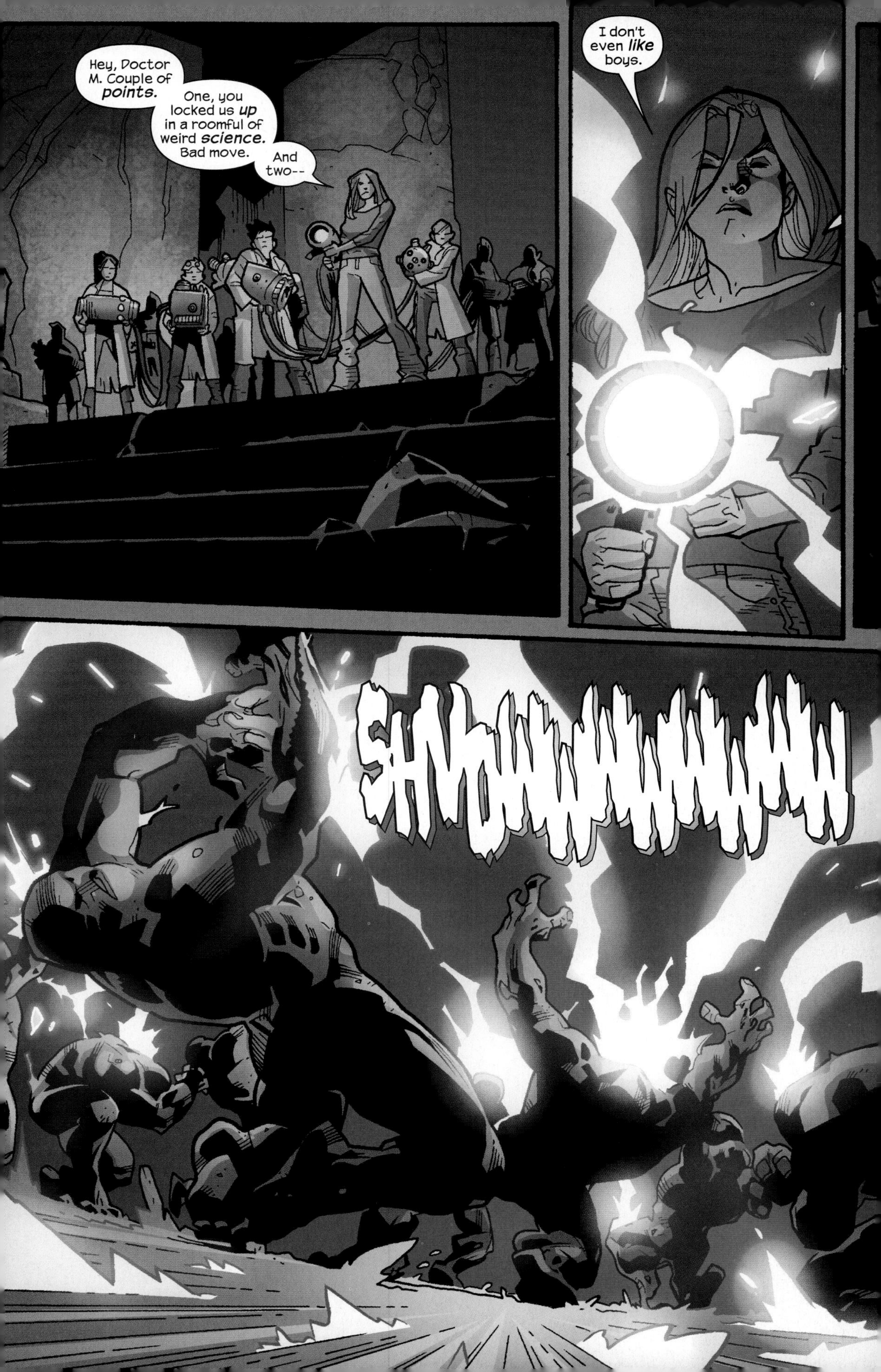
Hey, Doctor M. Couple of points.
One, you locked us up in a roomful of weird science. Bad move.
And two--
I don't even like boys.
SHMOWWWWWWWWW

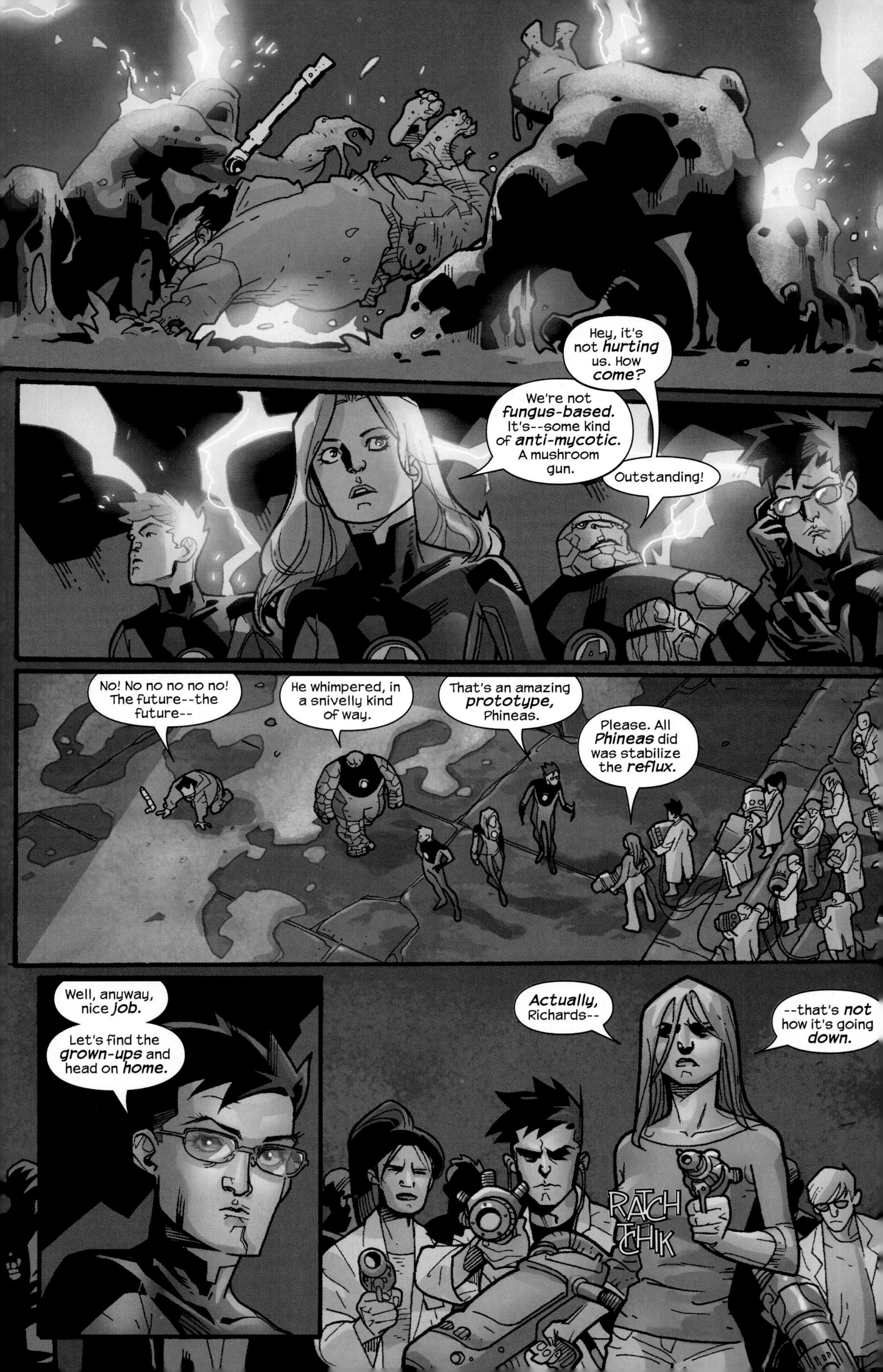

Hey, it's not hurting us. How come?
We're not fungus-based. It's--some kind of anti-mycotic. A mushroom gun.
Outstanding!
No! No no no no no! The future--the future--
He whimpered, in a snivelly kind of way.
That's an amazing prototype, Phineas.
Please. All Phineas did was stabilize the reflux.
Well, anyway, nice job.
Let's find the grown-ups and head on home.
Actually, Richards--
--that's not how it's going down.
RATCH CHIK

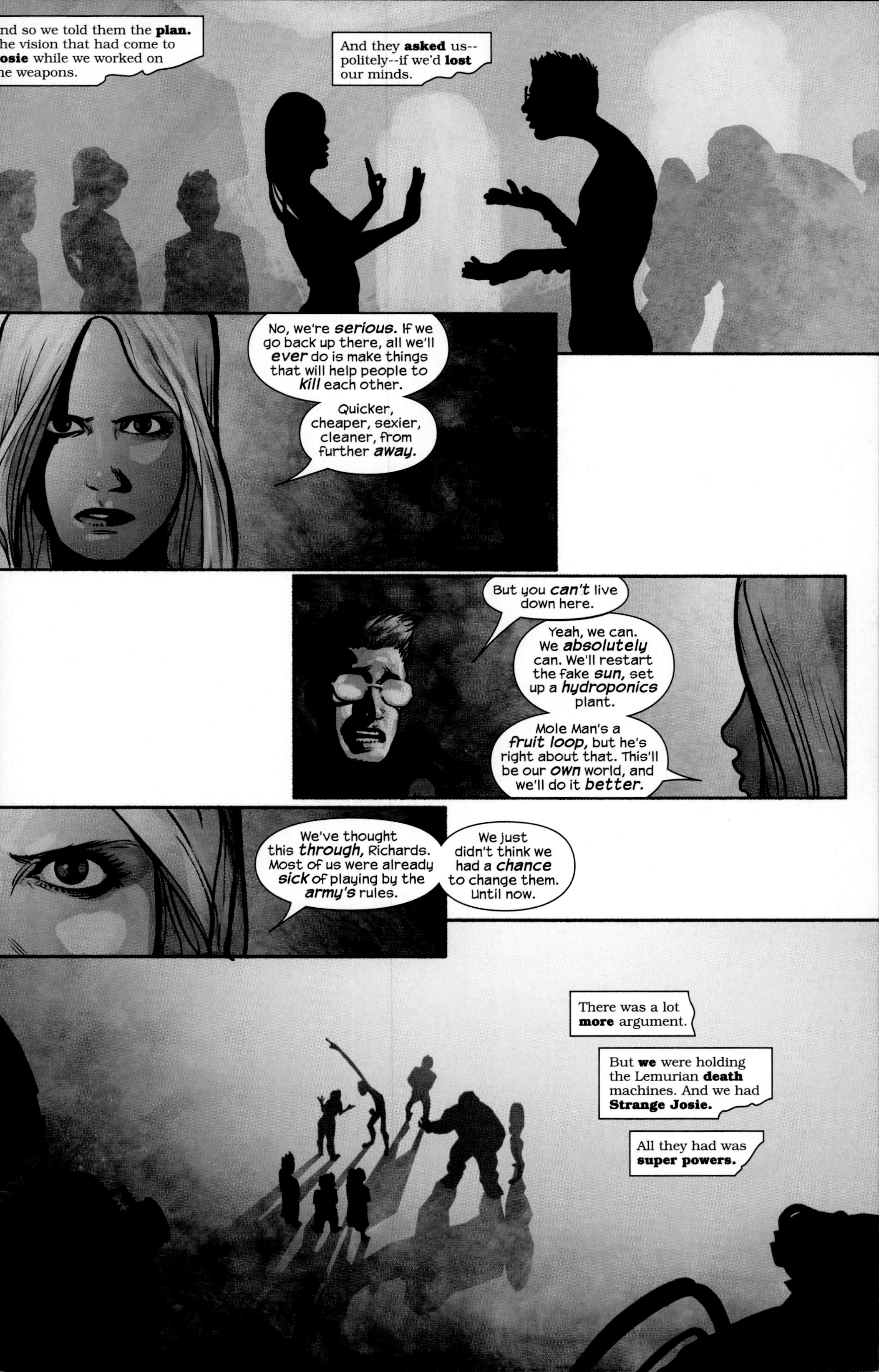

nd so we told them the **plan.** he vision that had come to osie while we worked on he weapons.
And they **asked** us--politely--if we'd **lost** our minds.
No, we're *serious.* If we go back up there, all we'll *ever* do is make things that will help people to *kill* each other.
Quicker, cheaper, sexier, cleaner, from further *away.*
But you *can't* live down here.
Yeah, we can. We *absolutely* can. We'll restart the fake *sun,* set up a *hydroponics* plant.
Mole Man's a *fruit loop,* but he's right about that. This'll be our *own* world, and we'll do it *better.*
We've thought this *through,* Richards. Most of us were already *sick* of playing by the *army's* rules.
We just didn't think we had a *chance* to change them. Until now.
There was a lot **more** argument.
But **we** were holding the Lemurian **death** machines. And we had **Strange Josie.**
All they had was **super powers.**

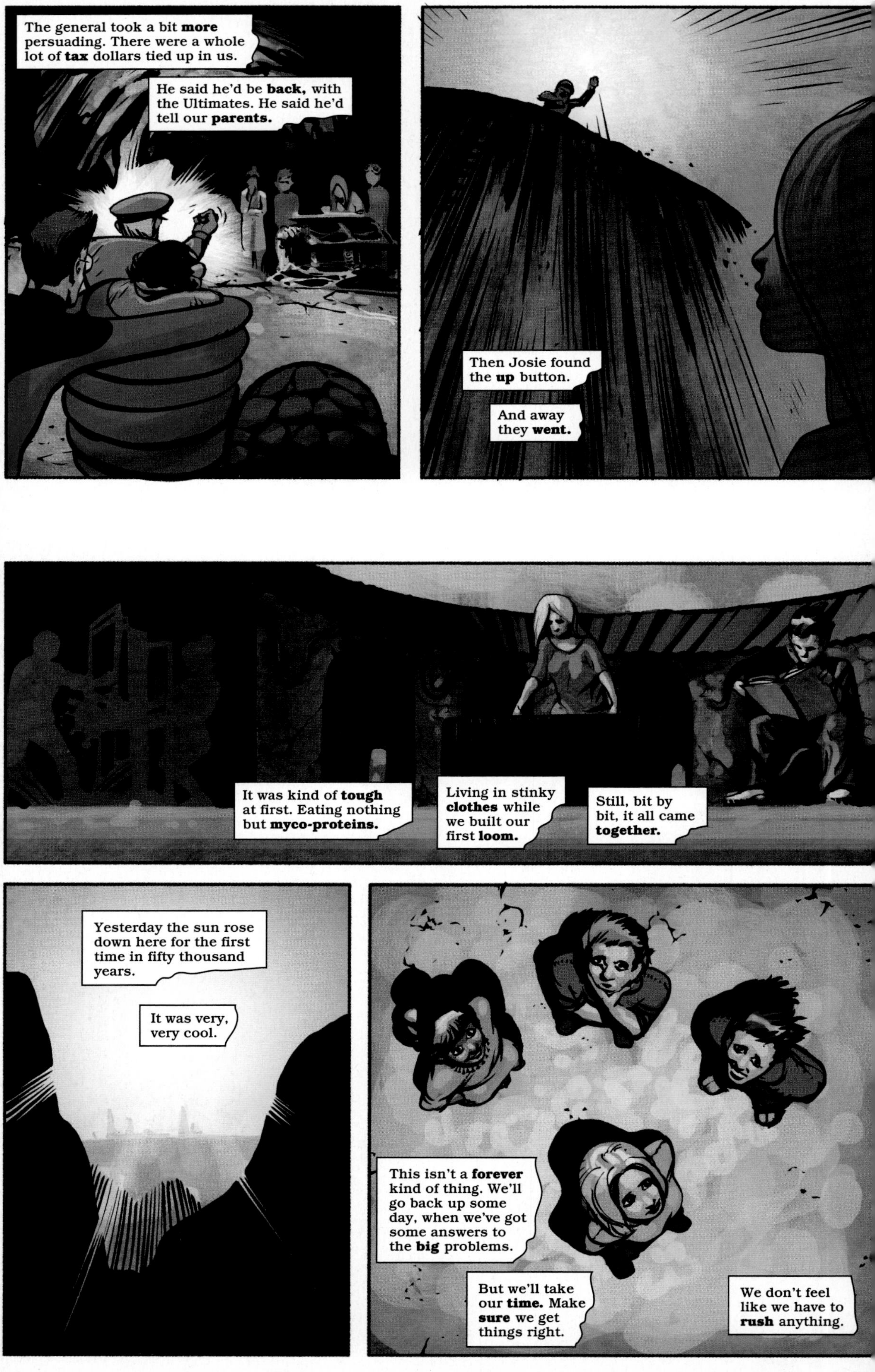
The general took a bit more persuading. There were a whole lot of tax dollars tied up in us.
He said he'd be back, with the Ultimates. He said he'd tell our parents.
Then Josie found the up button.
And away they went.
It was kind of tough at first. Eating nothing but myco-proteins.
Living in stinky clothes while we built our first loom.
Still, bit by bit, it all came together.
Yesterday the sun rose down here for the first time in fifty thousand years.
It was very, very cool.
This isn't a forever kind of thing. We'll go back up some day, when we've got some answers to the big problems.
But we'll take our time. Make sure we get things right.
We don't feel like we have to rush anything.

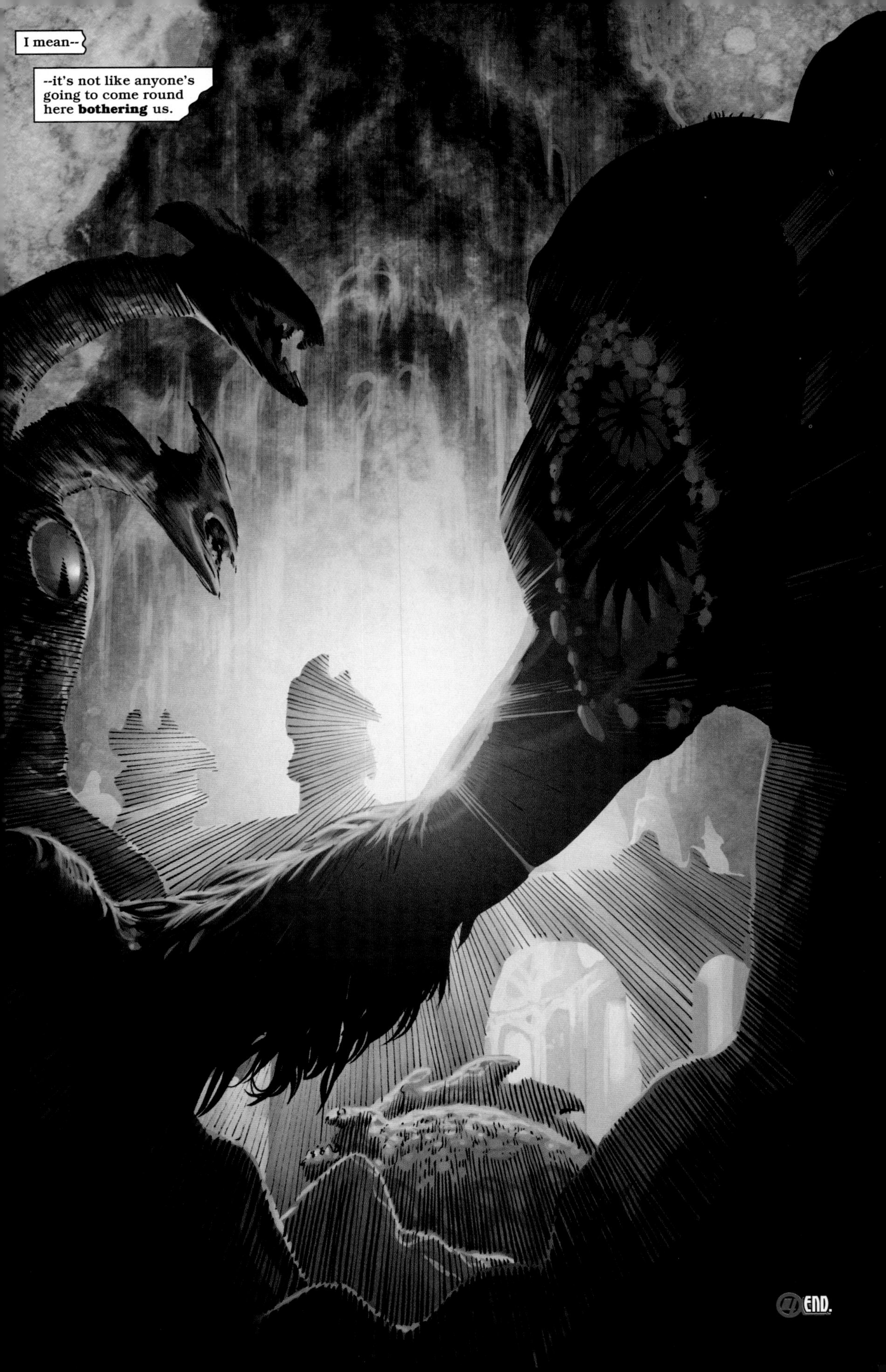
I mean--
--it's not like anyone's going to come round here **bothering** us.
END.

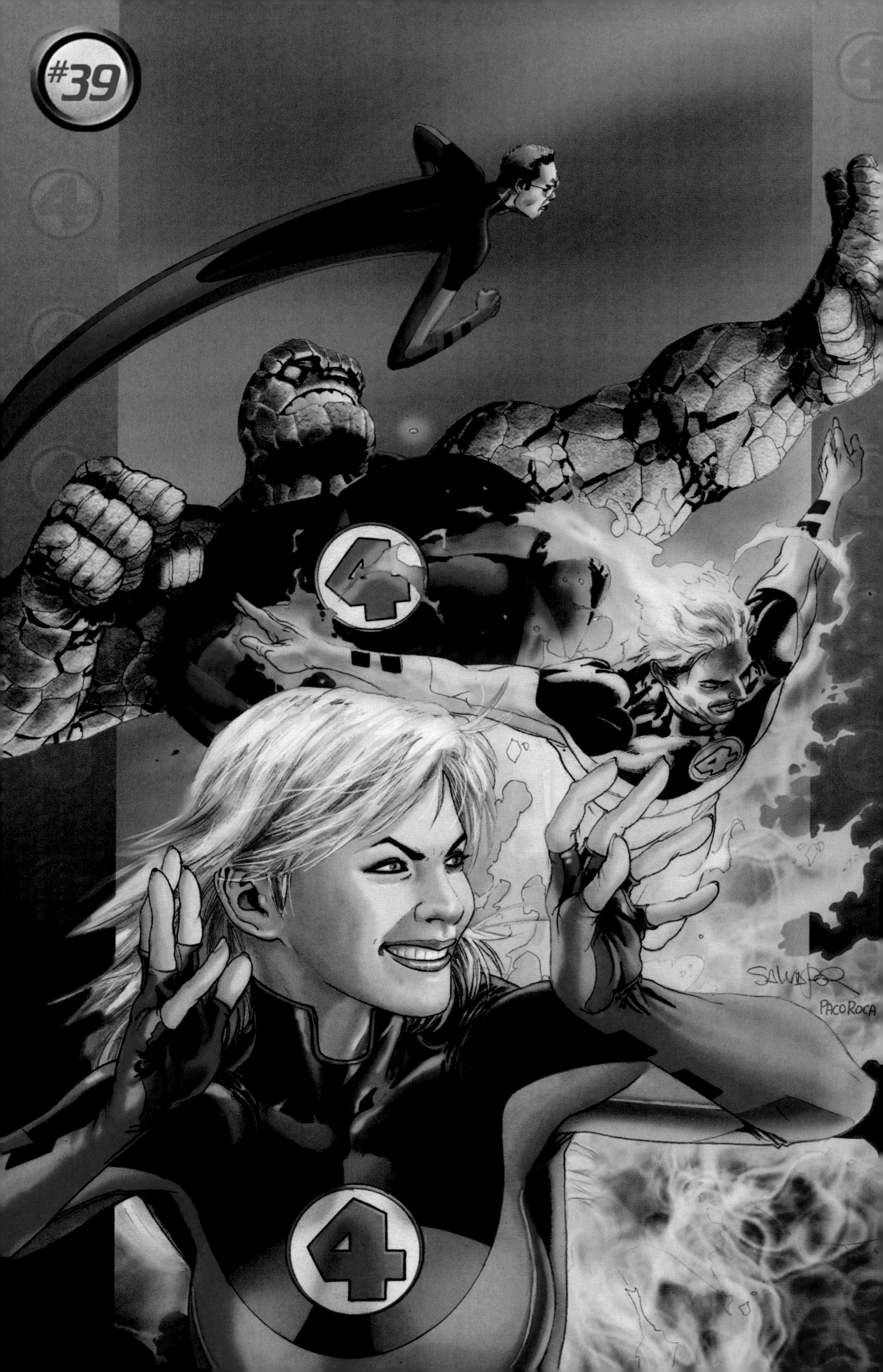
#39
SALVADOR
PACO ROCA

PREVIOUSLY IN ULTIMATE FANTASTIC FOUR:

Reed Richards, handpicked to join the Baxter Building think tank of young geniuses, spent his youth developing a teleport system that transported solid matter into a parallel universe called the N-Zone. Its first full-scale test was witnessed by Reed, fellow think tank members Sue Storm and her brother Johnny, as well as Reed's childhood friend Ben Grimm.

There was an accident. The quartet's genetic structures were scrambled and recombined in a fantastically strange way. Reed's body stretches and flows like water. Ben looks like a thing carved from desert rock. Sue can become invisible. Johnny generates flame. Together, they are the Fantastic Four!

After travelling to another dimension and becoming caught in the midst of an interstellar war, the Fantastic Four have returned to Earth. While Reed obsesses over plans for a powerful cosmic device—plans that were planted in his mind by an alien force—the rest of the FF try to resume their "normal" lives...

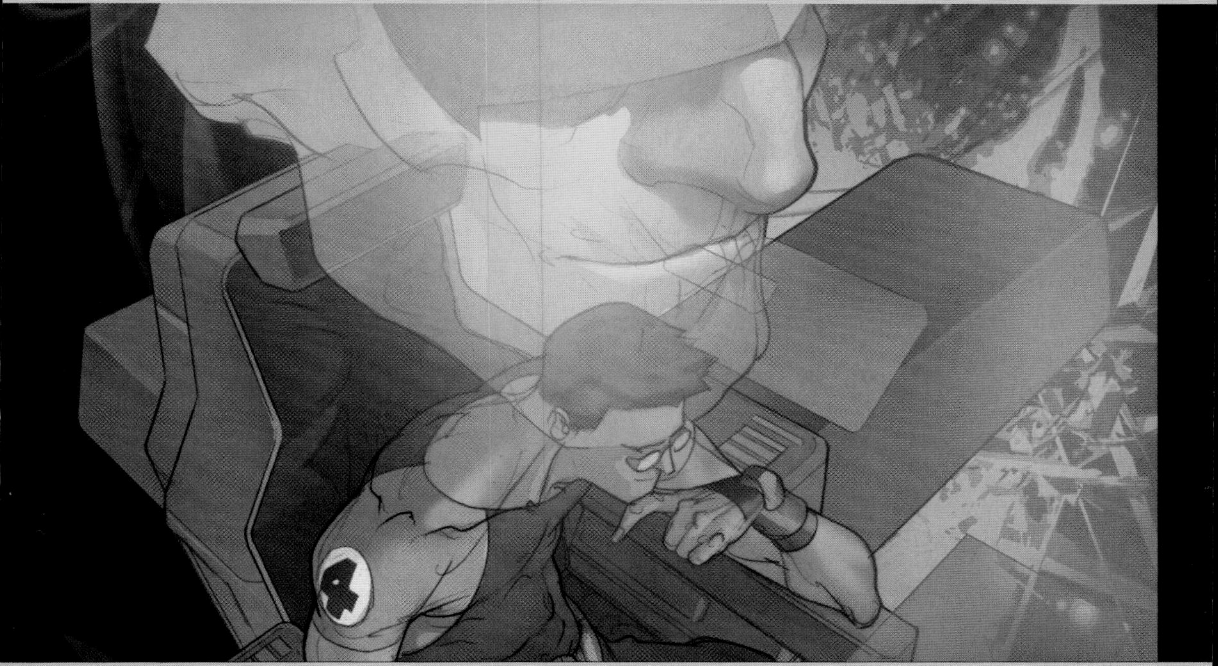

DEVILS

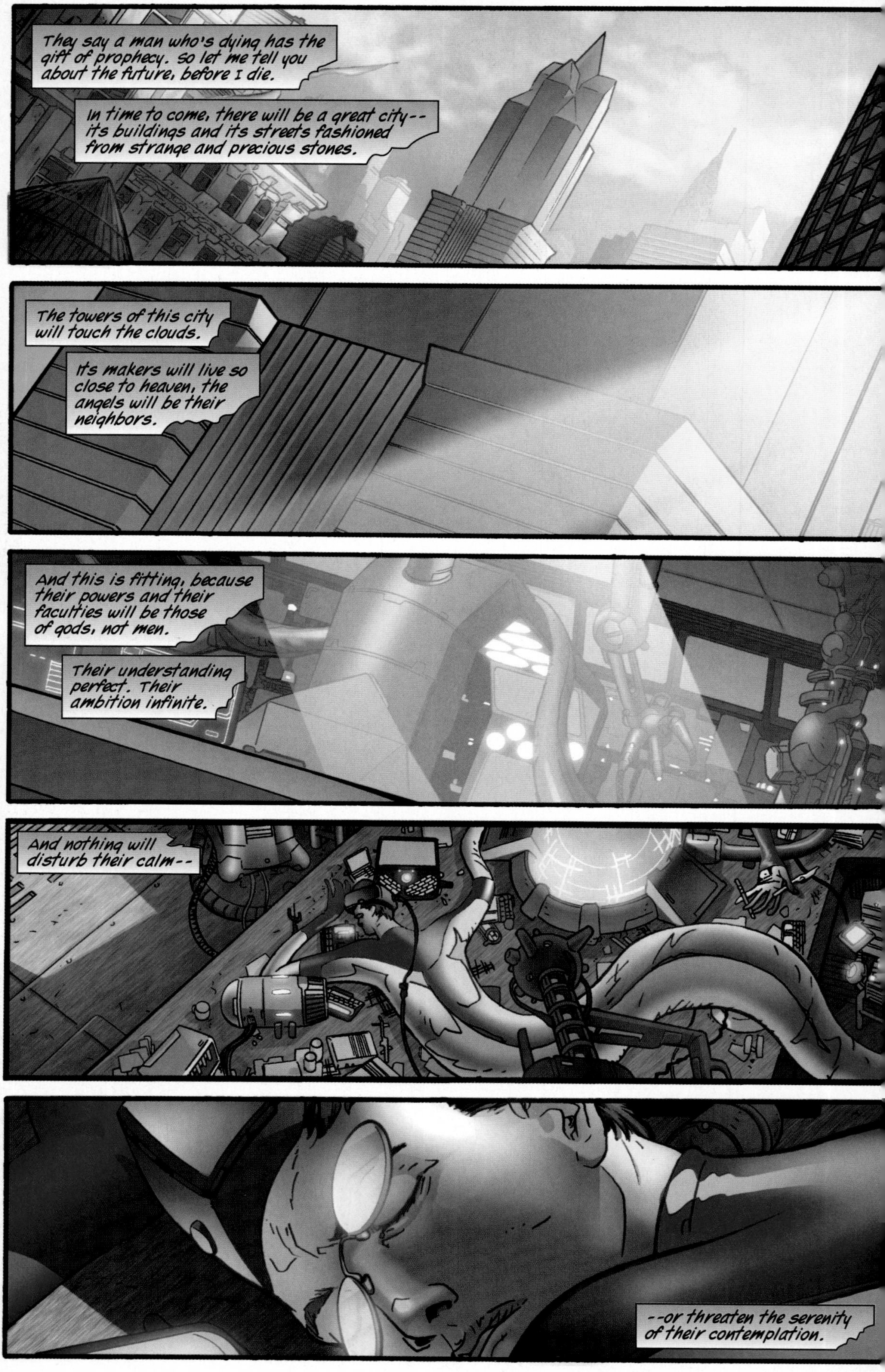
They say a man who's dying has the gift of prophecy. So let me tell you about the future, before I die.
In time to come, there will be a great city--its buildings and its streets fashioned from strange and precious stones.
The towers of this city will touch the clouds.
Its makers will live so close to heaven, the angels will be their neighbors.
And this is fitting, because their powers and their faculties will be those of gods, not men.
Their understanding perfect. Their ambition infinite.
And nothing will disturb their calm--
--or threaten the serenity of their contemplation.

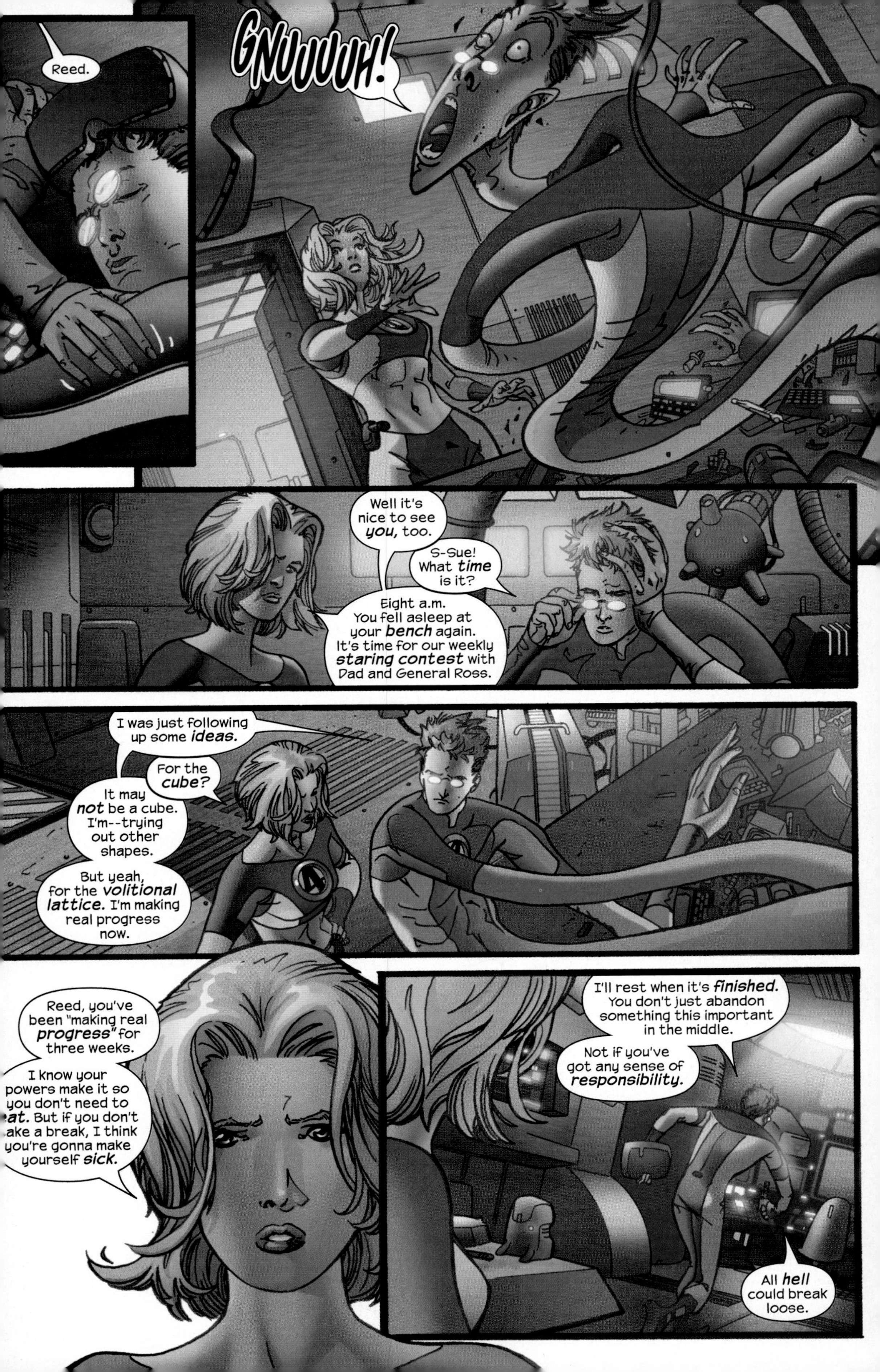

Reed.
GNUUUUH!
Well it's nice to see you, too.
S-Sue! What time is it?
Eight a.m. You fell asleep at your bench again. It's time for our weekly staring contest with Dad and General Ross.
I was just following up some ideas.
For the cube?
It may not be a cube. I'm--trying out other shapes.
But yeah, for the volitional lattice. I'm making real progress now.
Reed, you've been "making real progress" for three weeks.
I know your powers make it so you don't need to eat. But if you don't take a break, I think you're gonna make yourself sick.
I'll rest when it's finished. You don't just abandon something this important in the middle.
Not if you've got any sense of responsibility.
All hell could break loose.

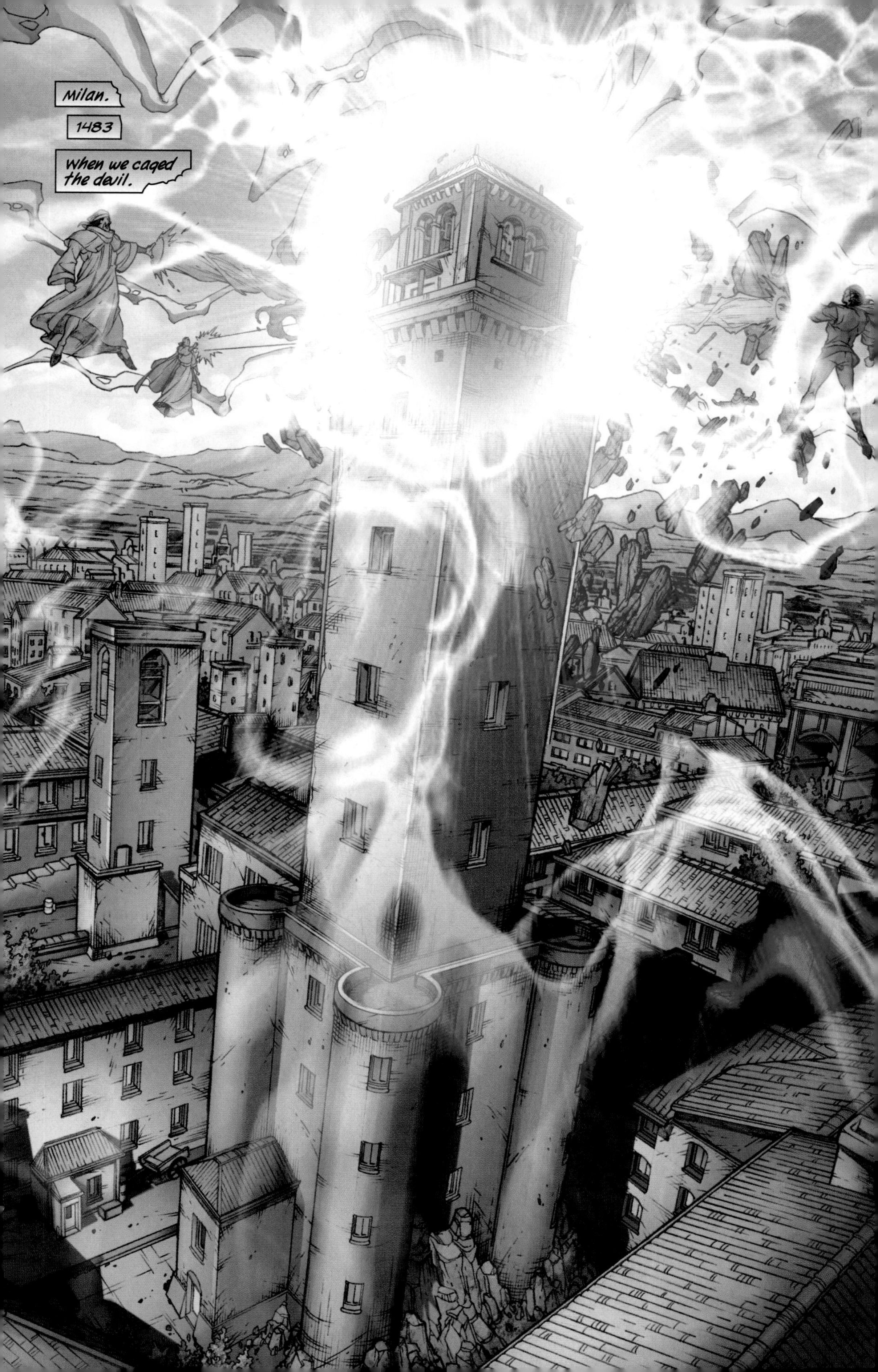
Milan.
1483
When we caged the devil.

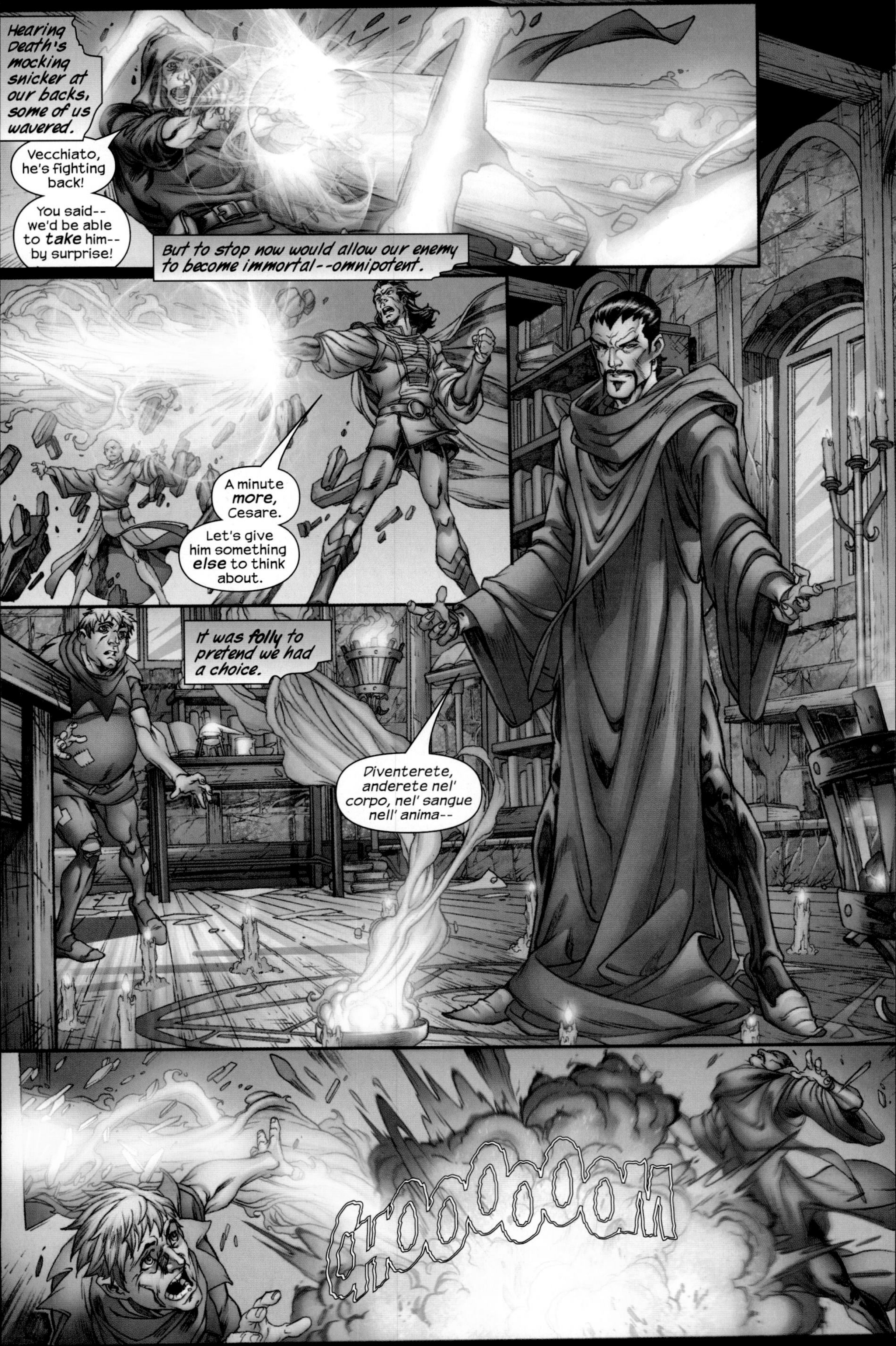
Hearing Death's mocking snicker at our backs, some of us wavered.
Vecchiato, he's fighting back!
You said-- we'd be able to take him-- by surprise!
But to stop now would allow our enemy to become immortal--omnipotent.
A minute more, Cesare.
Let's give him something else to think about.
It was folly to pretend we had a choice.
Diventerete, anderete nel' corpo, nel' sangue nell' anima--
CHOOOOOOOM

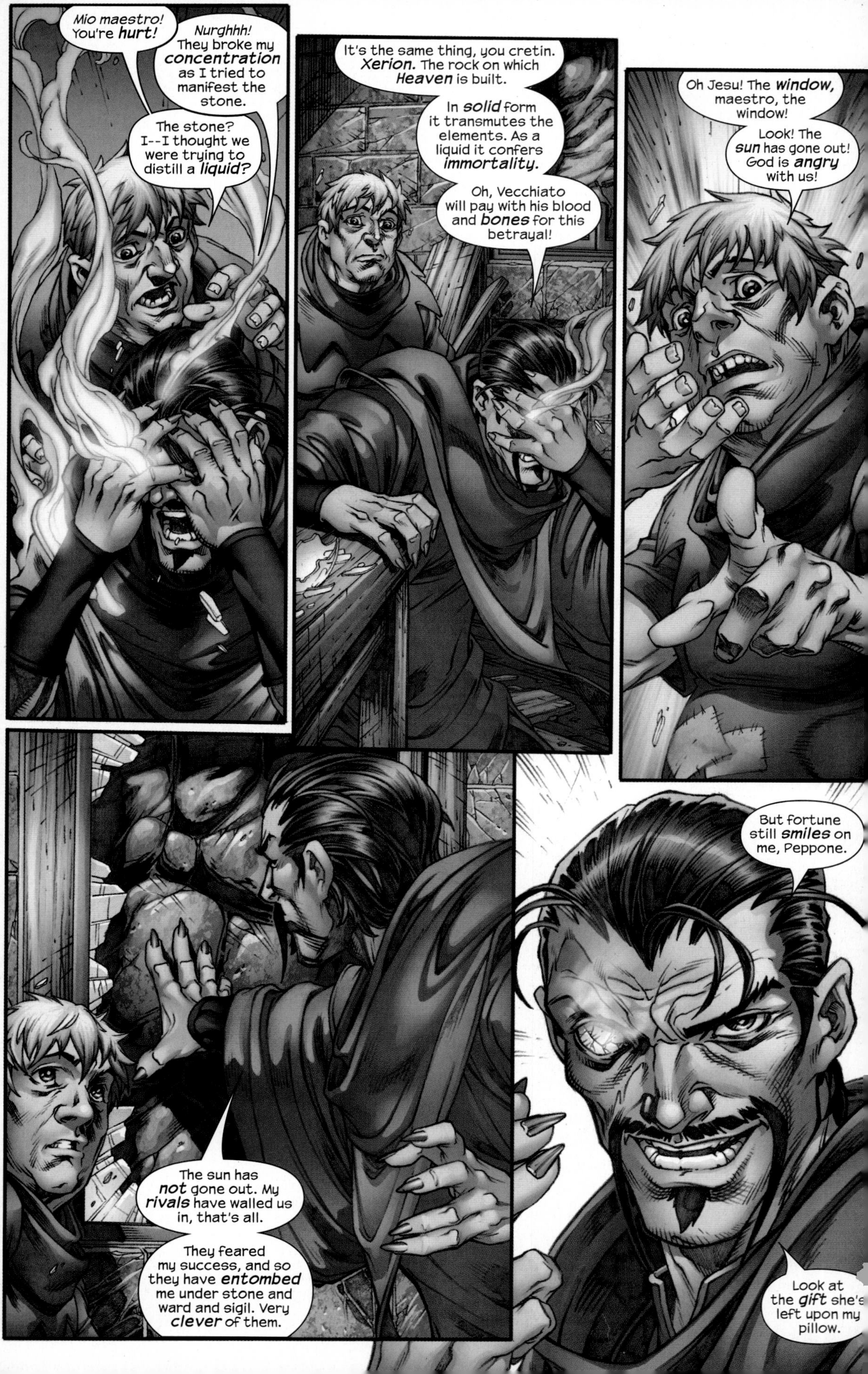
Mio maestro! You're hurt!
Nurghhh! They broke my concentration as I tried to manifest the stone.
The stone? I--I thought we were trying to distill a liquid?
It's the same thing, you cretin. Xerion. The rock on which Heaven is built.
In solid form it transmutes the elements. As a liquid it confers immortality.
Oh, Vecchiato will pay with his blood and bones for this betrayal!
Oh Jesu! The window, maestro, the window!
Look! The sun has gone out! God is angry with us!
The sun has not gone out. My rivals have walled us in, that's all.
They feared my success, and so they have entombed me under stone and ward and sigil. Very clever of them.
But fortune still smiles on me, Peppone.
Look at the gift she's left upon my pillow.

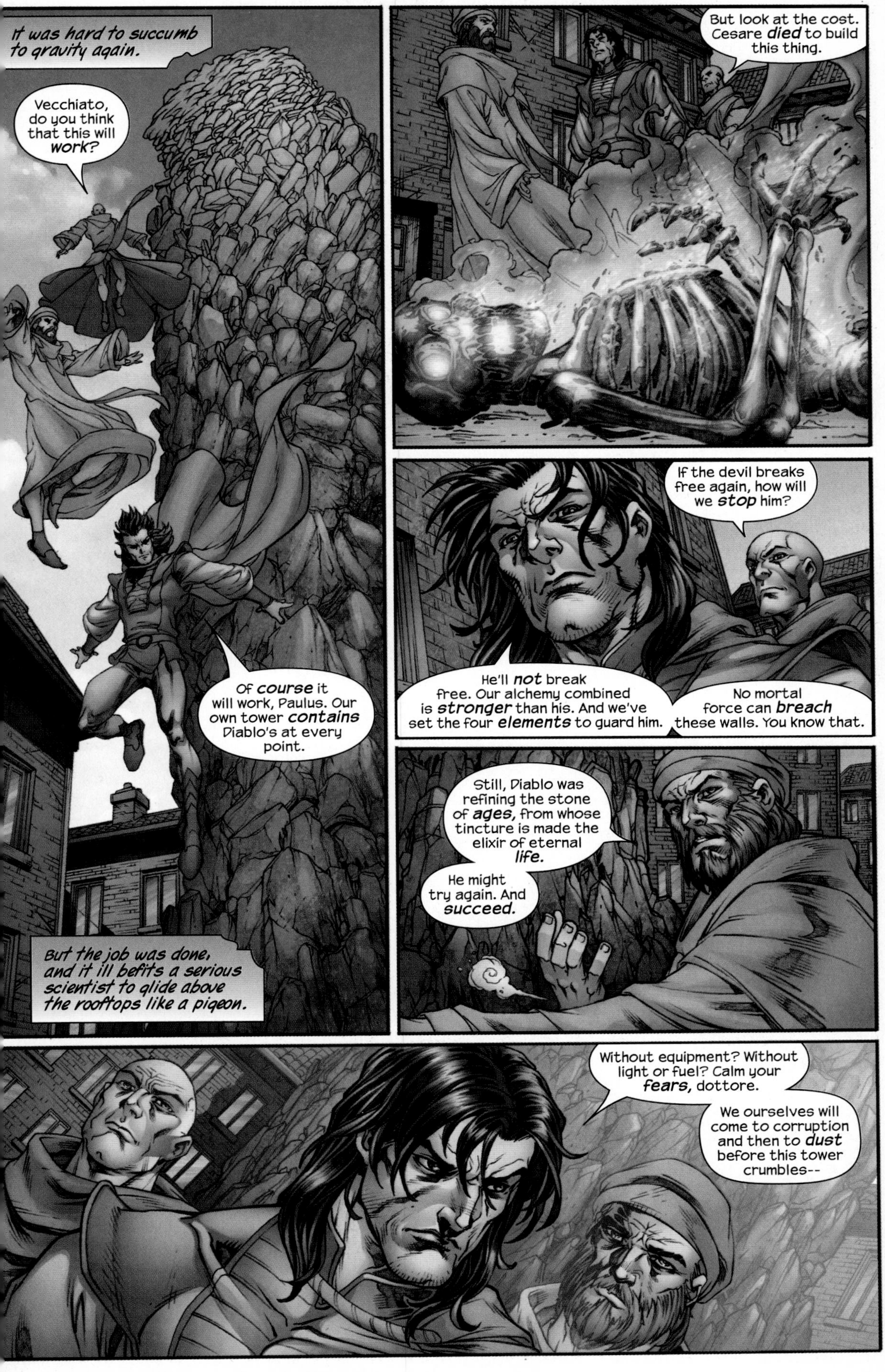
It was hard to succumb to gravity again.
Vecchiato, do you think that this will work?
Of course it will work, Paulus. Our own tower contains Diablo's at every point.
But the job was done, and it ill befits a serious scientist to glide above the rooftops like a pigeon.
But look at the cost. Cesare died to build this thing.
If the devil breaks free again, how will we stop him?
He'll not break free. Our alchemy combined is stronger than his. And we've set the four elements to guard him.
No mortal force can breach these walls. You know that.
Still, Diablo was refining the stone of ages, from whose tincture is made the elixir of eternal life.
He might try again. And succeed.
Without equipment? Without light or fuel? Calm your fears, dottore.
We ourselves will come to corruption and then to dust before this tower crumbles--

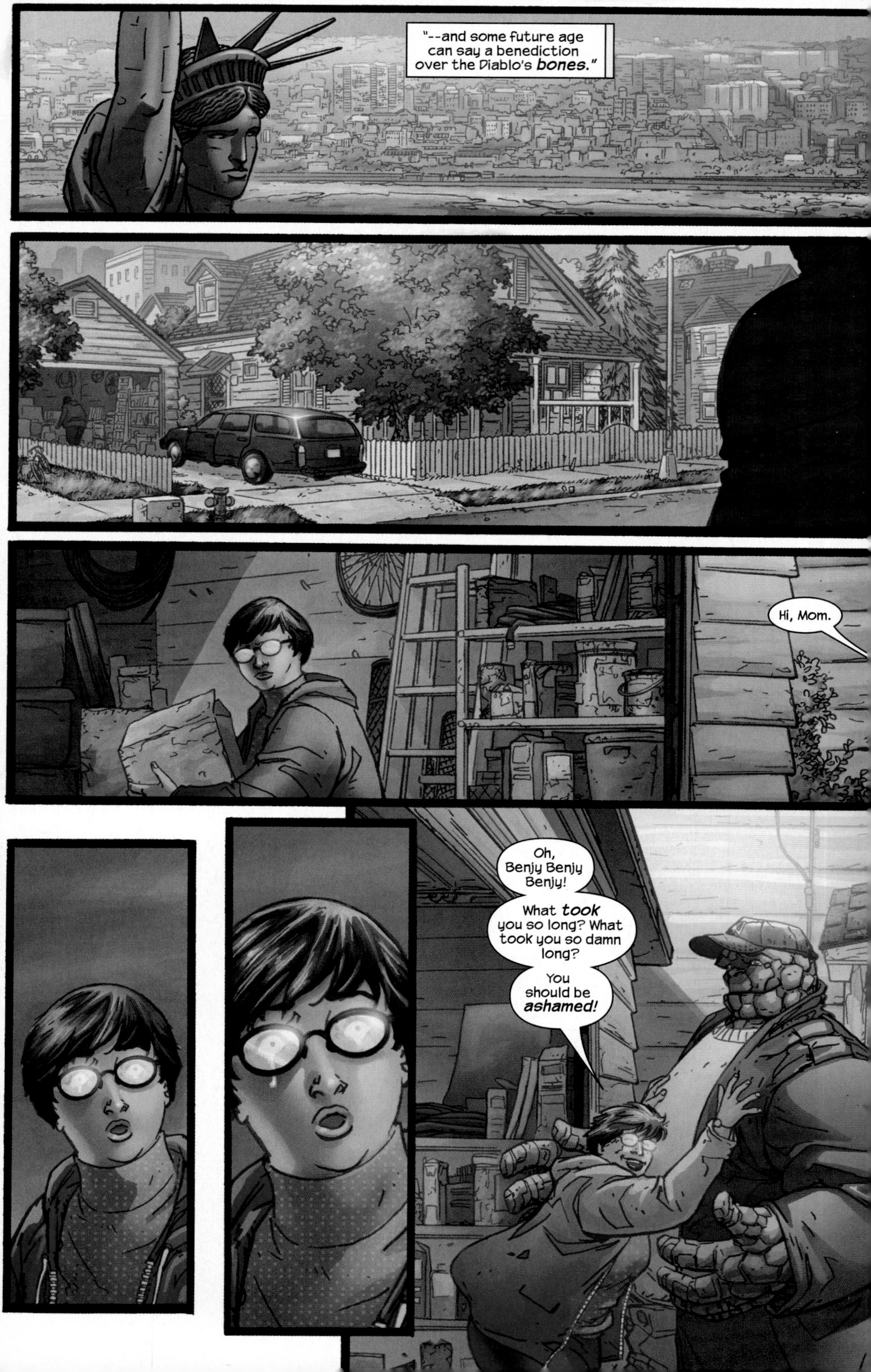
"--and some future age can say a benediction over the Diablo's *bones.*"
Hi, Mom.
Oh, Benjy Benjy Benjy!
What *took* you so long? What took you so damn long?
You should be *ashamed!*

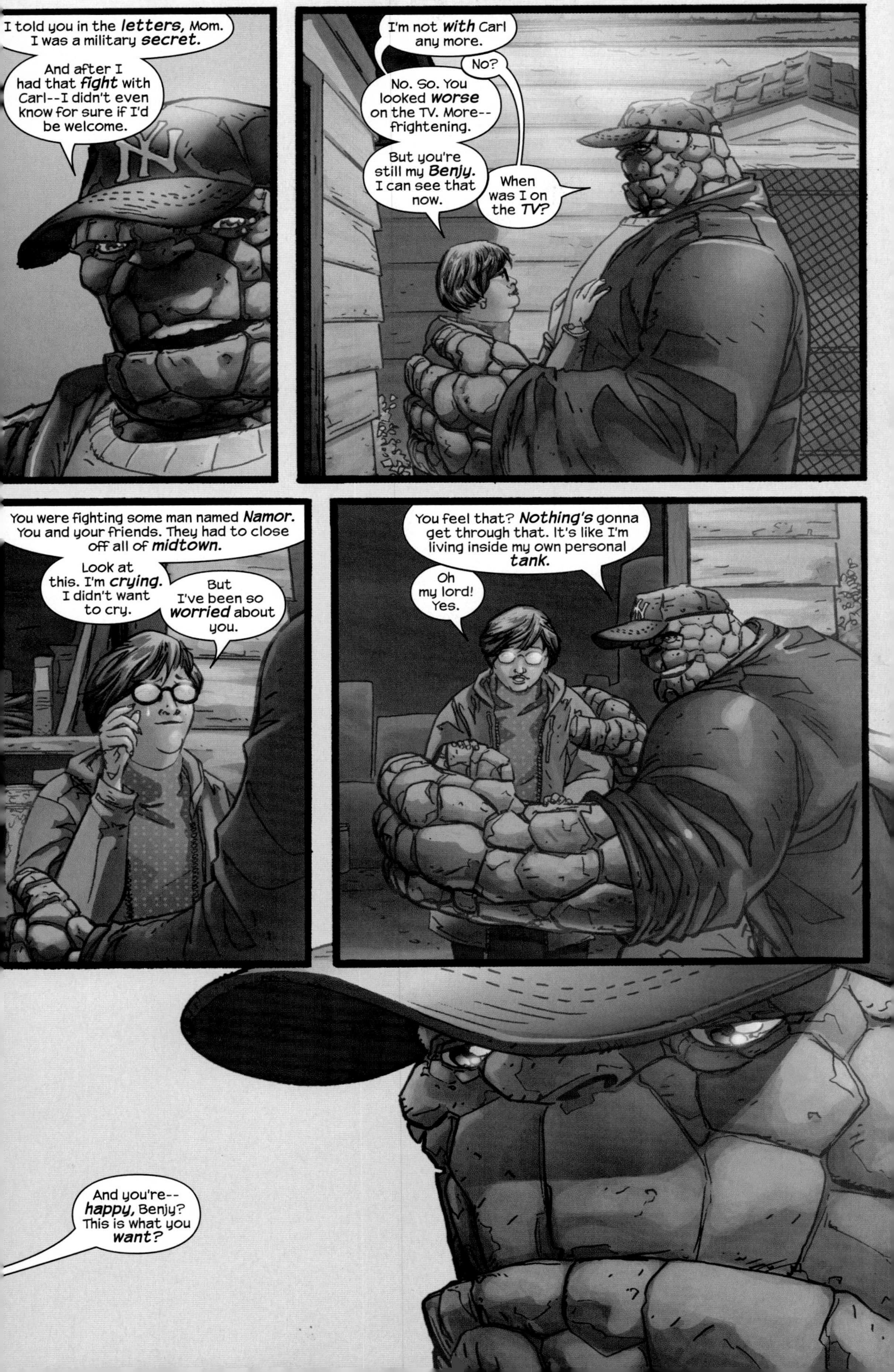
I told you in the letters, Mom. I was a military secret.
And after I had that fight with Carl--I didn't even know for sure if I'd be welcome.
I'm not with Carl any more.
No?
No. So. You looked worse on the TV. More--frightening.
But you're still my Benjy. I can see that now.
When was I on the TV?
You were fighting some man named Namor. You and your friends. They had to close off all of midtown.
Look at this. I'm crying. I didn't want to cry.
But I've been so worried about you.
You feel that? Nothing's gonna get through that. It's like I'm living inside my own personal tank.
Oh my lord! Yes.
And you're--happy, Benjy? This is what you want?

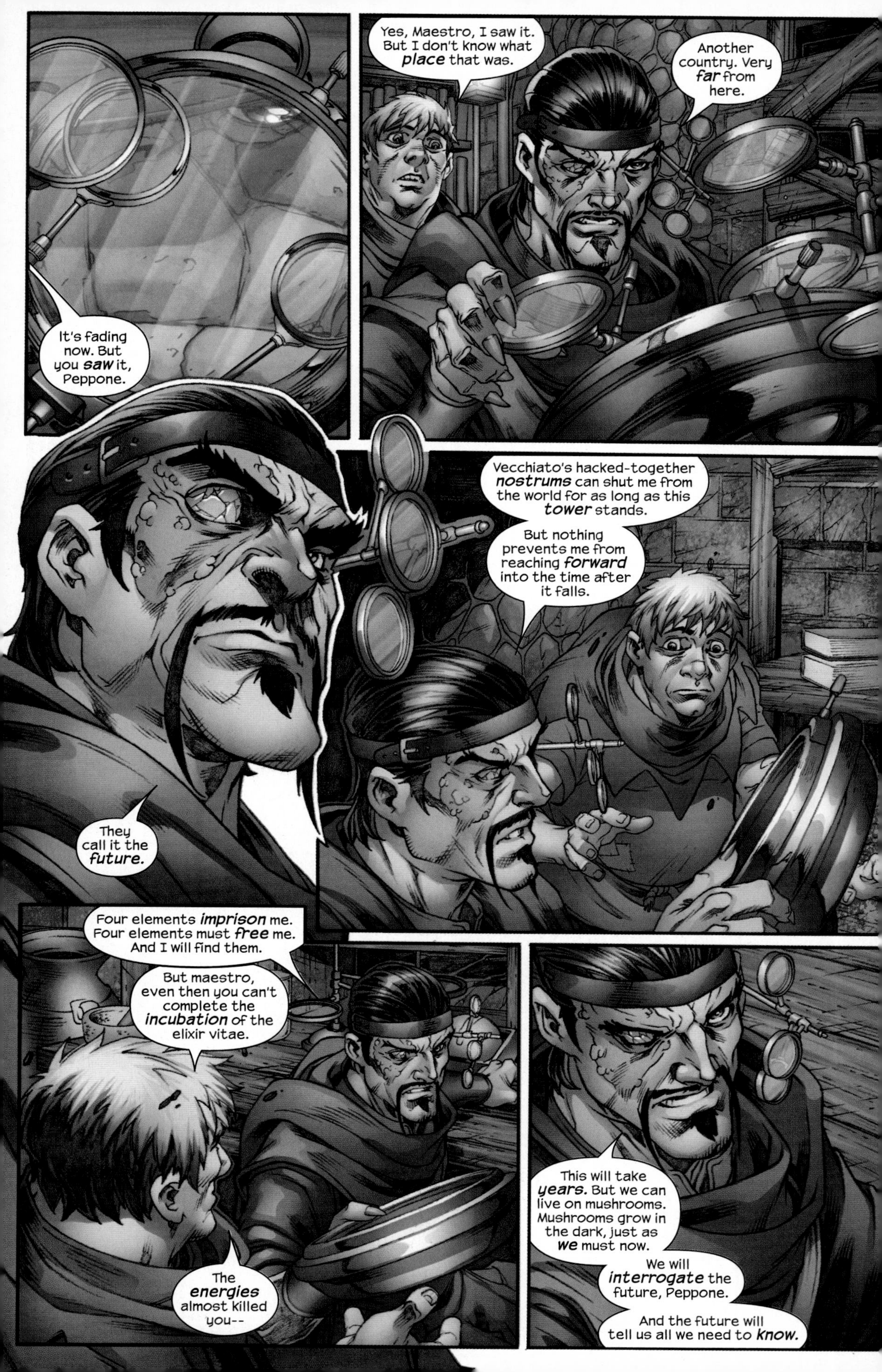
It's fading now. But you *saw* it, Peppone.
Yes, Maestro, I saw it. But I don't know what *place* that was.
Another country. Very *far* from here.
They call it the *future.*
Vecchiato's hacked-together *nostrums* can shut me from the world for as long as this *tower* stands.
But nothing prevents me from reaching *forward* into the time after it falls.
Four elements *imprison* me. Four elements must *free* me. And I will find them.
But maestro, even then you can't complete the *incubation* of the elixir vitae.
The *energies* almost killed you--
This will take *years*. But we can live on mushrooms. Mushrooms grow in the dark, just as *we* must now.
We will *interrogate* the future, Peppone.
And the future will tell us all we need to *know.*

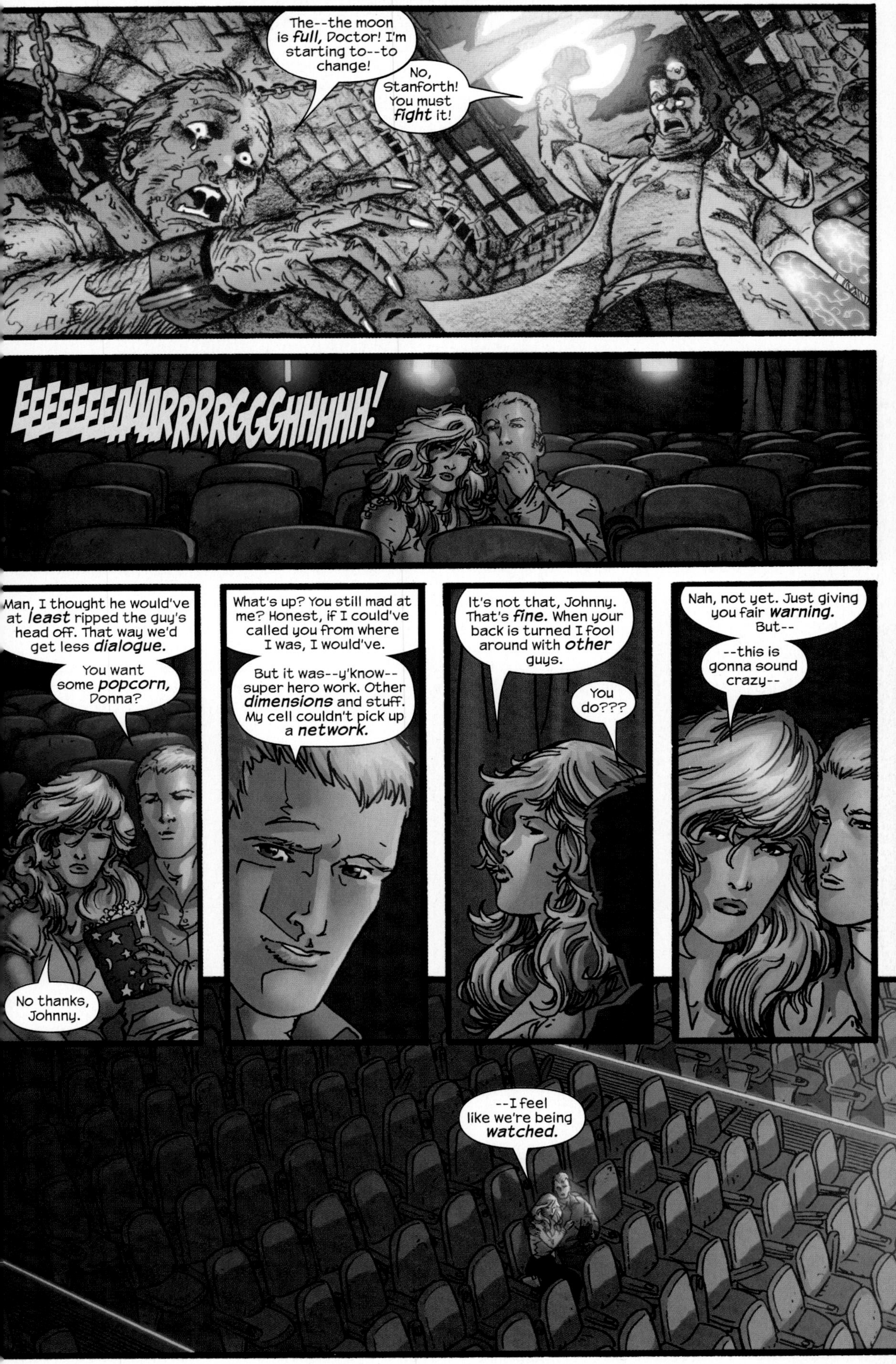

The--the moon is full, Doctor! I'm starting to--to change!
No, Stanforth! You must fight it!
EEEEEEEAAARRRRGGGHHHHH!
Man, I thought he would've at least ripped the guy's head off. That way we'd get less dialogue.
You want some popcorn, Donna?
No thanks, Johnny.
What's up? You still mad at me? Honest, if I could've called you from where I was, I would've.
But it was--y'know--super hero work. Other dimensions and stuff. My cell couldn't pick up a network.
It's not that, Johnny. That's fine. When your back is turned I fool around with other guys.
You do???
Nah, not yet. Just giving you fair warning. But--
--this is gonna sound crazy--
--I feel like we're being watched.

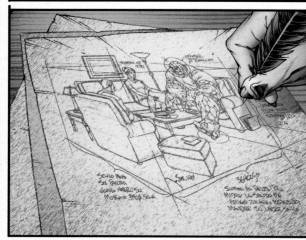

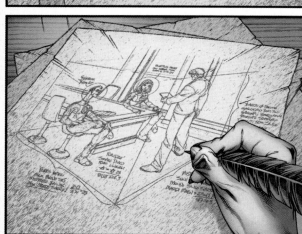

Bueno.

Buenissimo.

*

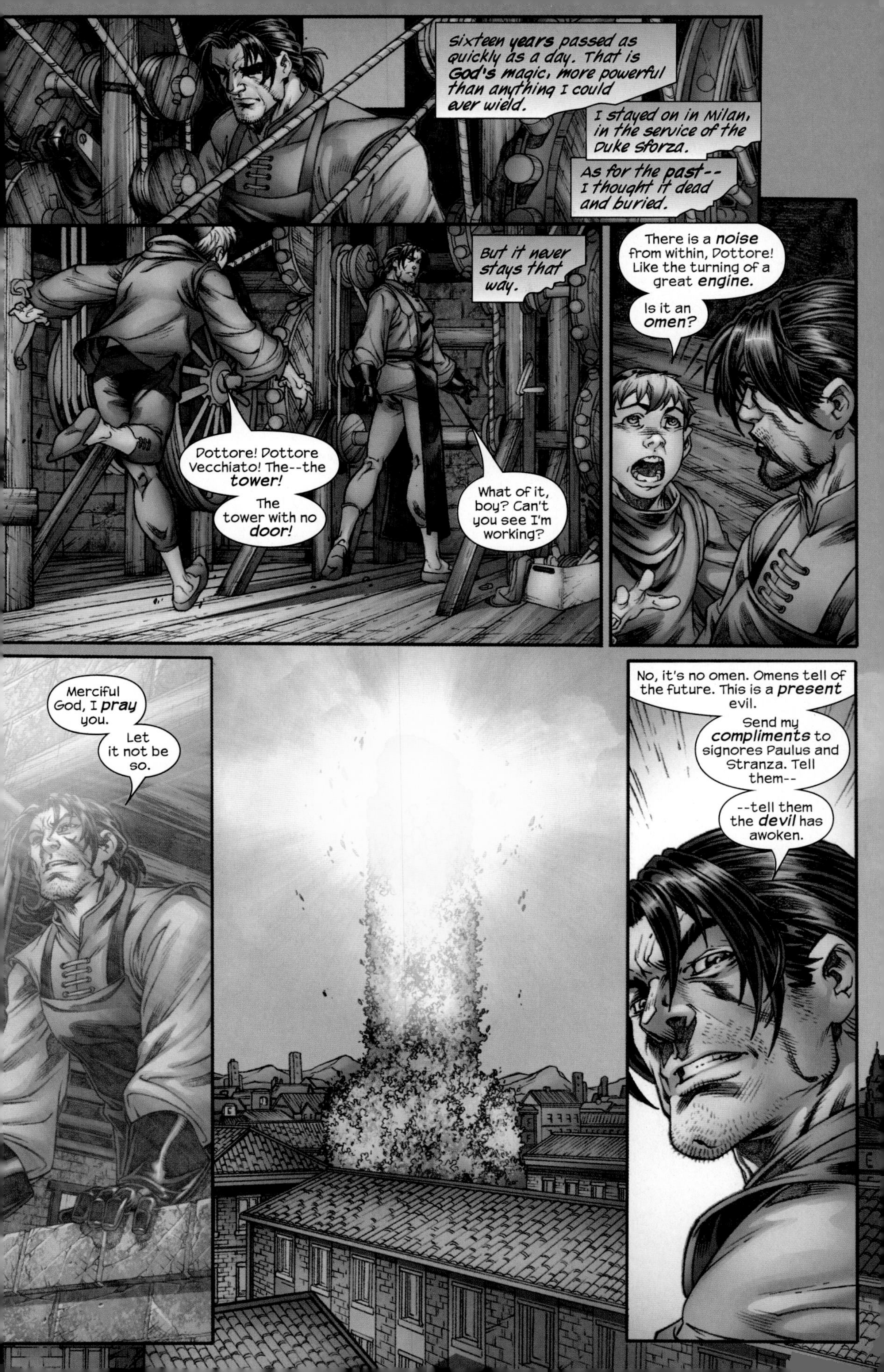
Sixteen years passed as quickly as a day. That is God's magic, more powerful than anything I could ever wield.
I stayed on in Milan, in the service of the Duke Sforza.
As for the past-- I thought it dead and buried.
But it never stays that way.
Dottore! Dottore Vecchiato! The--the tower!
The tower with no door!
What of it, boy? Can't you see I'm working?
There is a noise from within, Dottore! Like the turning of a great engine.
Is it an omen?
Merciful God, I pray you.
Let it not be so.
No, it's no omen. Omens tell of the future. This is a present evil.
Send my compliments to signores Paulus and Stranza. Tell them--
--tell them the devil has awoken.

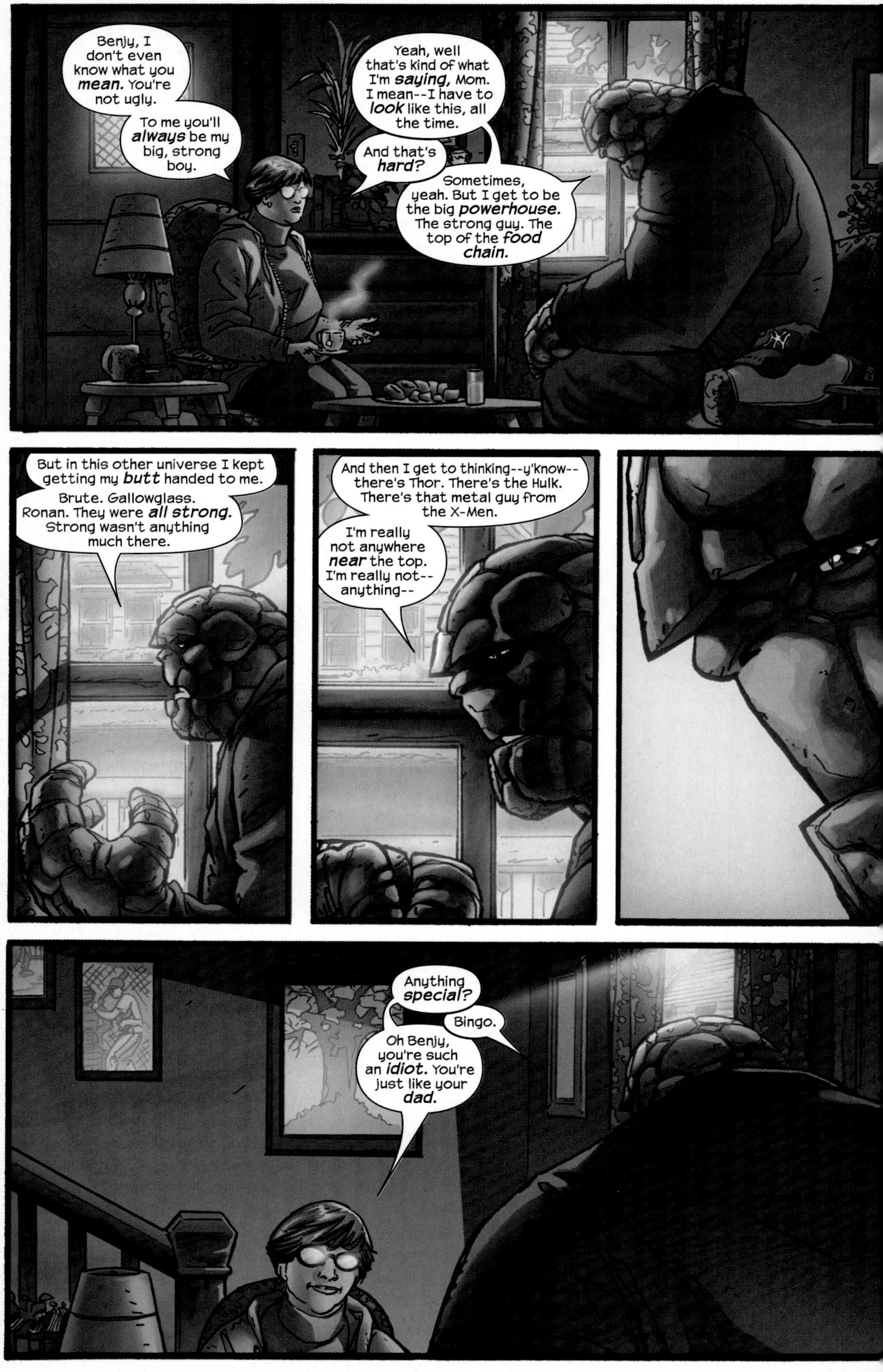

Benjy, I don't even know what you *mean.* You're not ugly.
To me you'll *always* be my big, strong boy.
Yeah, well that's kind of what I'm *saying,* Mom. I mean--I have to *look* like this, all the time.
And that's *hard?*
Sometimes, yeah. But I get to be the big *powerhouse.* The strong guy. The top of the *food chain.*
But in this other universe I kept getting my *butt* handed to me.
Brute. Gallowglass. Ronan. They were *all strong.* Strong wasn't anything much there.
And then I get to thinking--y'know--there's Thor. There's the Hulk. There's that metal guy from the X-Men.
I'm really not anywhere *near* the top. I'm really not--anything--
Anything *special?*
Bingo.
Oh Benjy, you're such an *idiot.* You're just like your *dad.*

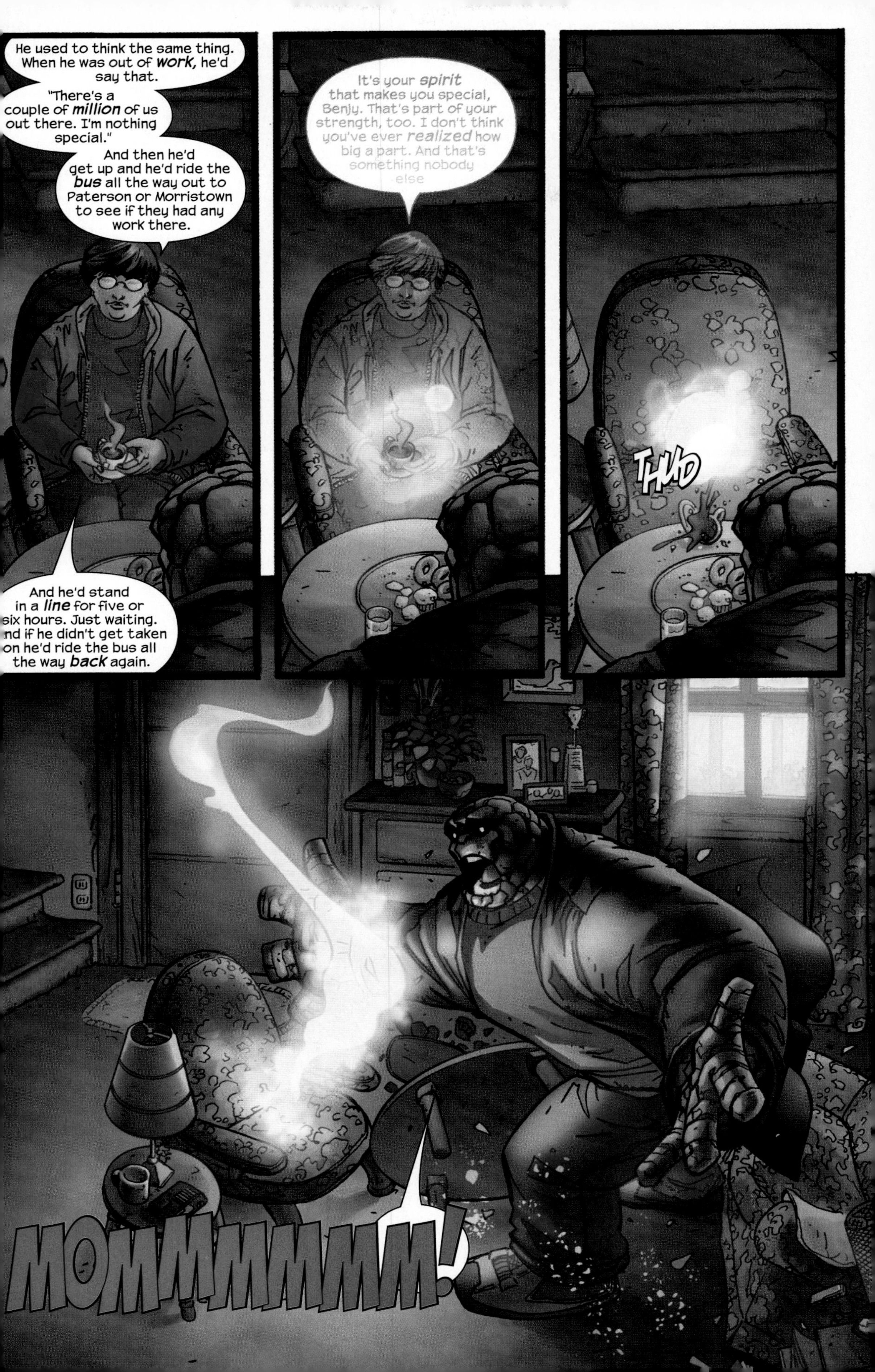
He used to think the same thing. When he was out of work, he'd say that.
"There's a couple of million of us out there. I'm nothing special."
And then he'd get up and he'd ride the bus all the way out to Paterson or Morristown to see if they had any work there.
And he'd stand in a line for five or six hours. Just waiting. nd if he didn't get taken on he'd ride the bus all the way back again.
It's your spirit that makes you special, Benjy. That's part of your strength, too. I don't think you've ever realized how big a part. And that's something nobody else
THUD
MOMMMMMMM!

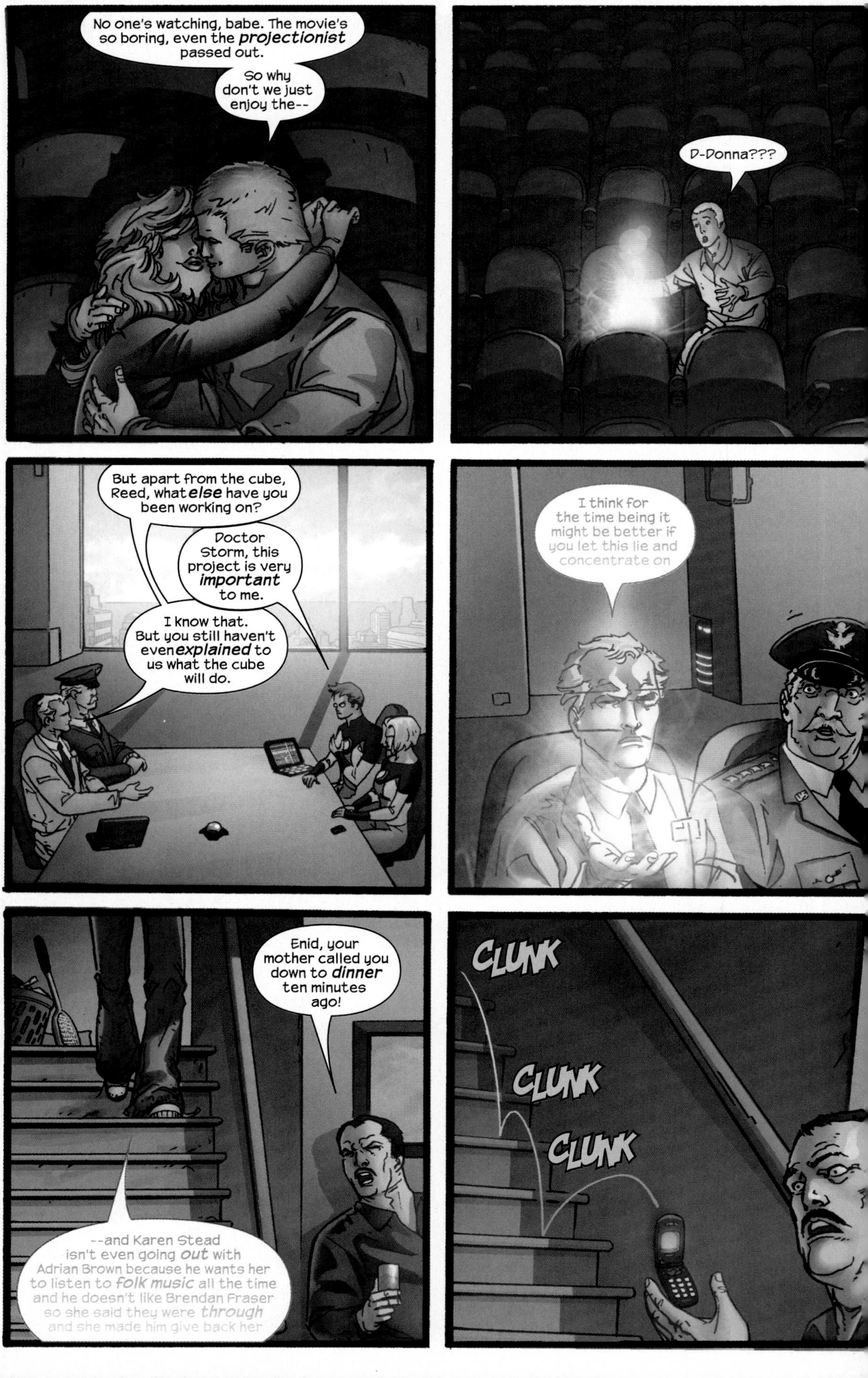
No one's watching, babe. The movie's so boring, even the *projectionist* passed out.
So why don't we just enjoy the--
D-Donna???
But apart from the cube, Reed, what *else* have you been working on?
Doctor Storm, this project is very *important* to me.
I know that. But you still haven't even *explained* to us what the cube will do.
I think for the time being it might be better if you let this lie and concentrate on
Enid, your mother called you down to *dinner* ten minutes ago!
--and Karen Stead isn't even going *out* with Adrian Brown because he wants her to listen to *folk music* all the time and he doesn't like Brendan Fraser so she said they were *through* and she made him give back her
CLUNK
CLUNK
CLUNK

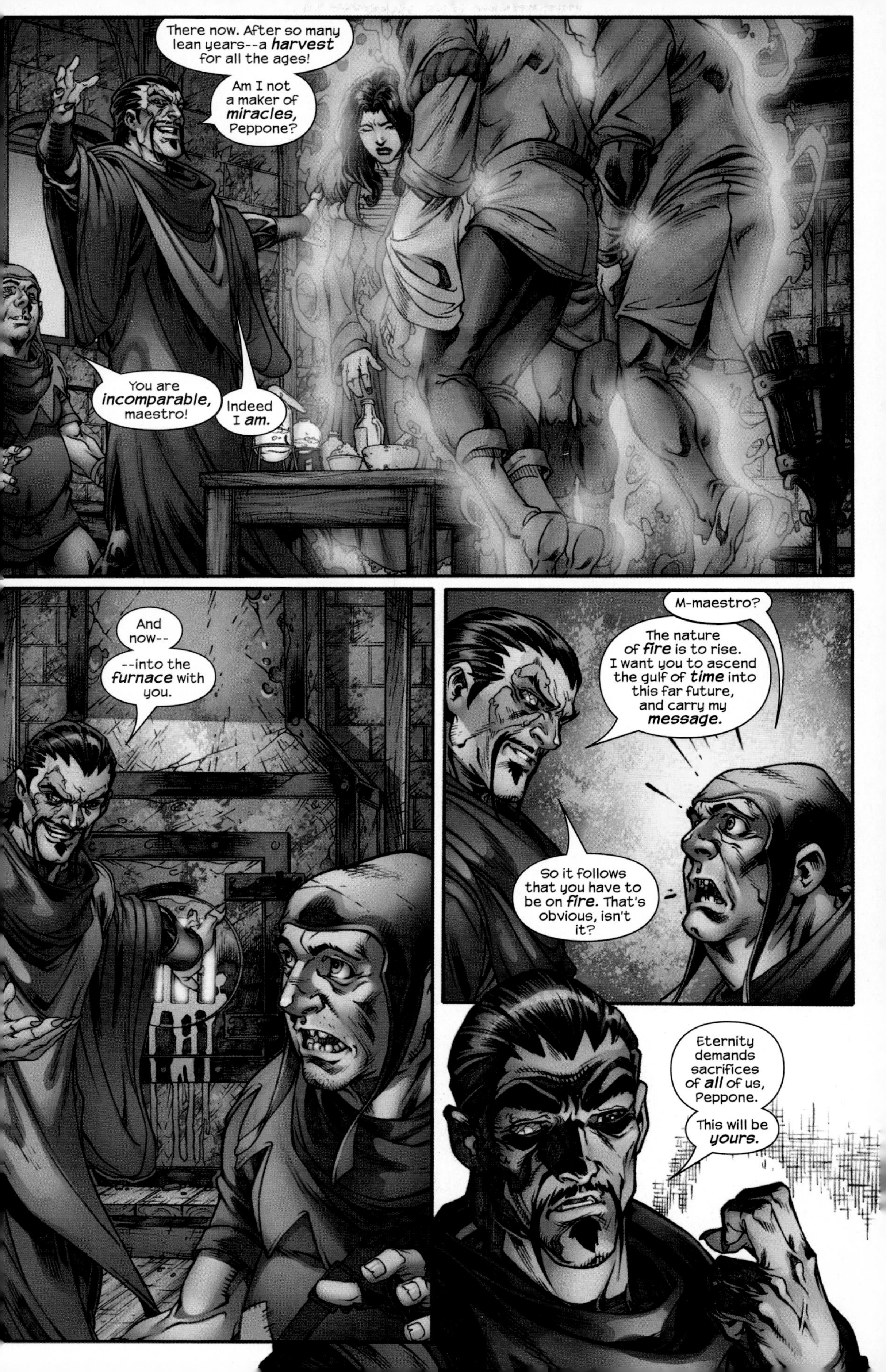
There now. After so many lean years--a *harvest* for all the ages!
Am I not a maker of *miracles,* Peppone?
You are *incomparable,* maestro!
Indeed I *am.*
And now--
--into the *furnace* with you.
M-maestro?
The nature of *fire* is to rise. I want you to ascend the gulf of *time* into this far future, and carry my *message.*
So it follows that you have to be on *fire.* That's obvious, isn't it?
Eternity demands sacrifices of *all* of us, Peppone.
This will be *yours.*

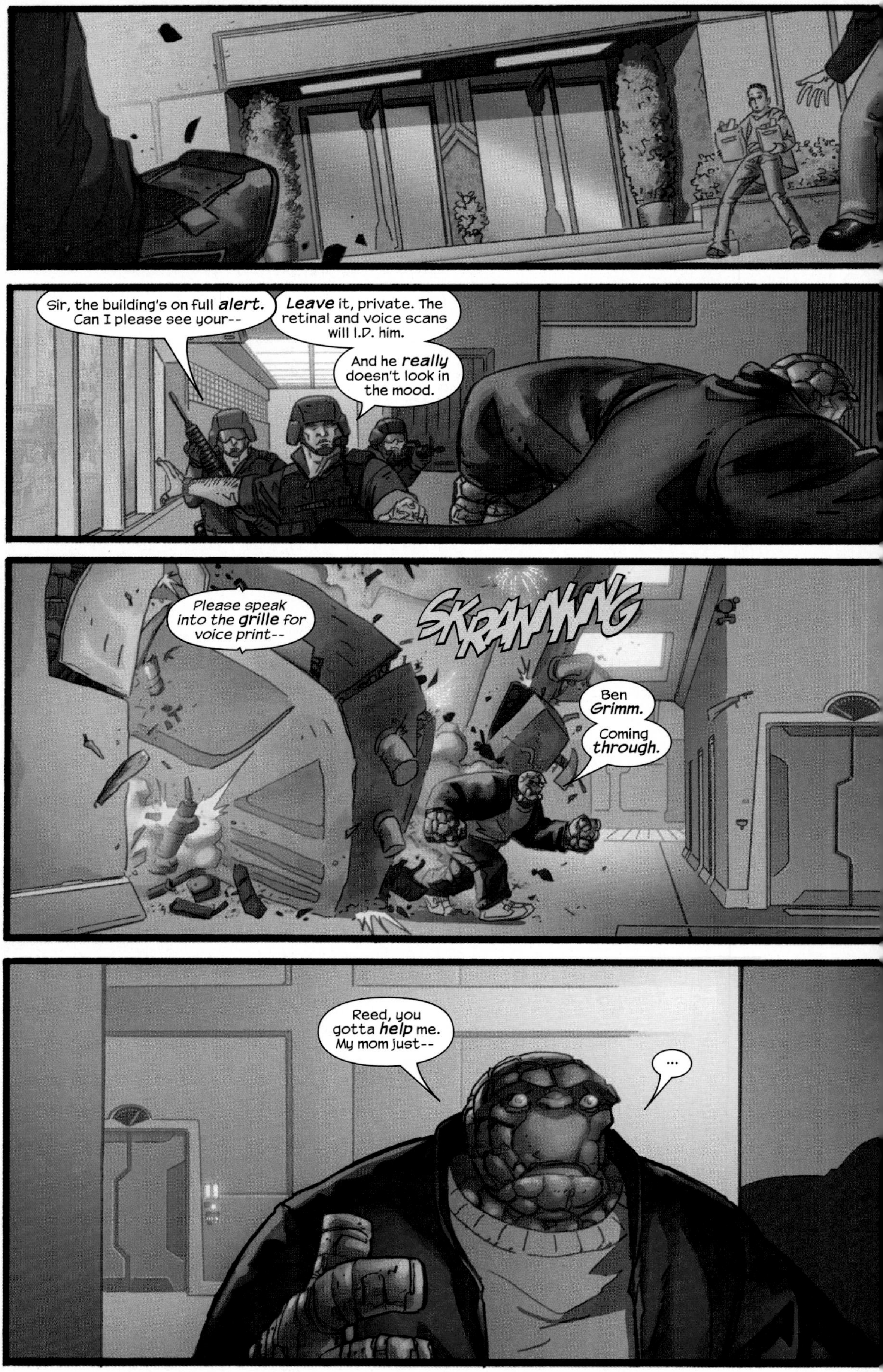

Sir, the building's on full alert. Can I please see your--
Leave it, private. The retinal and voice scans will I.D. him.
And he really doesn't look in the mood.
Please speak into the grille for voice print--
SKRANNNNG
Ben Grimm.
Coming through.
Reed, you gotta help me. My mom just--
...

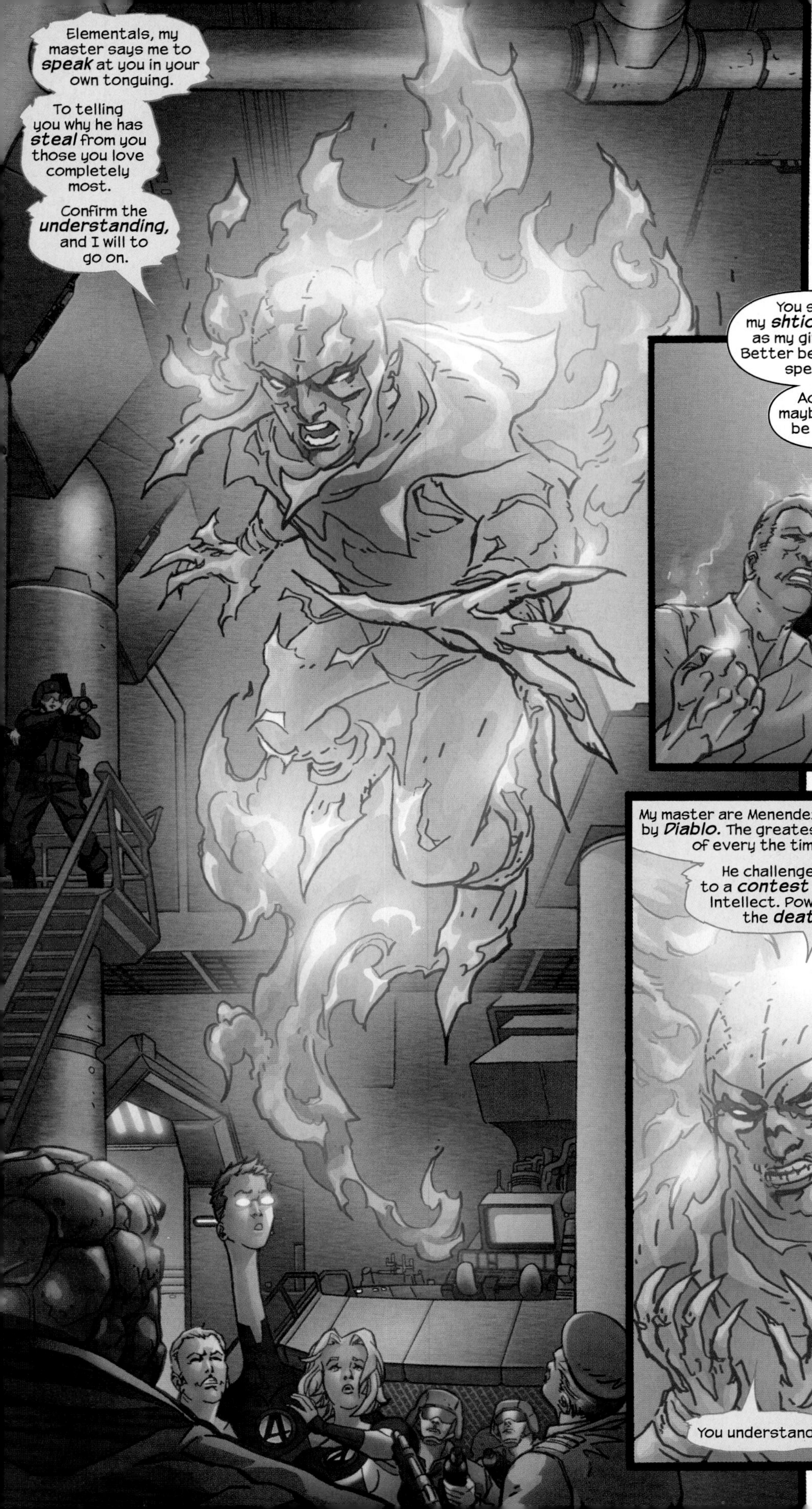
Elementals, my master says me to *speak* at you in your own tonguing.
To telling you why he has *steal* from you those you love completely most.
Confirm the *understanding,* and I will to go on.
You stole my *shtick* as well as my girlfriend. Better be a *short* speech.
Actually, maybe better be a *mime.*
My master are Menendez Flores, known by *Diablo.* The greatest *alchemist* of every the time lived.
He challenge you to a *contest* of skill. Intellect. Power. To the *death.*
You understand?

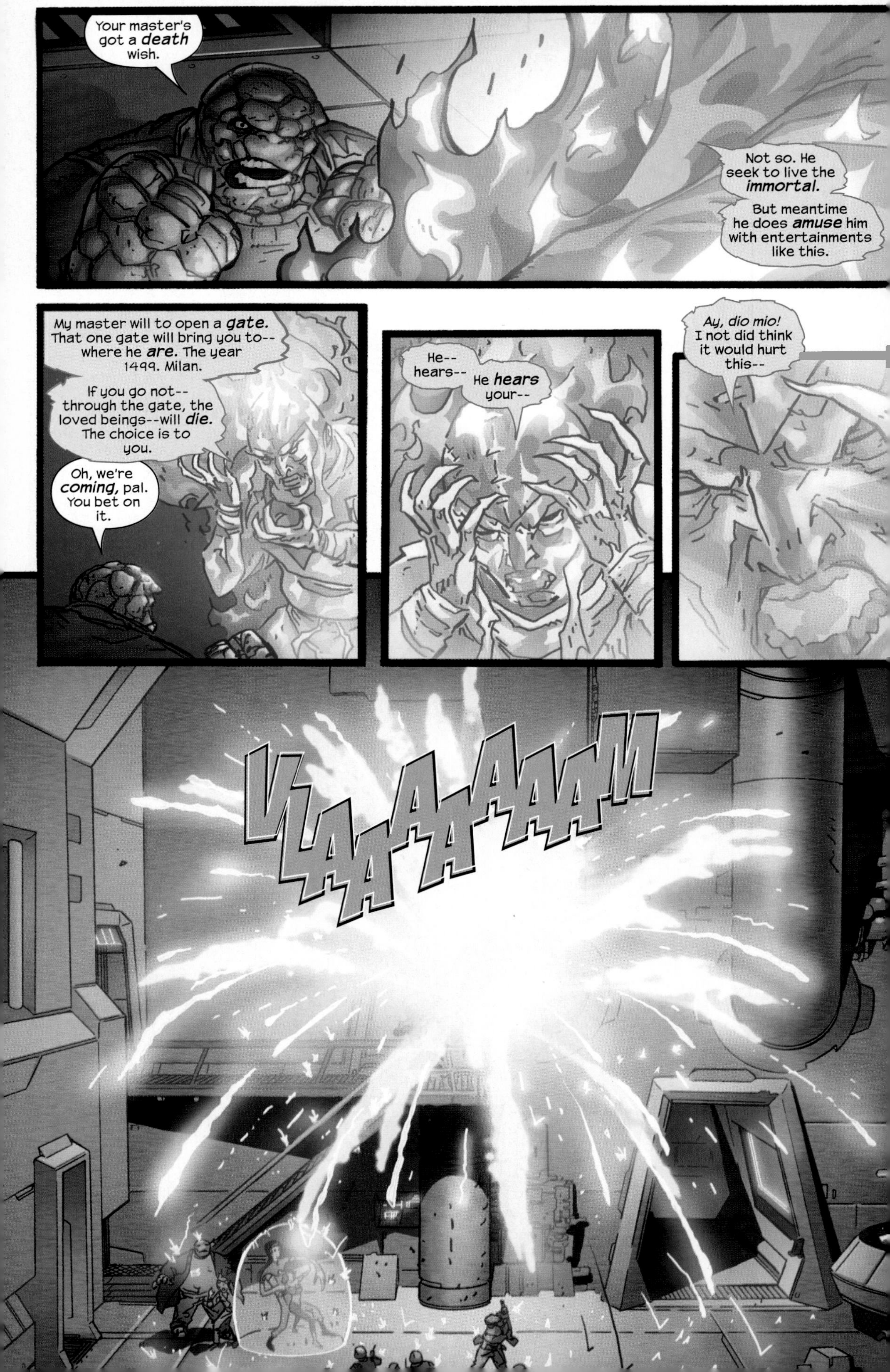
Your master's got a *death* wish.
Not so. He seek to live the *immortal.*
But meantime he does *amuse* him with entertainments like this.
My master will to open a *gate.* That one gate will bring you to--where he *are.* The year 1499. Milan.
If you go not--through the gate, the loved beings--will *die.* The choice is to you.
Oh, we're *coming,* pal. You bet on it.
He--hears--
He *hears* your--
Ay, dio mio! I not did think it would hurt this--
VLAAAAAAAAM

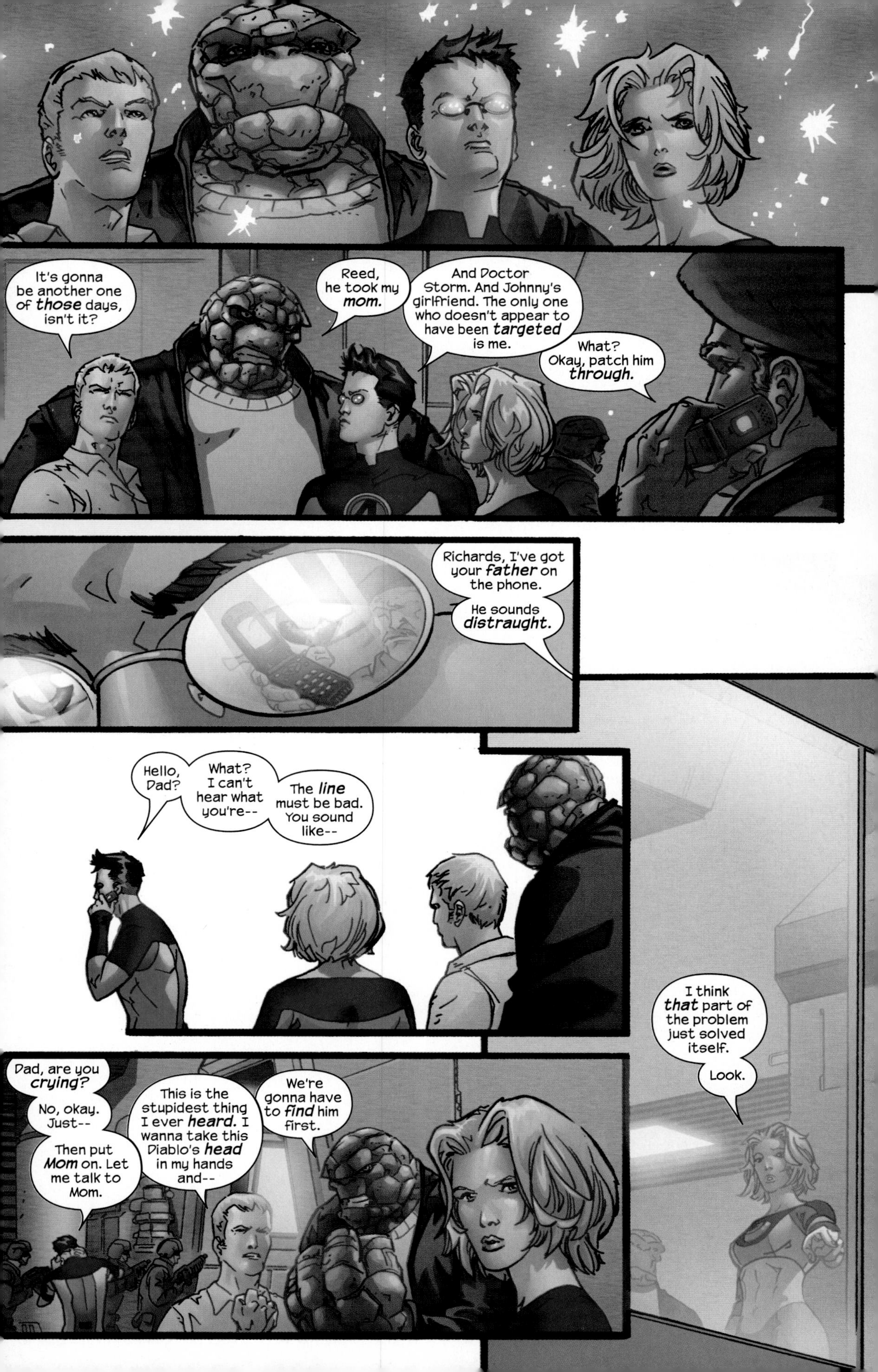

It's gonna be another one of *those* days, isn't it?
Reed, he took my *mom.*
And Doctor Storm. And Johnny's girlfriend. The only one who doesn't appear to have been *targeted* is me.
What? Okay, patch him *through.*
Richards, I've got your *father* on the phone.
He sounds *distraught.*
Hello, Dad?
What? I can't hear what you're--
The *line* must be bad. You sound like--
Dad, are you *crying?*
No, okay. Just--
Then put *Mom* on. Let me talk to Mom.
This is the stupidest thing I ever *heard.* I wanna take this Diablo's *head* in my hands and--
We're gonna have to *find* him first.
I think *that* part of the problem just solved itself.
Look.

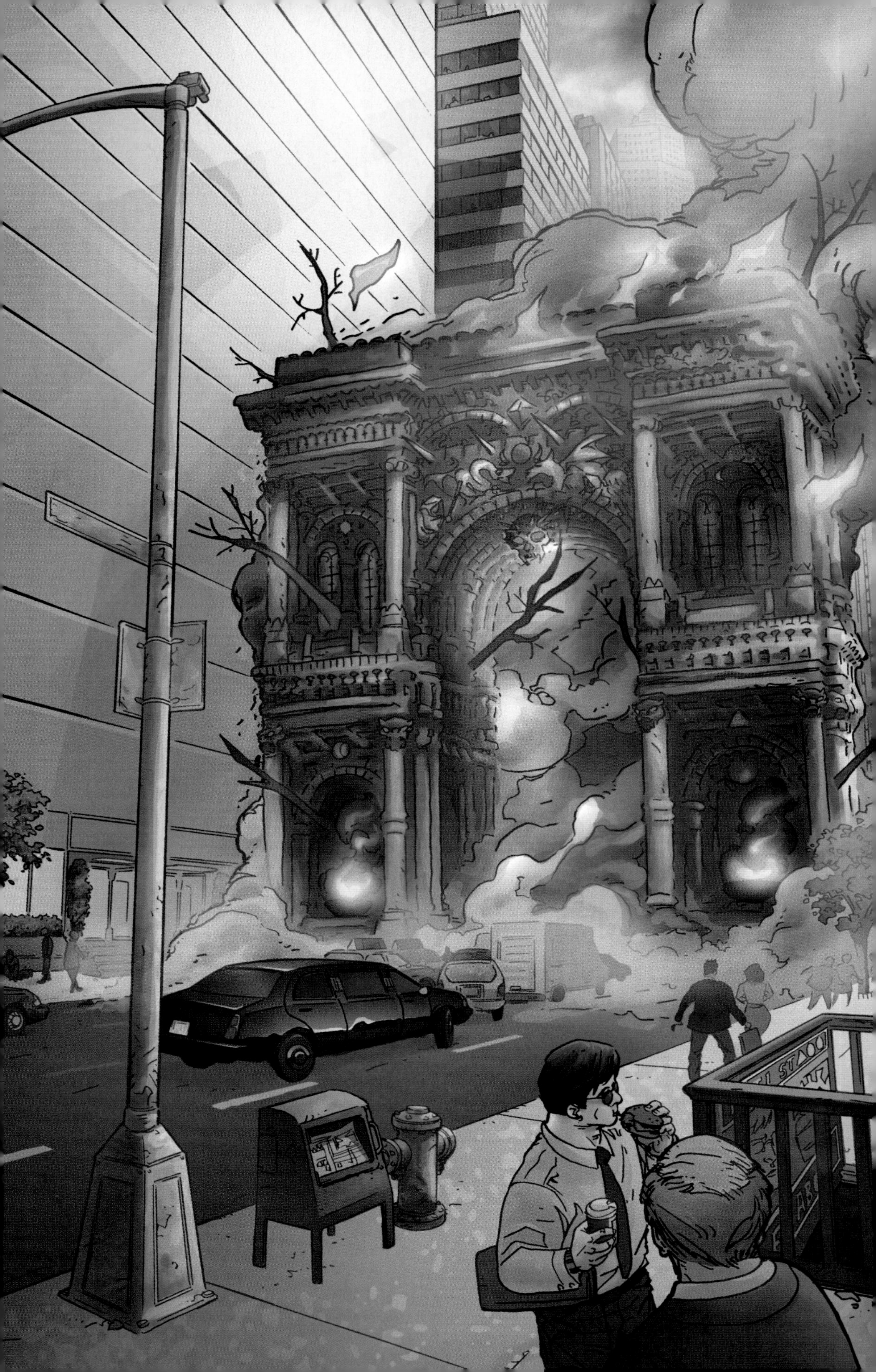

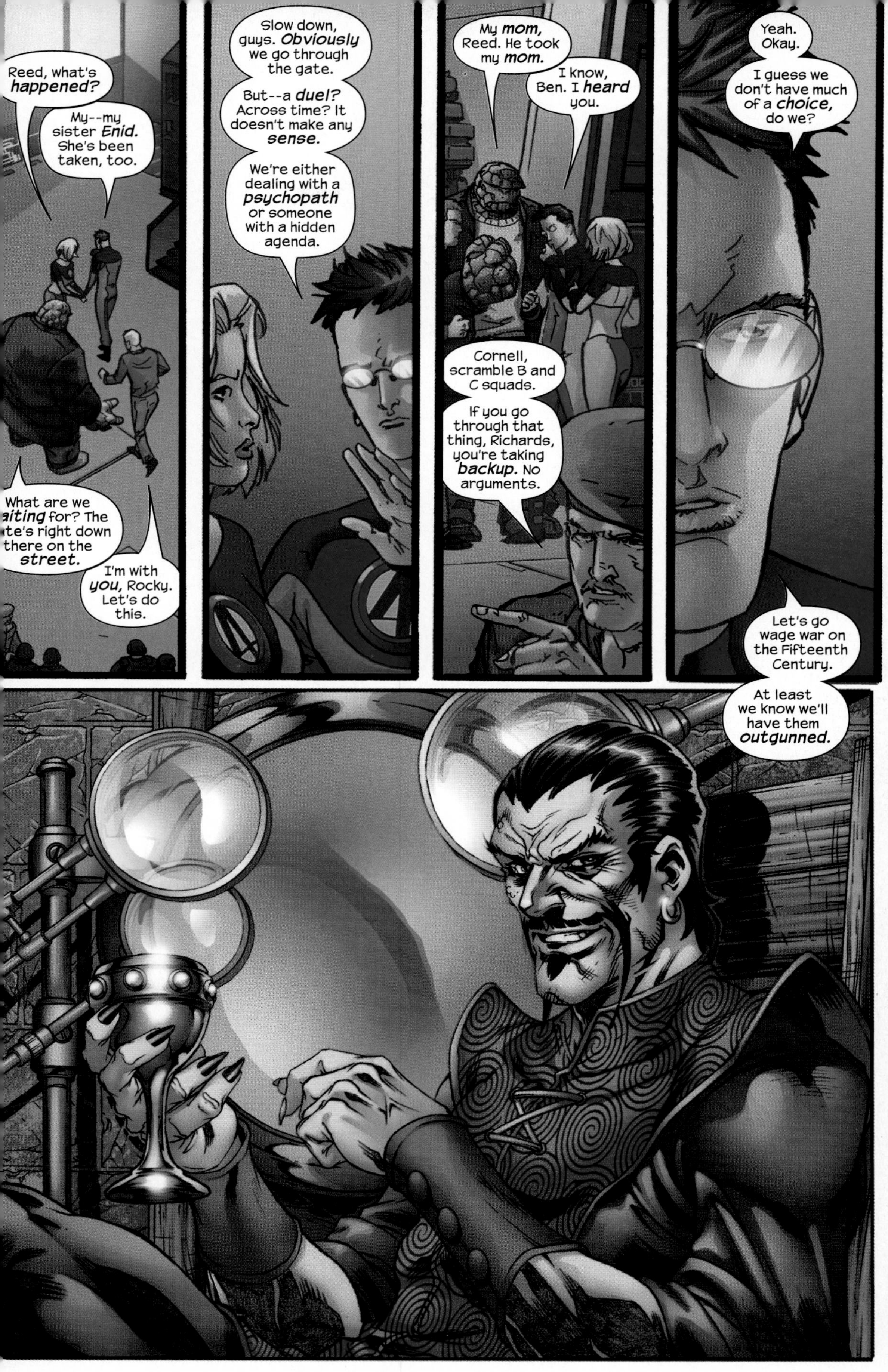

Reed, what's *happened?*
My--my sister *Enid.* She's been taken, too.
What are we aiting for? The te's right down there on the *street.*
I'm with *you,* Rocky. Let's do this.
Slow down, guys. *Obviously* we go through the gate.
But--a *duel?* Across time? It doesn't make any *sense.*
We're either dealing with a *psychopath* or someone with a hidden agenda.
My *mom,* Reed. He took my *mom.*
I know, Ben. I *heard* you.
Cornell, scramble B and C squads.
If you go through that thing, Richards, you're taking *backup.* No arguments.
Yeah. Okay.
I guess we don't have much of a *choice,* do we?
Let's go wage war on the Fifteenth Century.
At least we know we'll have them *outgunned.*

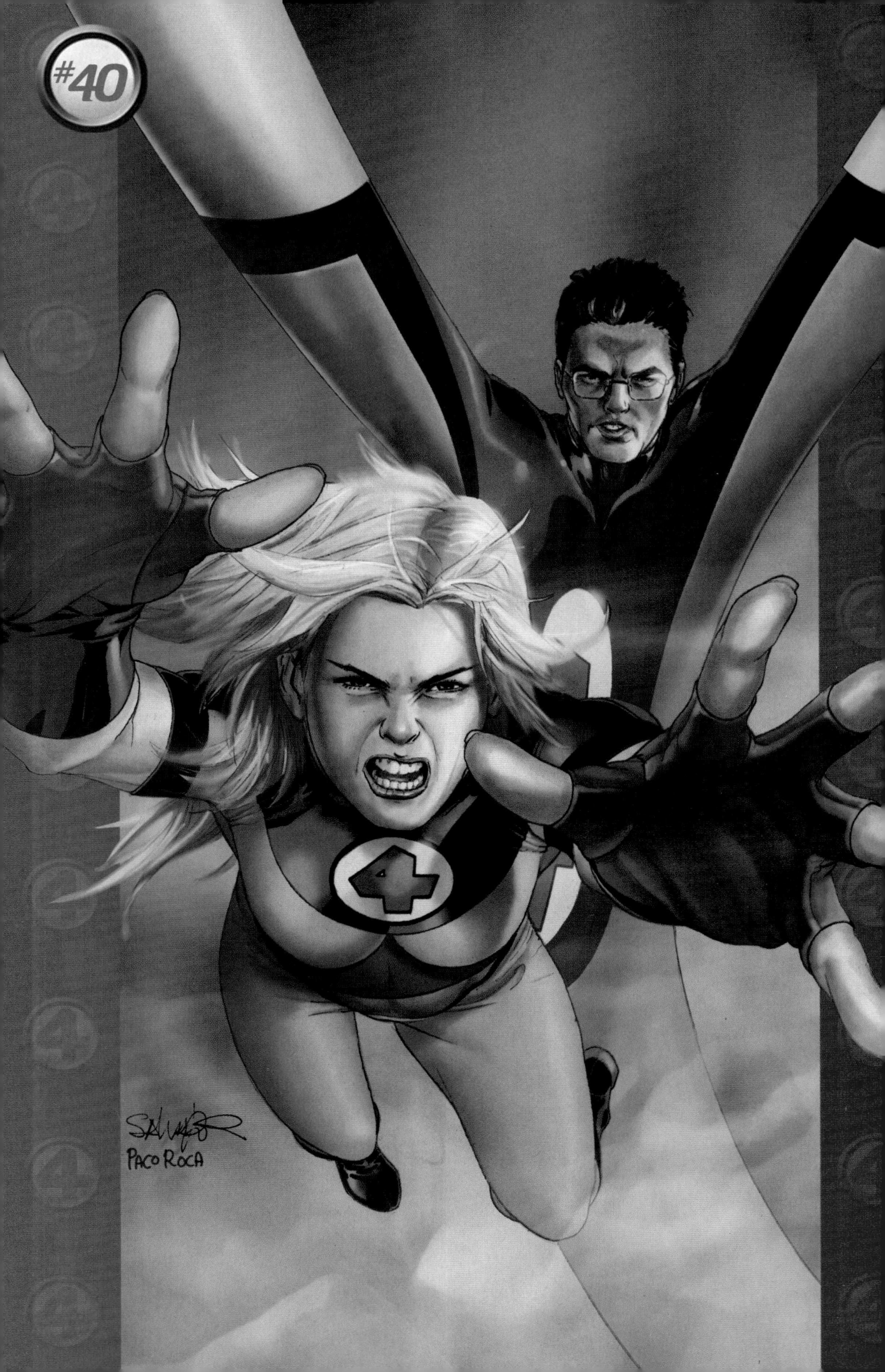
#40
SALVADOR
PACO ROCA

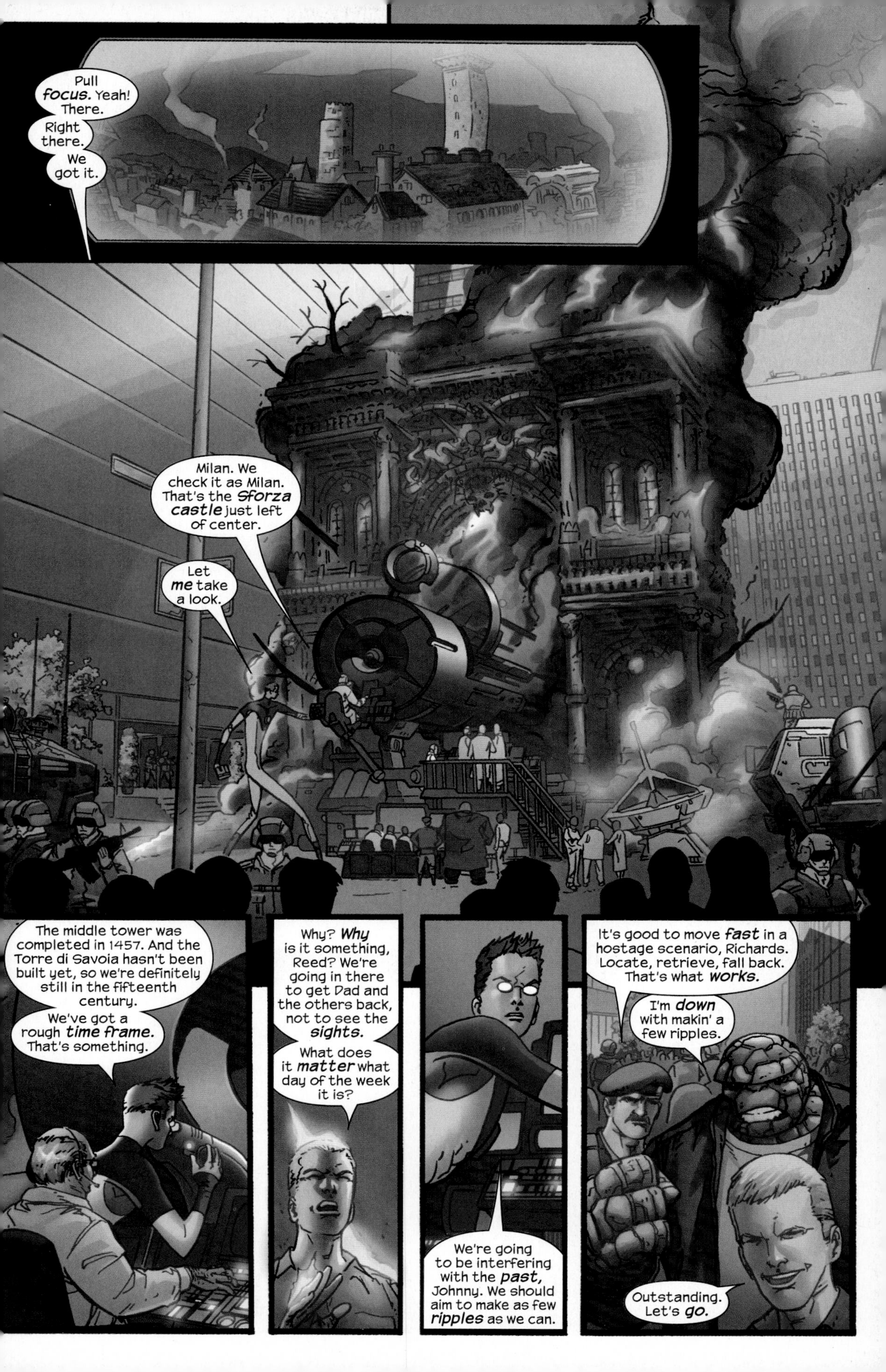
Pull *focus.* Yeah! There.
Right there.
We got it.
Milan. We check it as Milan. That's the *Sforza castle* just left of center.
Let *me* take a look.
The middle tower was completed in 1457. And the Torre di Savoia hasn't been built yet, so we're definitely still in the fifteenth century.
We've got a rough *time frame.* That's something.
Why? *Why* is it something, Reed? We're going in there to get Dad and the others back, not to see the *sights.*
What does it *matter* what day of the week it is?
We're going to be interfering with the *past,* Johnny. We should aim to make as few *ripples* as we can.
It's good to move *fast* in a hostage scenario, Richards. Locate, retrieve, fall back. That's what *works.*
I'm *down* with makin' a few ripples.
Outstanding. Let's *go.*

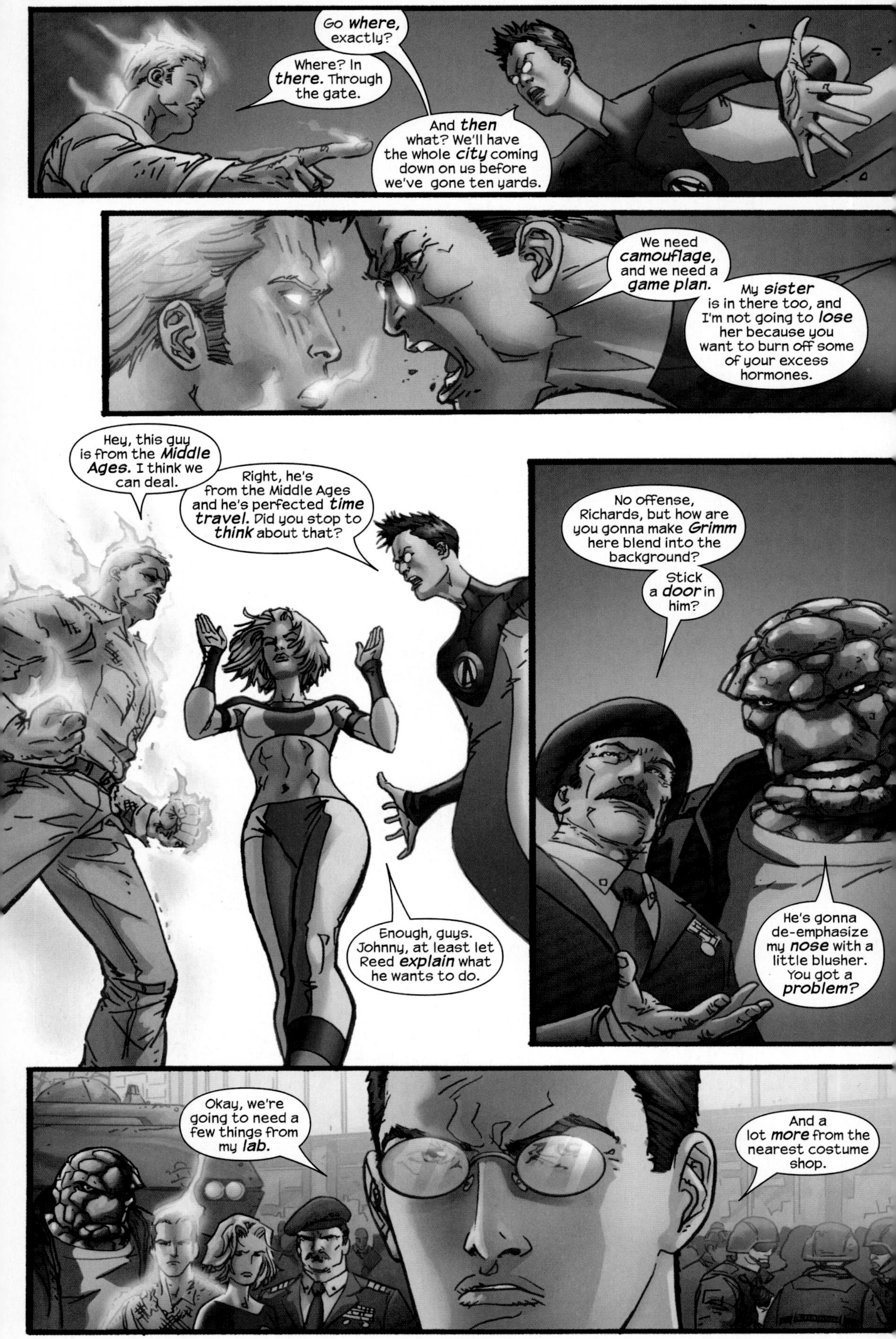

Where? In **there.** Through the gate.
Go **where,** exactly?
And **then** what? We'll have the whole **city** coming down on us before we've gone ten yards.
We need **camouflage,** and we need a **game plan.**
My **sister** is in there too, and I'm not going to **lose** her because you want to burn off some of your excess hormones.
Hey, this guy is from the **Middle Ages.** I think we can deal.
Right, he's from the Middle Ages and he's perfected **time travel.** Did you stop to **think** about that?
Enough, guys. Johnny, at least let Reed **explain** what he wants to do.
No offense, Richards, but how are you gonna make **Grimm** here blend into the background?
Stick a **door** in him?
He's gonna de-emphasize my **nose** with a little blusher. You got a **problem?**
Okay, we're going to need a few things from my **lab.**
And a lot **more** from the nearest costume shop.

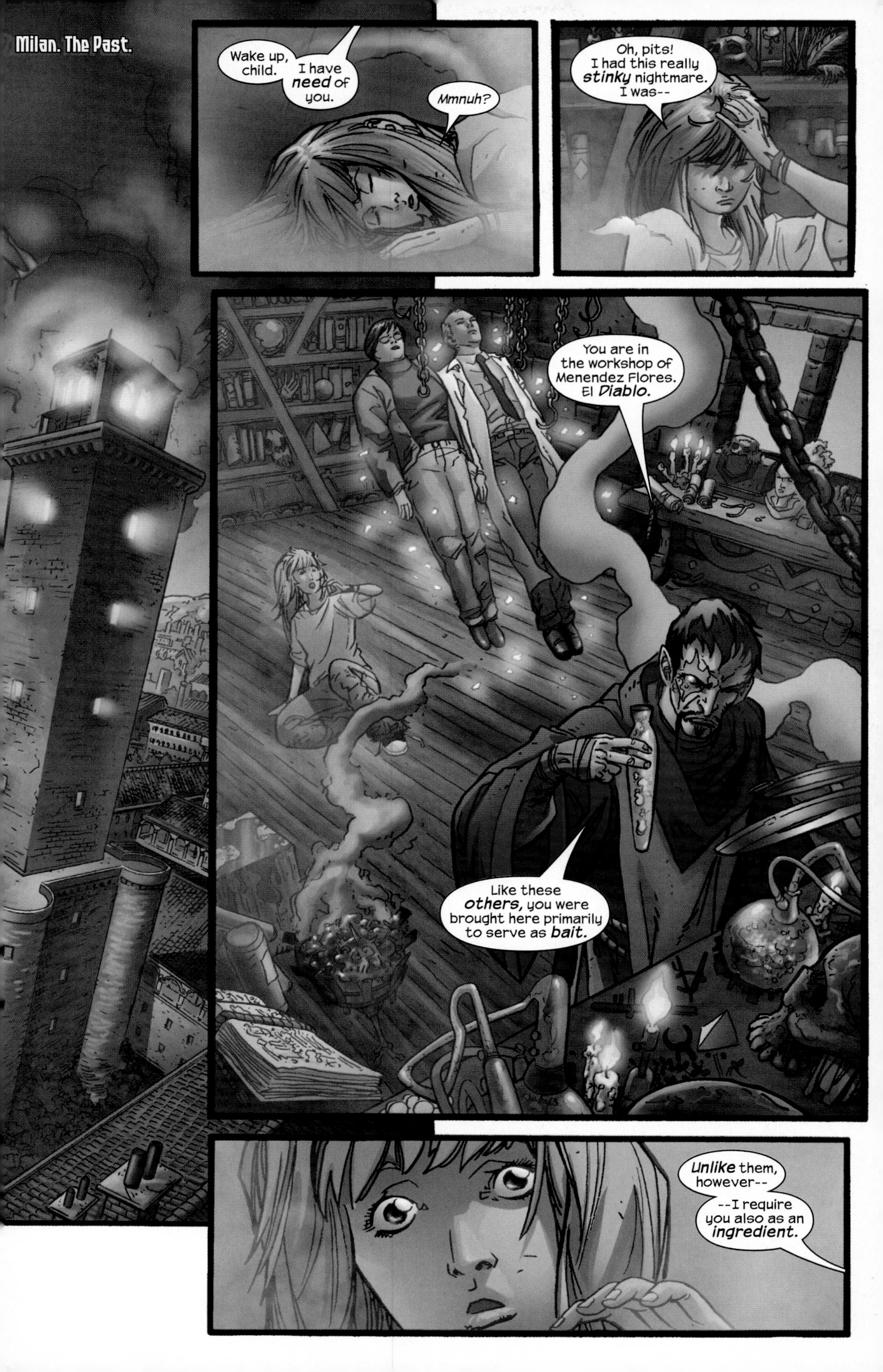
Milan. The Past.
Wake up, child.
I have need of you.
Mmnuh?
Oh, pits! I had this really stinky nightmare. I was--
You are in the workshop of Menendez Flores. El Diablo.
Like these others, you were brought here primarily to serve as bait.
Unlike them, however--
--I require you also as an ingredient.

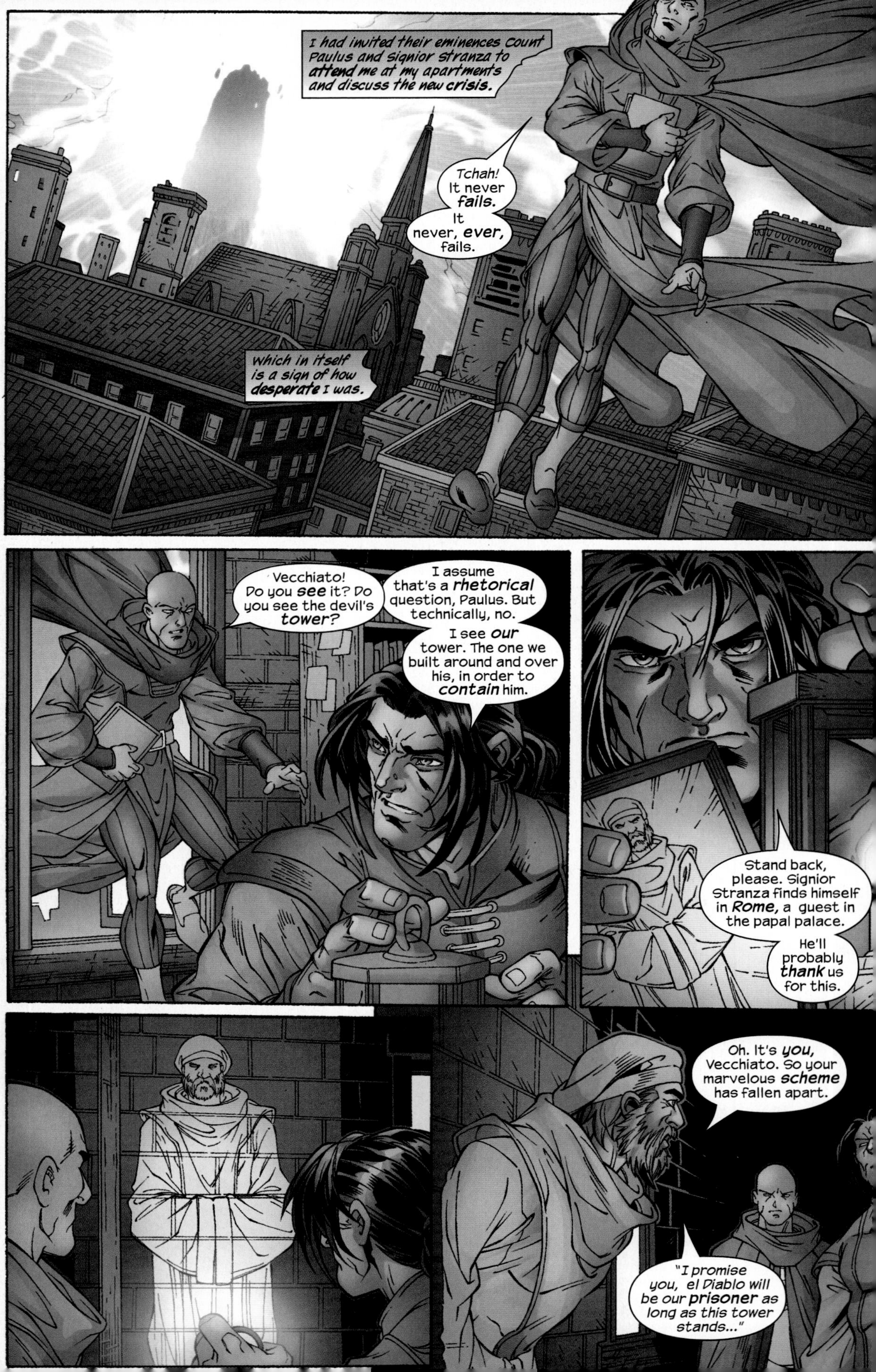
I had invited their eminences Count Paulus and Signior Stranza to attend me at my apartments and discuss the new crisis.
Tchah! It never fails.
It never, ever, fails.
Which in itself is a sign of how desperate I was.
Vecchiato! Do you see it? Do you see the devil's tower?
I assume that's a rhetorical question, Paulus. But technically, no.
I see our tower. The one we built around and over his, in order to contain him.
Stand back, please. Signior Stranza finds himself in Rome, a guest in the papal palace.
He'll probably thank us for this.
Oh. It's you, Vecchiato. So your marvelous scheme has fallen apart.
"I promise you, el Diablo will be our prisoner as long as this tower stands..."

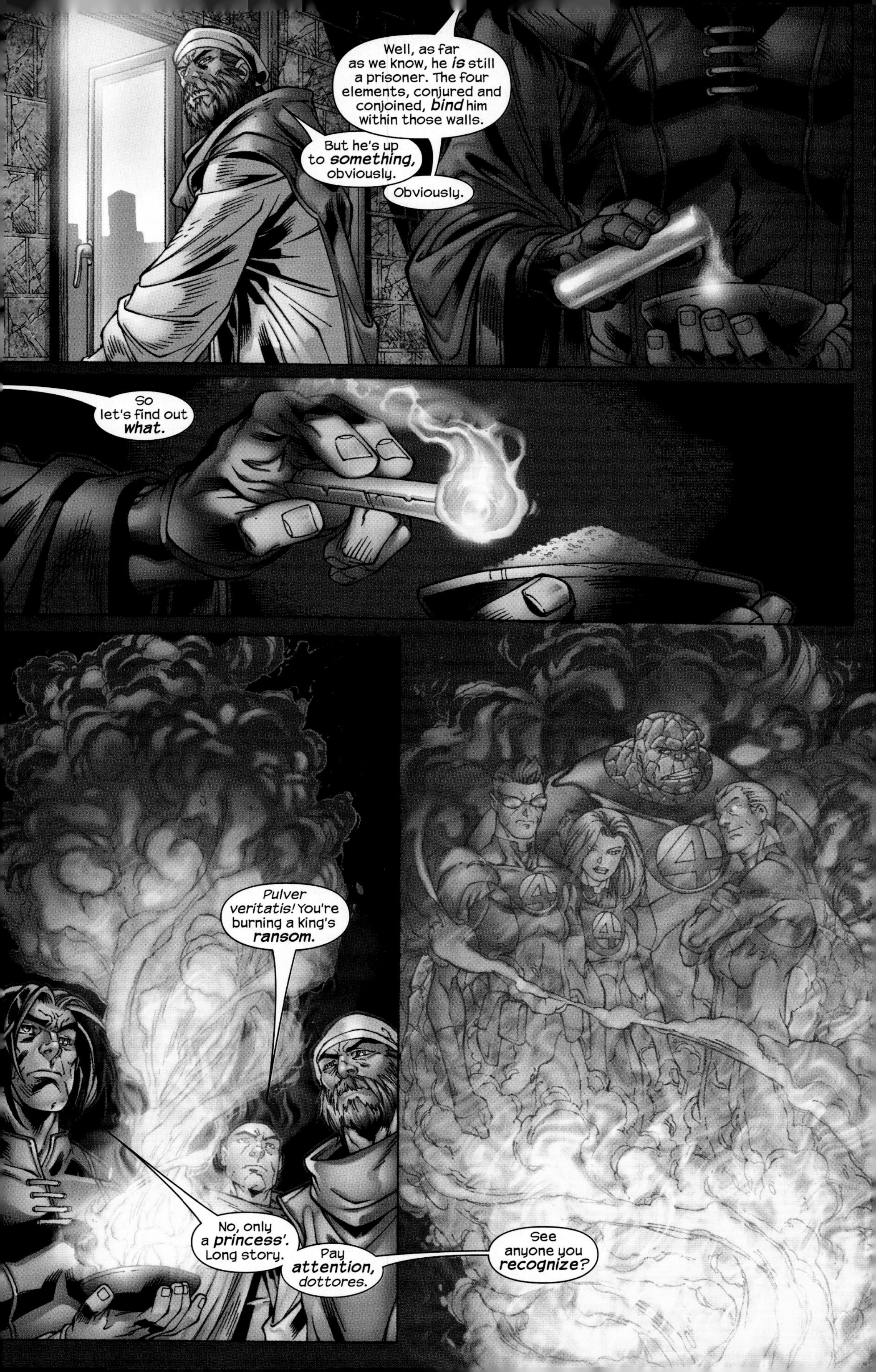
Well, as far as we know, he *is* still a prisoner. The four elements, conjured and conjoined, ***bind*** him within those walls.
But he's up to ***something,*** obviously.
Obviously.
So let's find out ***what.***
Pulver veritatis! You're burning a king's ***ransom.***
No, only a ***princess'.*** Long story.
Pay ***attention,*** dottores.
See anyone you ***recognize?***

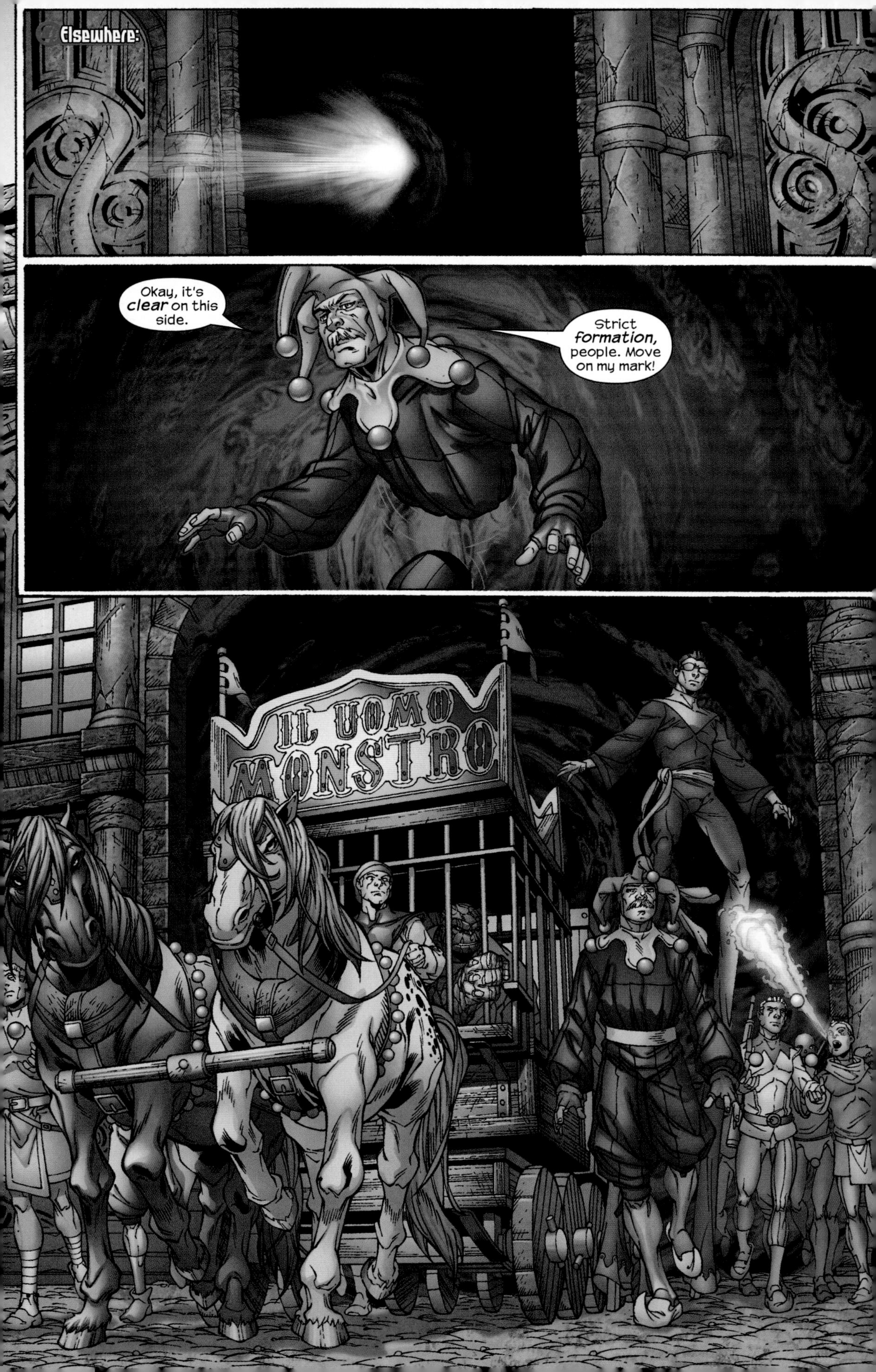
Elsewhere:
Okay, it's clear on this side.
Strict formation, people. Move on my mark!
IL UOMO MONSTRO

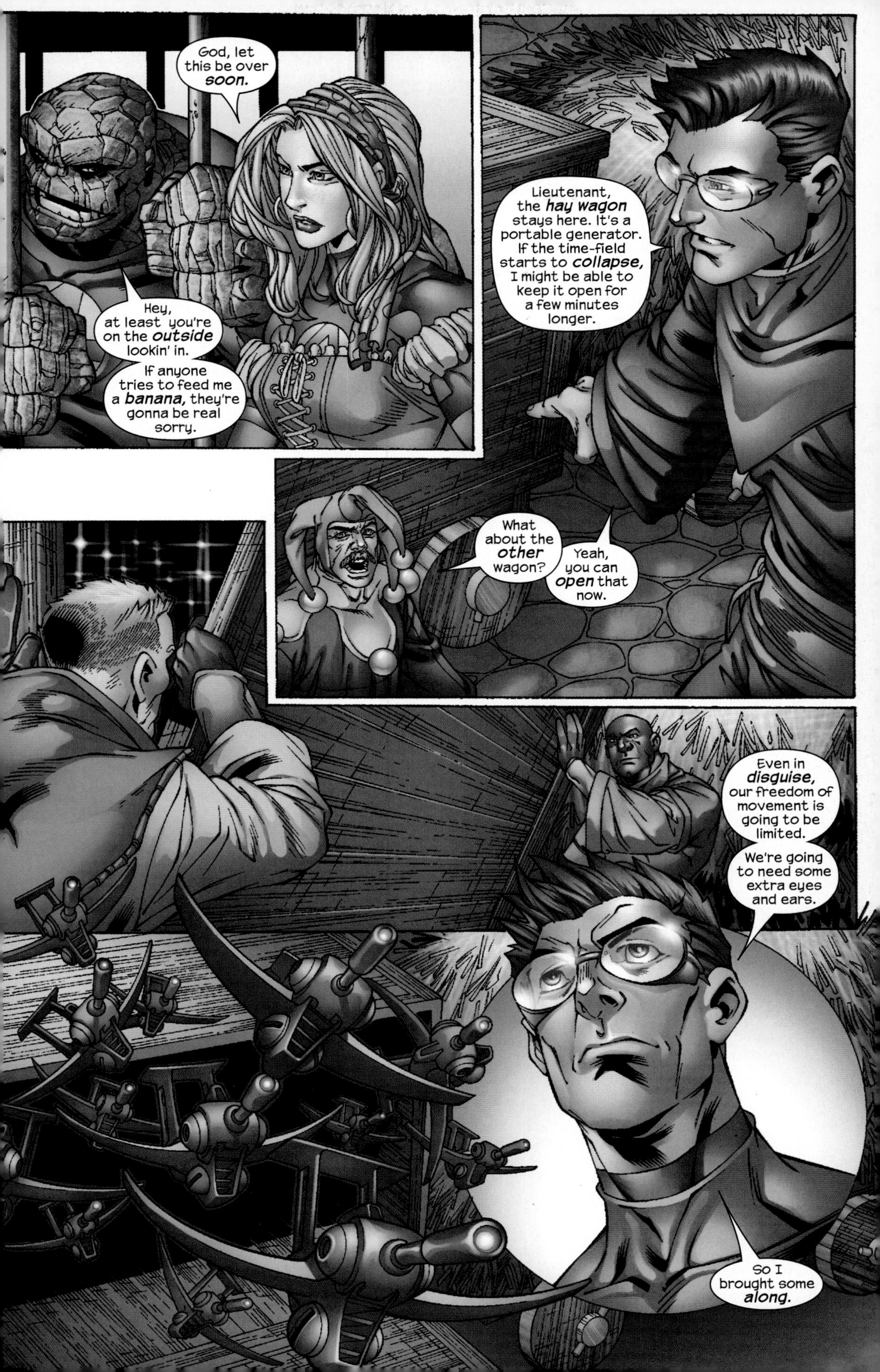
God, let this be over *soon.*
Hey, at least you're on the *outside* lookin' in.
If anyone tries to feed me a *banana,* they're gonna be real sorry.
Lieutenant, the *hay wagon* stays here. It's a portable generator. If the time-field starts to *collapse,* I might be able to keep it open for a few minutes longer.
What about the *other* wagon?
Yeah, you can *open* that now.
Even in *disguise,* our freedom of movement is going to be limited.
We're going to need some extra eyes and ears.
So I brought some *along.*

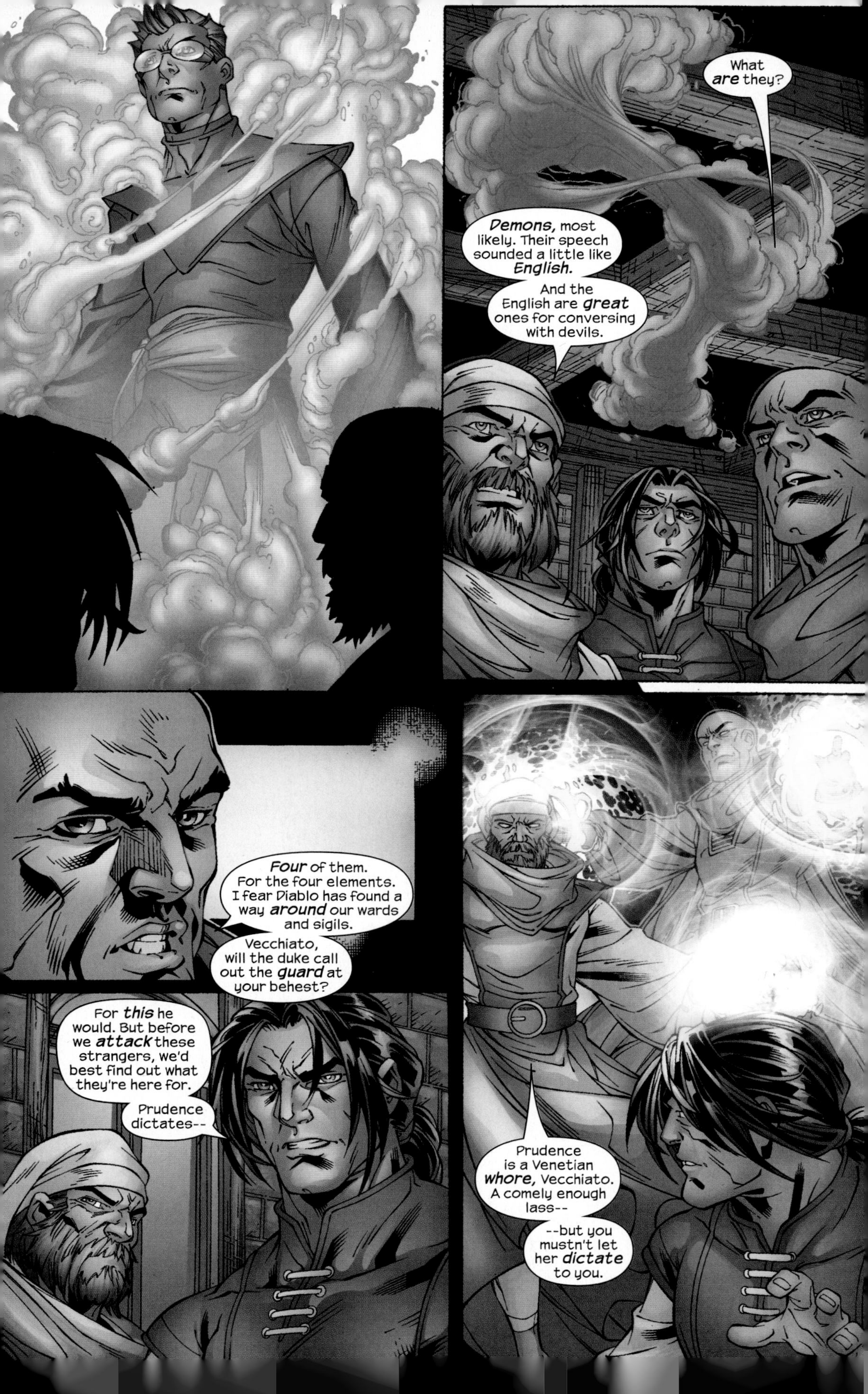
What are they?
Demons, most likely. Their speech sounded a little like English.
And the English are great ones for conversing with devils.
Four of them. For the four elements. I fear Diablo has found a way around our wards and sigils.
Vecchiato, will the duke call out the guard at your behest?
For this he would. But before we attack these strangers, we'd best find out what they're here for.
Prudence dictates--
Prudence is a Venetian whore, Vecchiato. A comely enough lass--
--but you mustn't let her dictate to you.

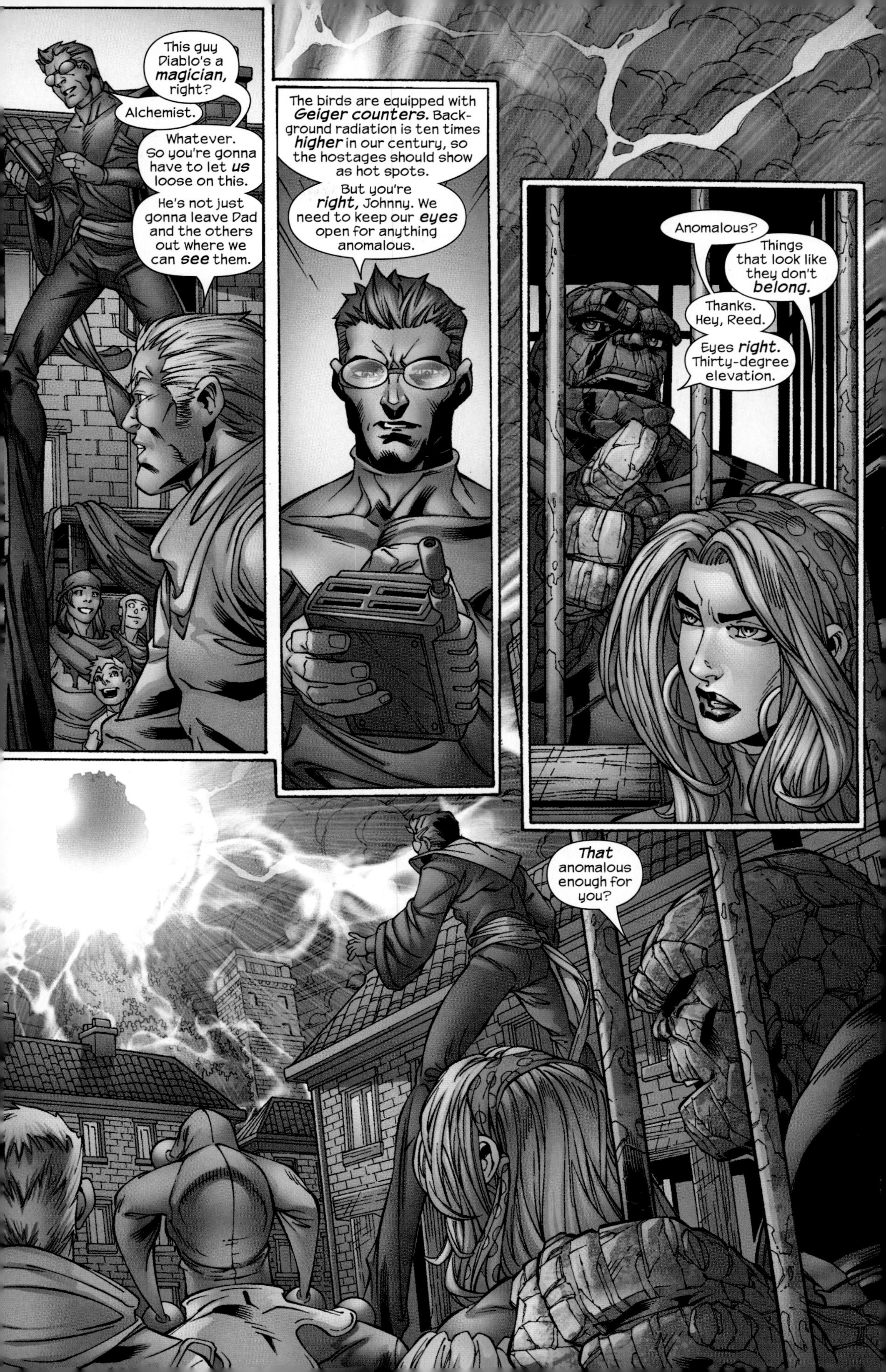
This guy Diablo's a *magician*, right?
Alchemist.
Whatever. So you're gonna have to let *us* loose on this.
He's not just gonna leave Dad and the others out where we can *see* them.
The birds are equipped with *Geiger counters.* Background radiation is ten times *higher* in our century, so the hostages should show as hot spots.
But you're *right,* Johnny. We need to keep our *eyes* open for anything anomalous.
Anomalous?
Things that look like they don't *belong.*
Thanks. Hey, Reed.
Eyes *right.* Thirty-degree elevation.
That anomalous enough for you?

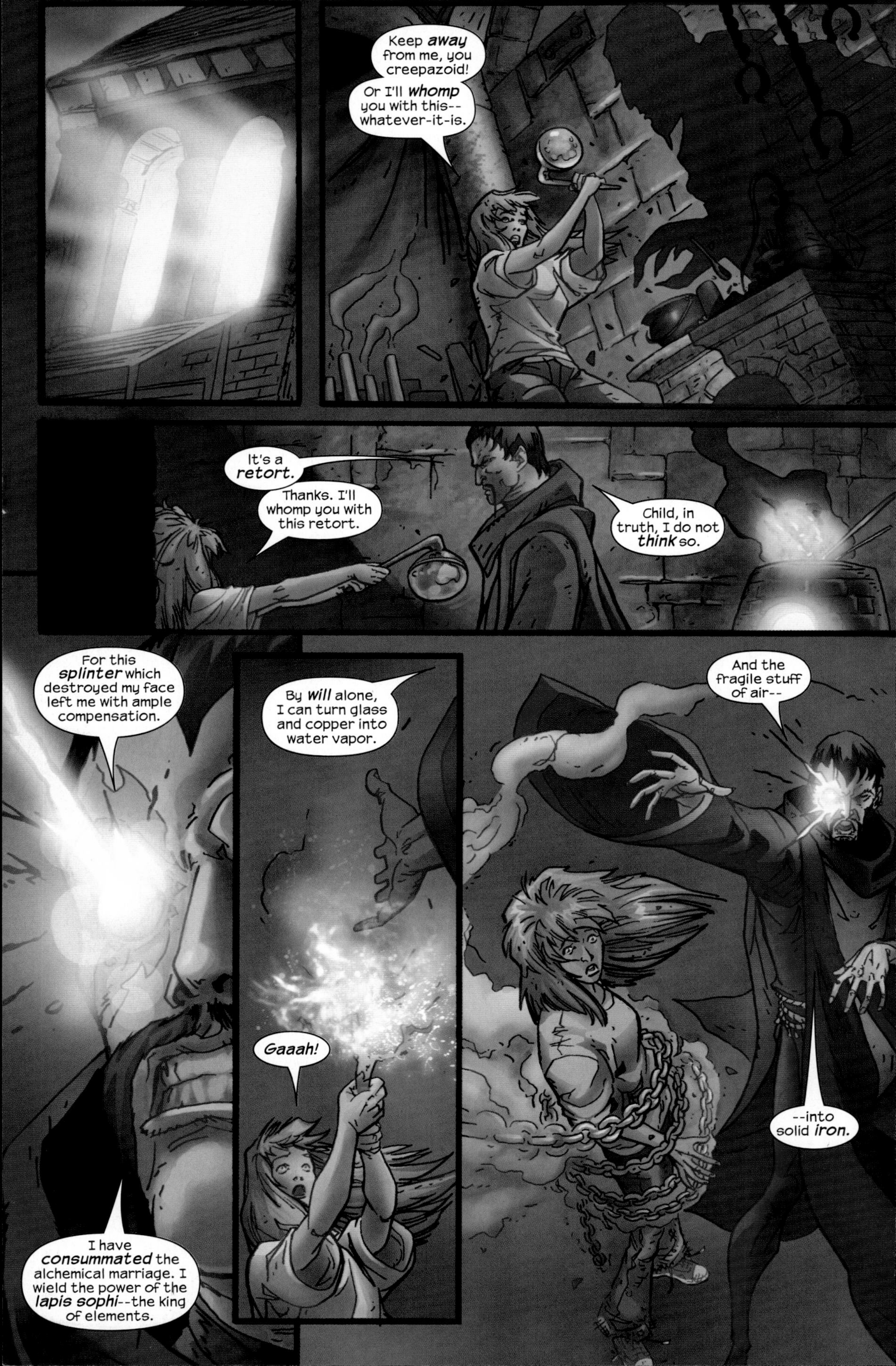

Keep *away* from me, you creepazoid!
Or I'll *whomp* you with this-- whatever-it-is.
It's a *retort.*
Thanks. I'll whomp you with this retort.
Child, in truth, I do not *think* so.
For this *splinter* which destroyed my face left me with ample compensation.
I have *consummated* the alchemical marriage. I wield the power of the *lapis sophi*--the king of elements.
By *will* alone, I can turn glass and copper into water vapor.
Gaaah!
And the fragile stuff of air--
--into solid *iron.*

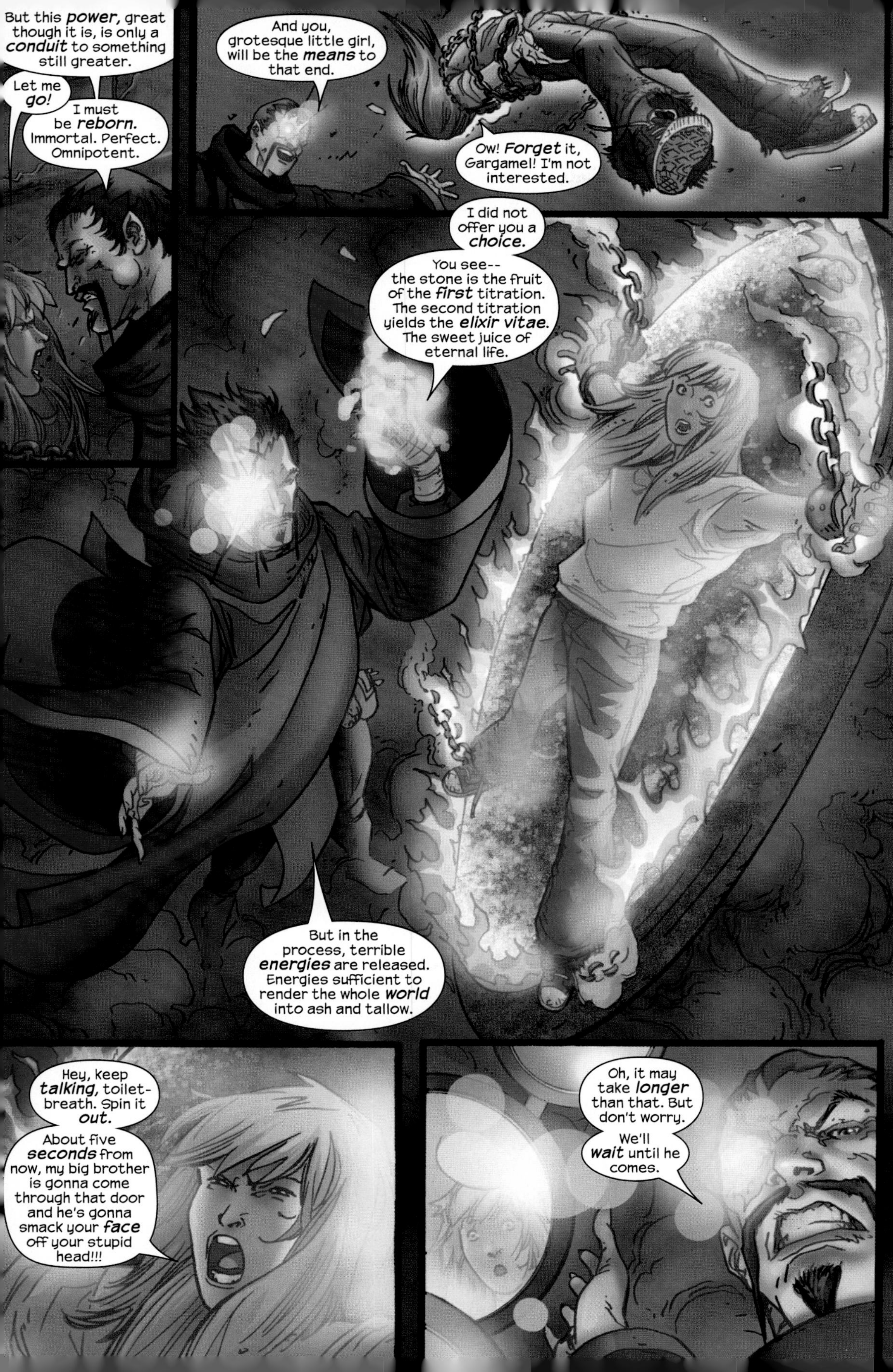

But this *power*, great though it is, is only a *conduit* to something still greater.
Let me *go!*
I must be *reborn.* Immortal. Perfect. Omnipotent.
And you, grotesque little girl, will be the *means* to that end.
Ow! *Forget* it, Gargamel! I'm not interested.
I did not offer you a *choice.*
You see-- the stone is the fruit of the *first* titration. The second titration yields the *elixir vitae*. The sweet juice of eternal life.
But in the process, terrible *energies* are released. Energies sufficient to render the whole *world* into ash and tallow.
Hey, keep *talking,* toilet-breath. Spin it *out.*
About five *seconds* from now, my big brother is gonna come through that door and he's gonna smack your *face* off your stupid head!!!
Oh, it may take *longer* than that. But don't worry.
We'll *wait* until he comes.

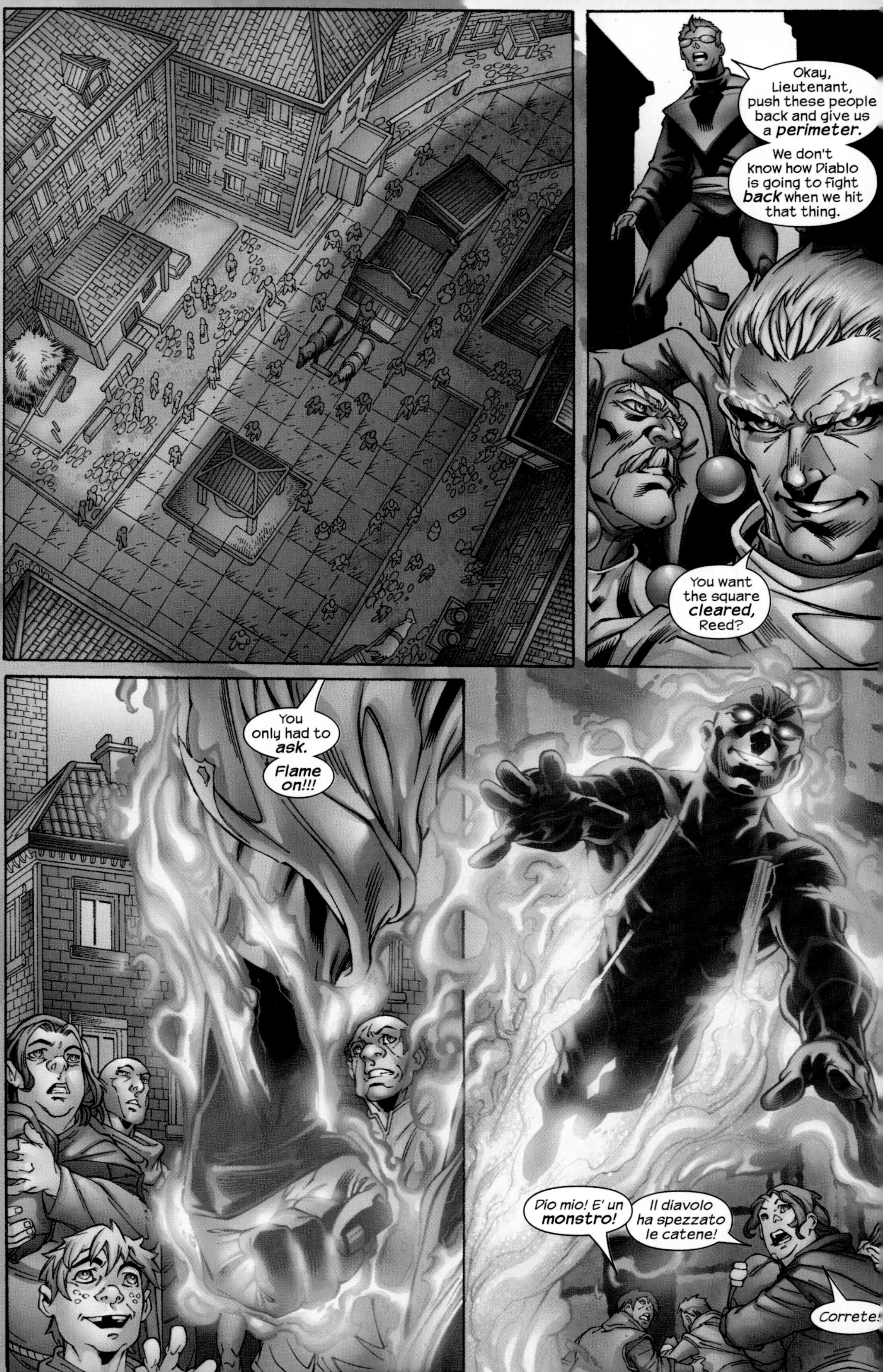
Okay, Lieutenant, push these people back and give us a *perimeter.*
We don't know how Diablo is going to fight *back* when we hit that thing.
You want the square *cleared,* Reed?
You only had to *ask.*
Flame on!!!
*Dio mio! E' un **monstro!***
Il diavolo ha spezzato le catene!
Correte!

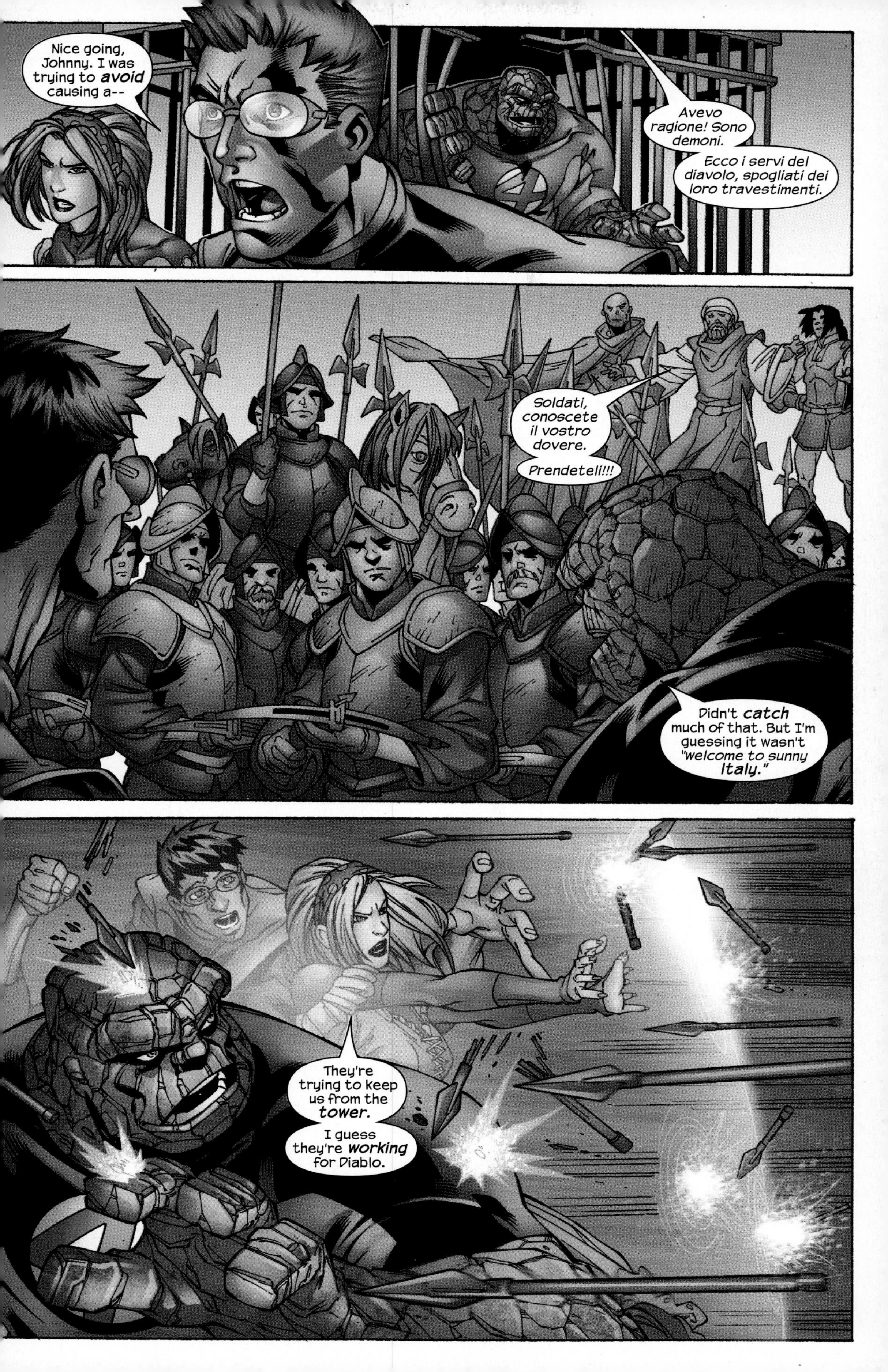
Nice going, Johnny. I was trying to **avoid** causing a--
Avevo ragione! Sono demoni.
Ecco i servi del diavolo, spogliati dei loro travestimenti.
Soldati, conoscete il vostro dovere.
Prendeteli!!!
Didn't **catch** much of that. But I'm guessing it wasn't "welcome to sunny **Italy.**"
They're trying to keep us from the **tower.**
I guess they're **working** for Diablo.

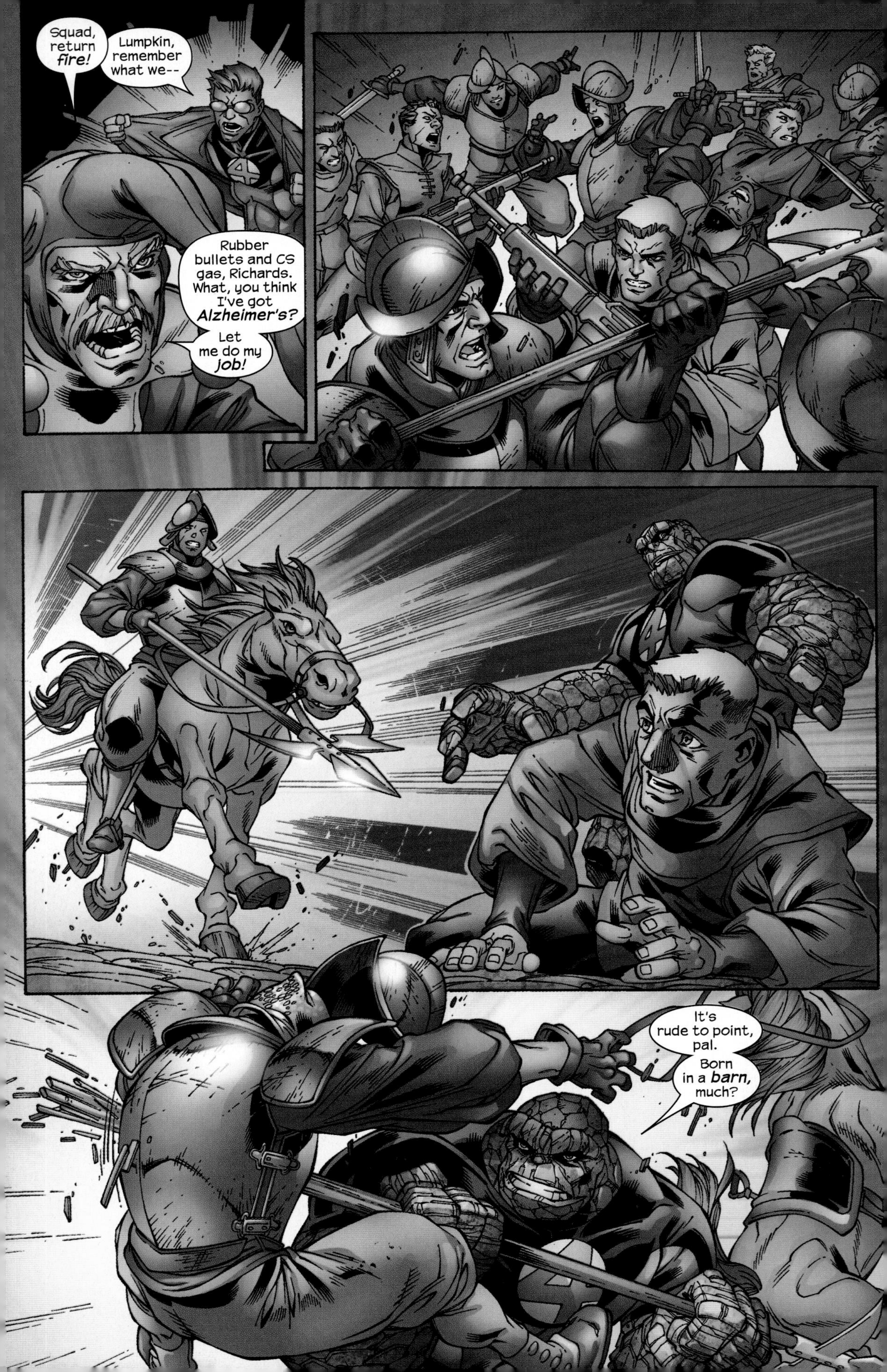
Squad, return *fire!*
Lumpkin, remember what we--
Rubber bullets and CS gas, Richards. What, you think I've got ***Alzheimer's?***
Let me do my ***job!***
It's rude to point, pal.
Born in a ***barn,*** much?

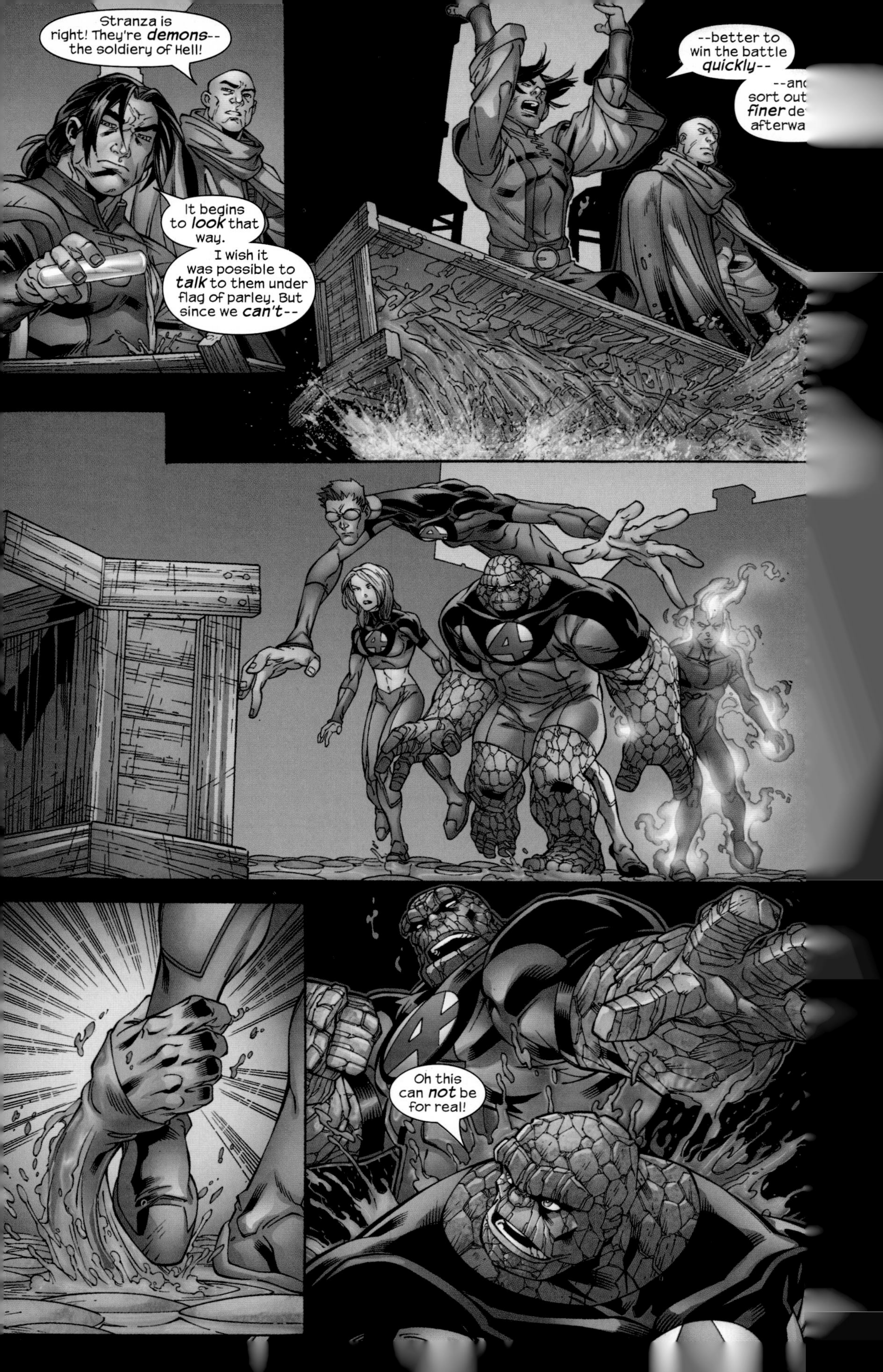

Stranza is right! They're *demons*-- the soldiery of Hell!
It begins to *look* that way.
I wish it was possible to *talk* to them under flag of parley. But since we *can't*--
--better to win the battle *quickly*--
Oh this can *not* be for real!

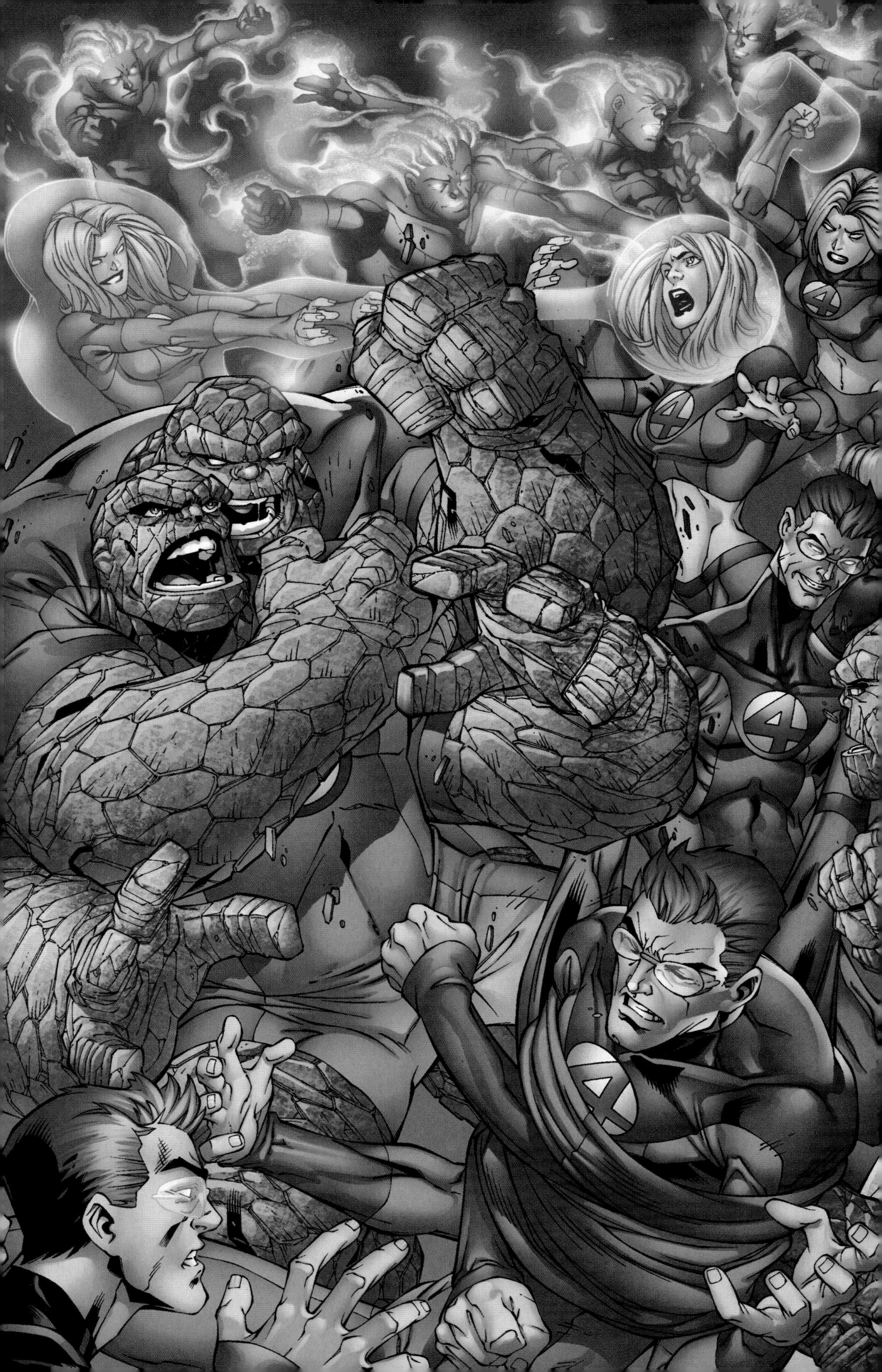

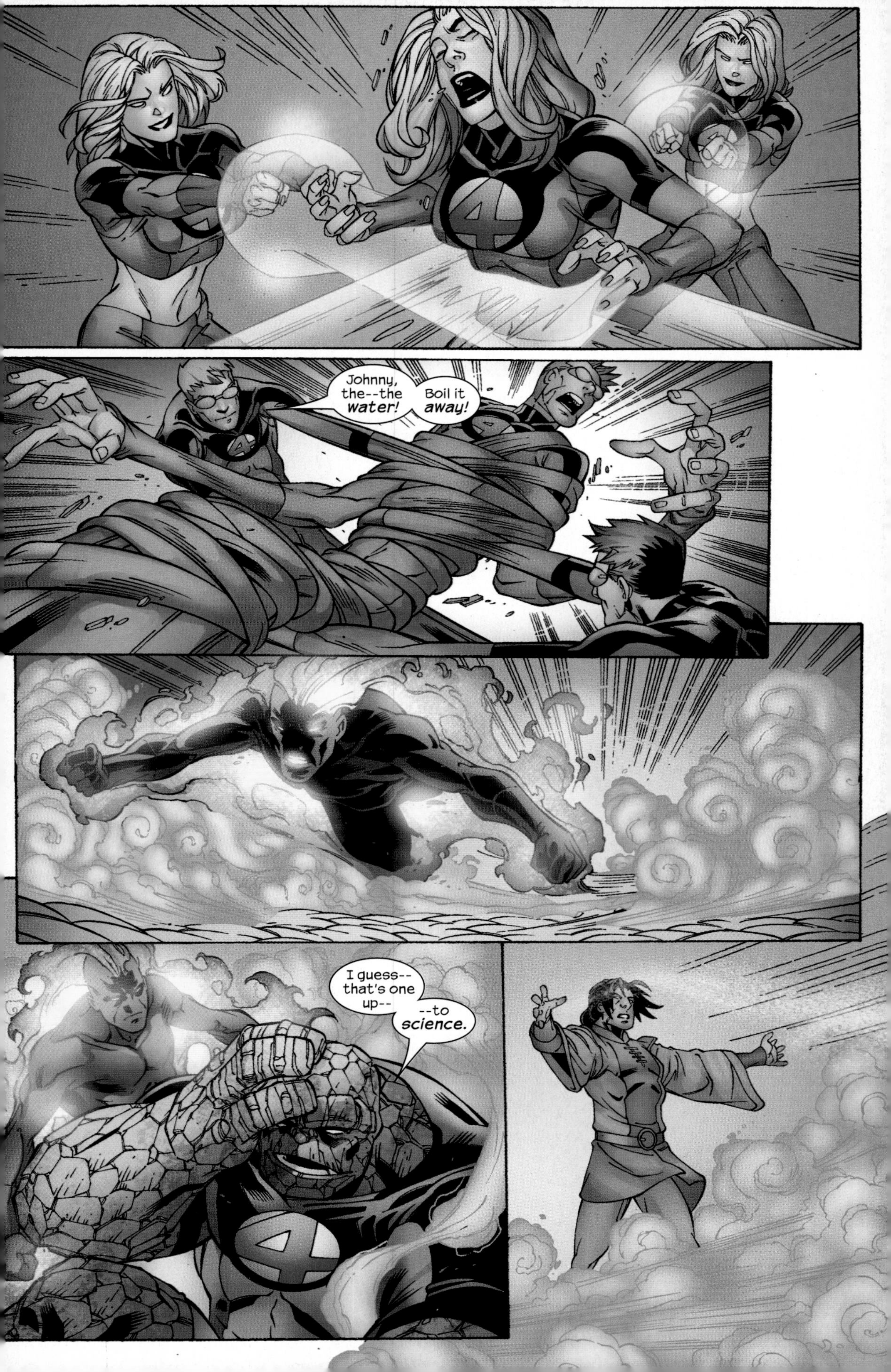

Johnny, the--the water!
Boil it away!
I guess--that's one up--
--to science.

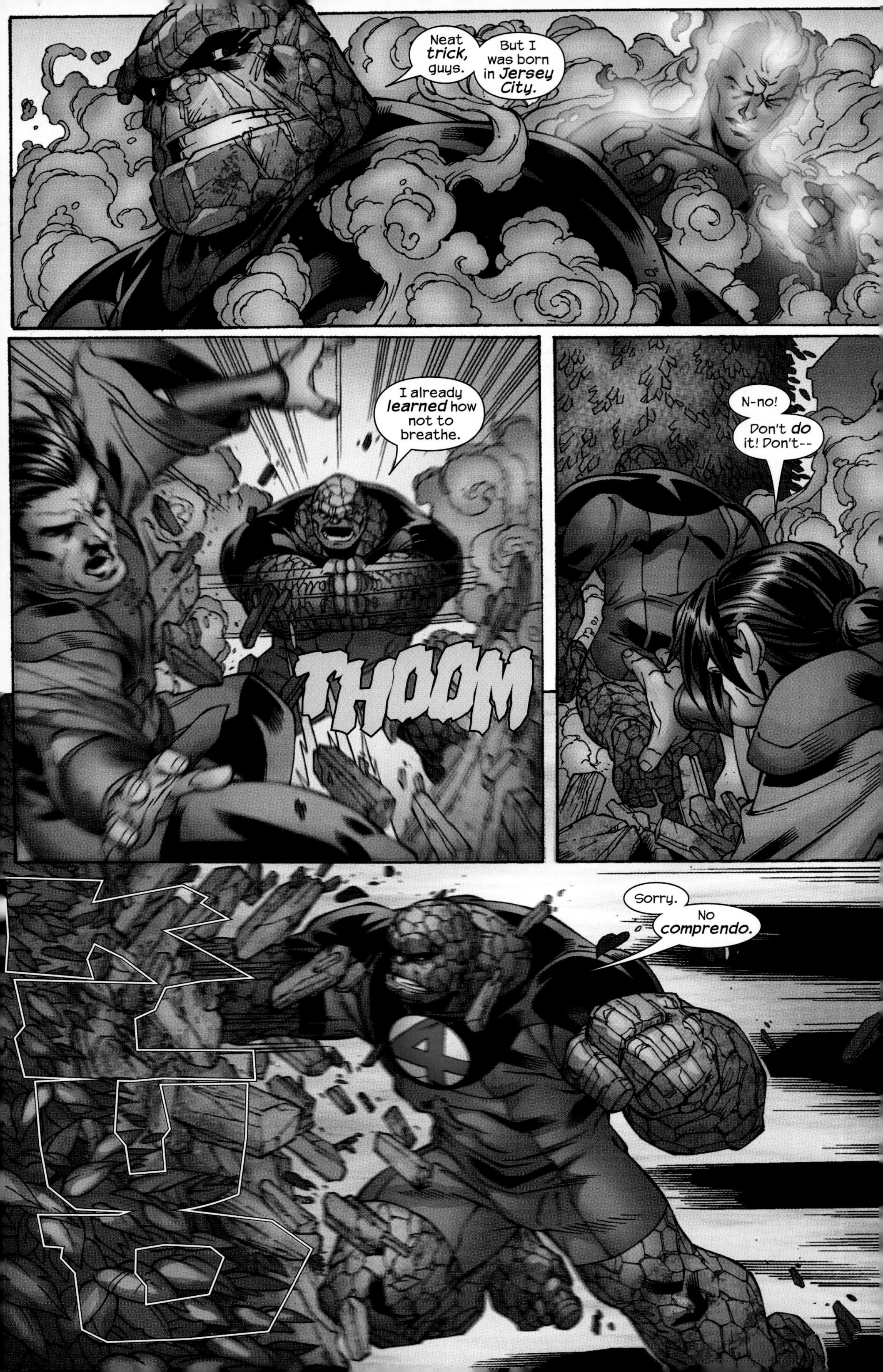
Neat trick, guys.
But I was born in Jersey City.
I already learned how not to breathe.
THOOM
N-no!
Don't do it! Don't--
Sorry.
No comprendo.

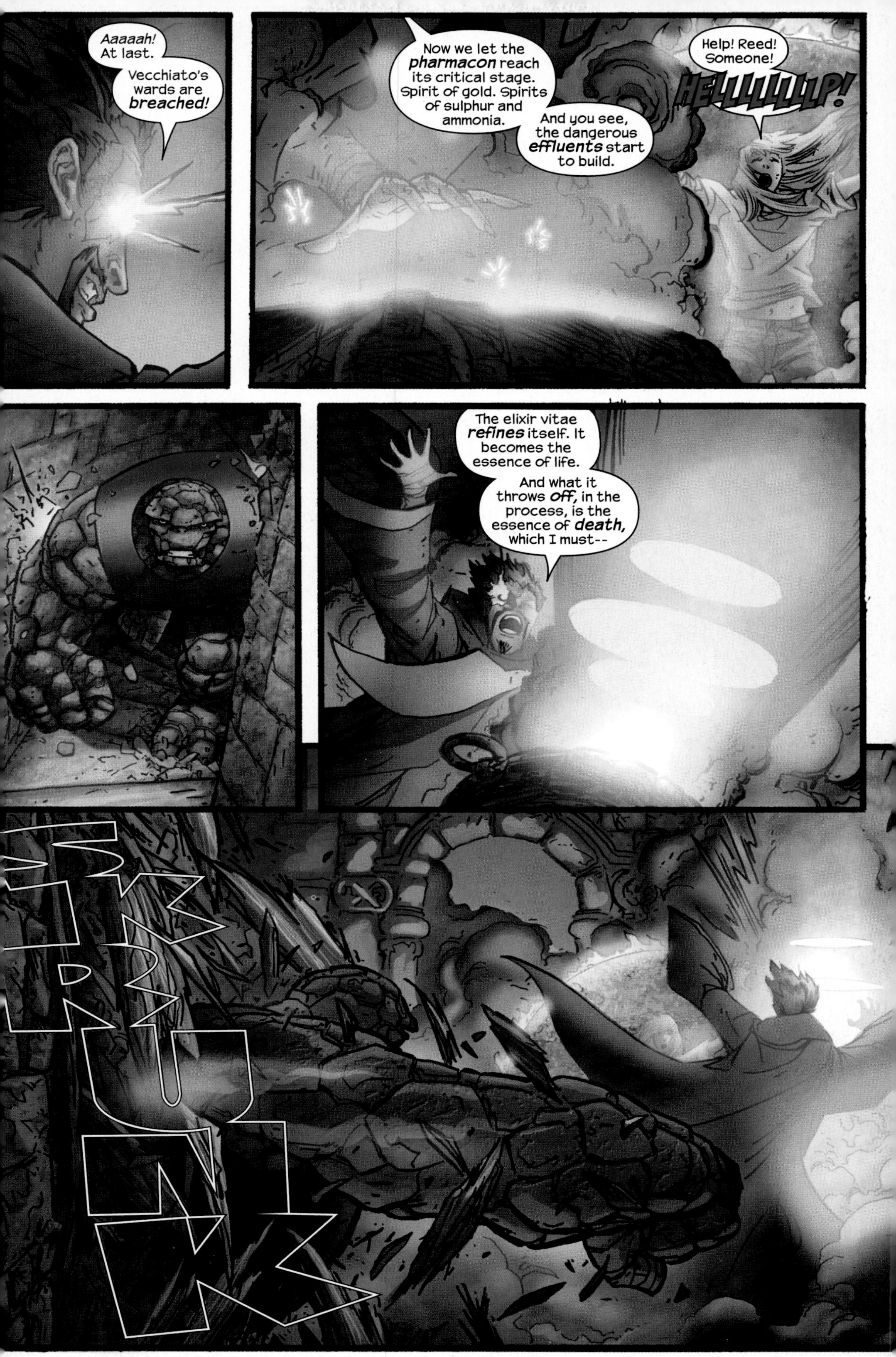
Aaaaah! At last.
Vecchiato's wards are *breached!*
Now we let the *pharmacon* reach its critical stage. Spirit of gold. Spirits of sulphur and ammonia.
And you see, the dangerous *effluents* start to build.
Help! Reed! Someone!
HELLLLLLLLP!
The elixir vitae *refines* itself. It becomes the essence of life.
And what it throws *off,* in the process, is the essence of *death,* which I must--
SKRUNK

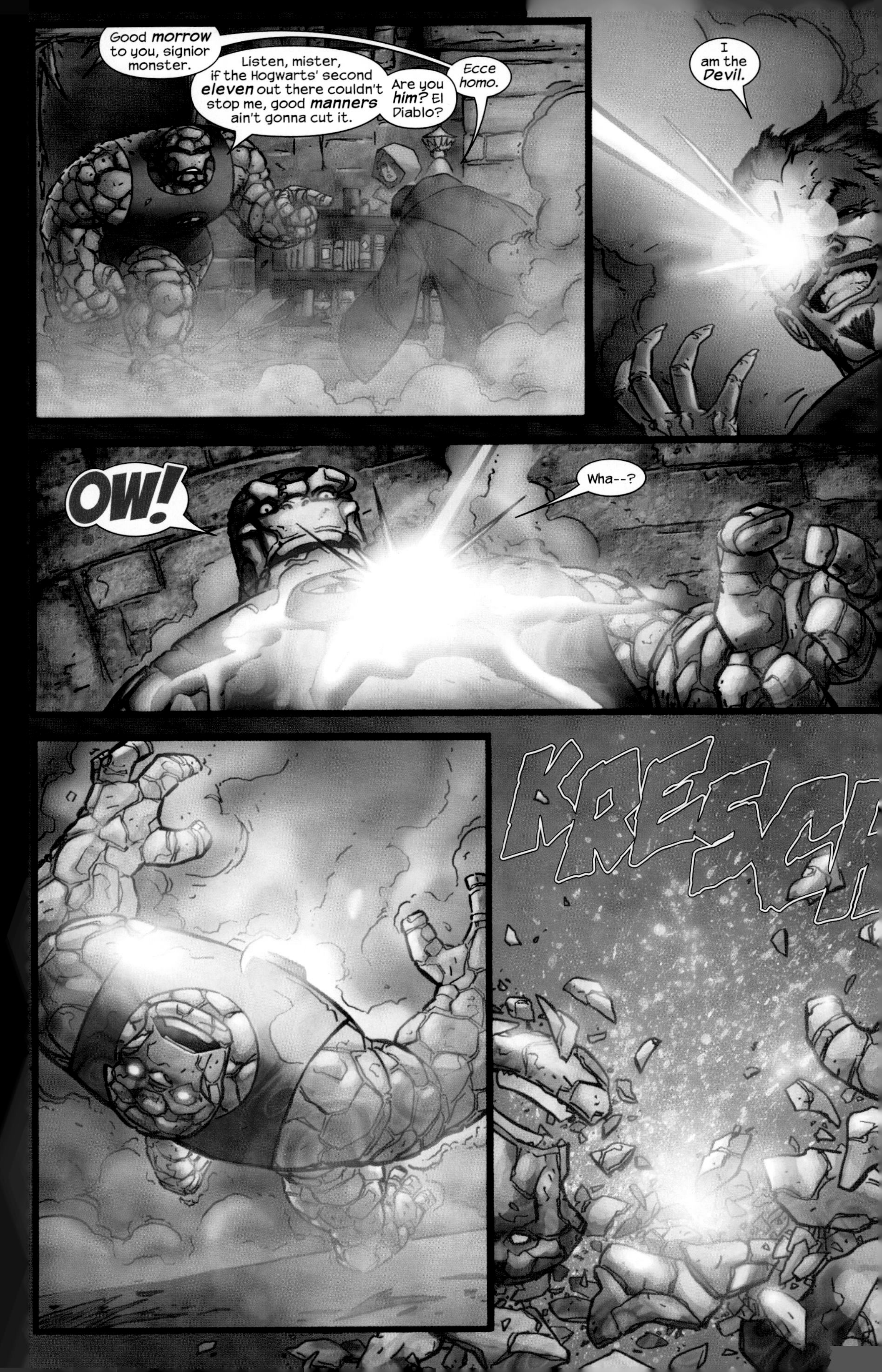
Good morrow to you, signior monster.
Listen, mister, if the Hogwarts' second eleven out there couldn't stop me, good manners ain't gonna cut it.
Are you him? El Diablo?
Ecce homo.
I am the Devil.
OW!
Wha--?

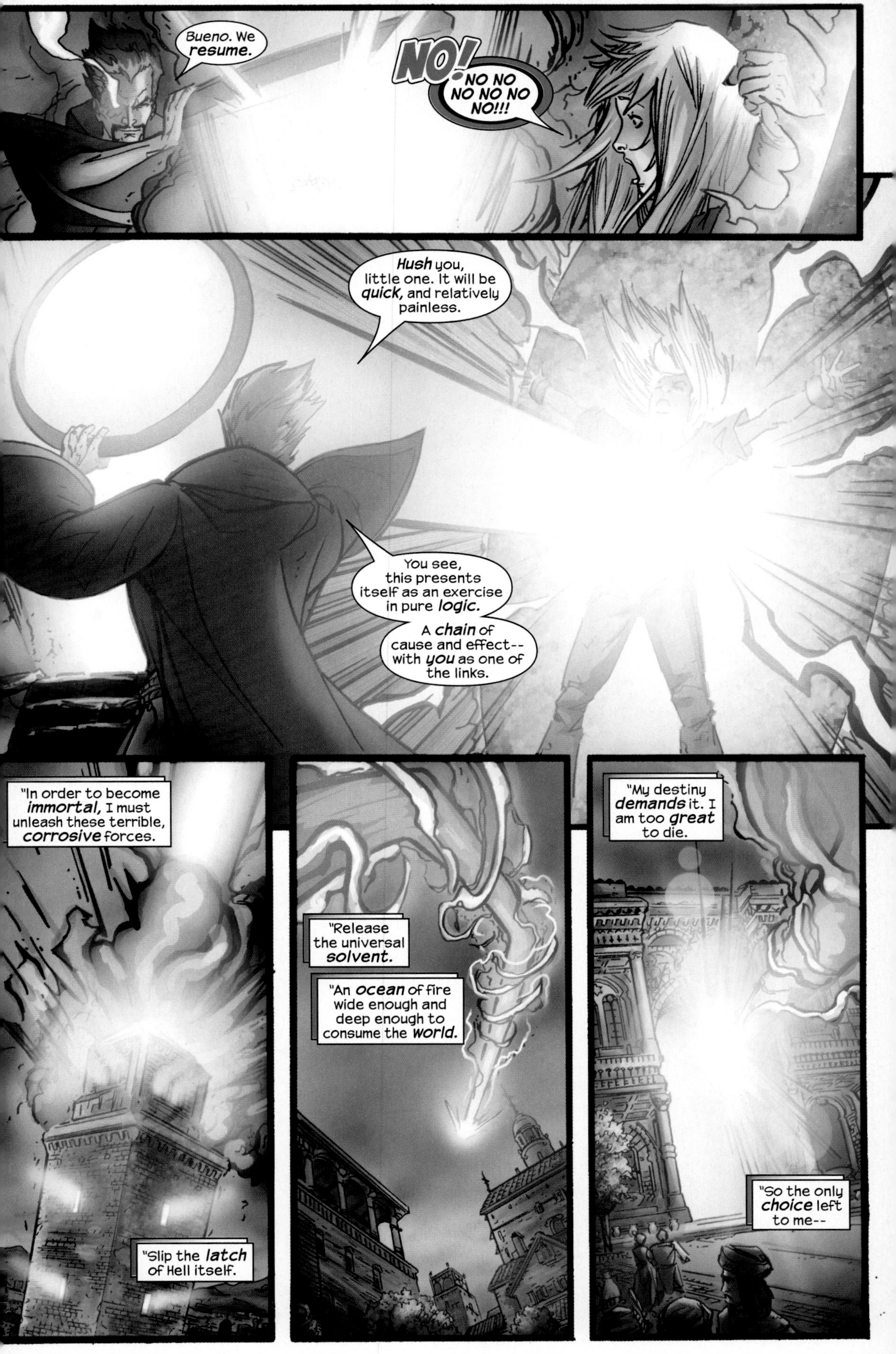
Bueno. We resume.
NO!
NO NO NO NO NO NO!!!
Hush you, little one. It will be quick, and relatively painless.
You see, this presents itself as an exercise in pure logic.
A chain of cause and effect-- with you as one of the links.
"In order to become immortal, I must unleash these terrible, corrosive forces.
"Slip the latch of Hell itself.
"Release the universal solvent.
"An ocean of fire wide enough and deep enough to consume the world.
"My destiny demands it. I am too great to die.
"So the only choice left to me--

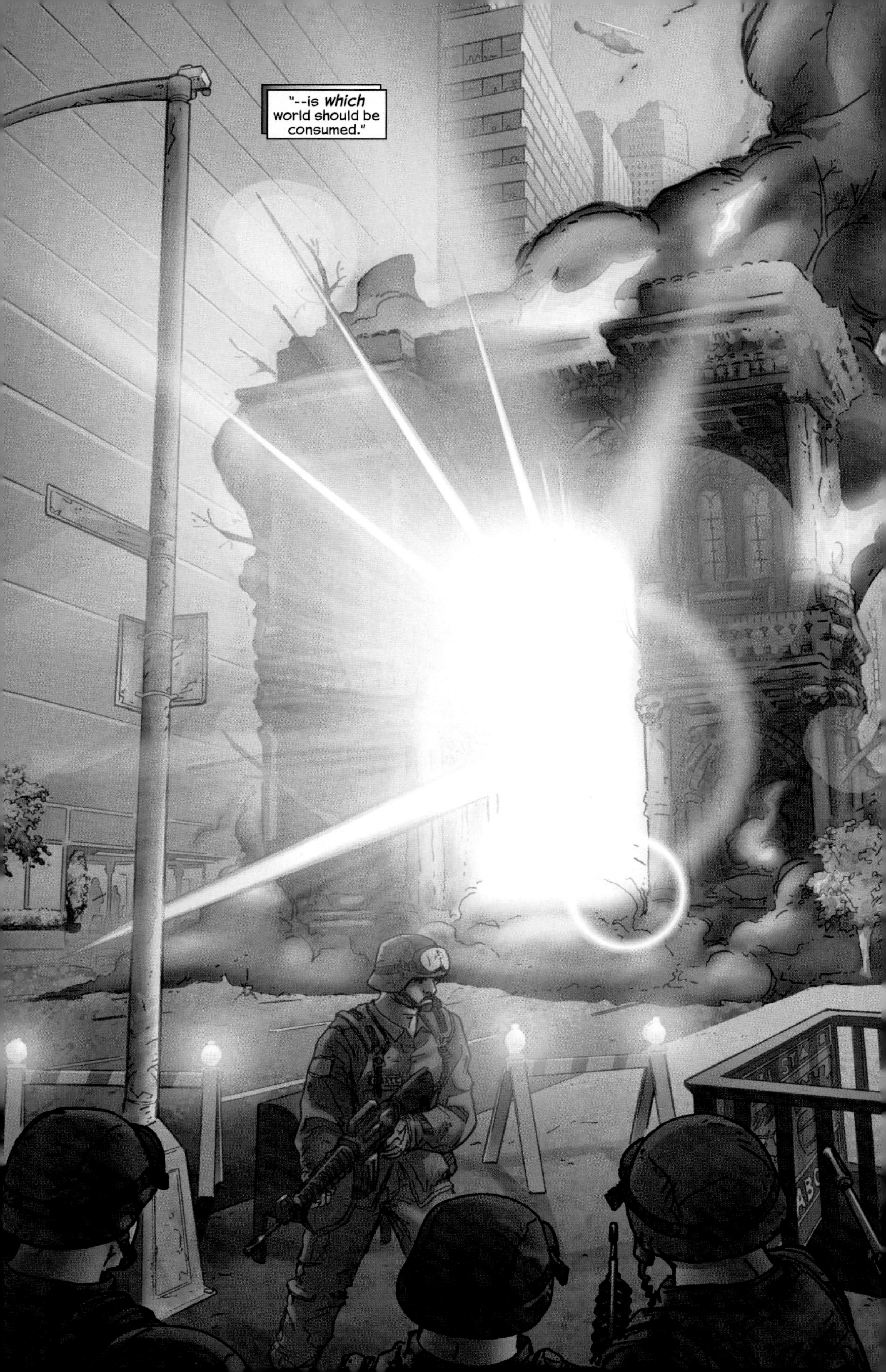
"--is *which* world should be consumed."

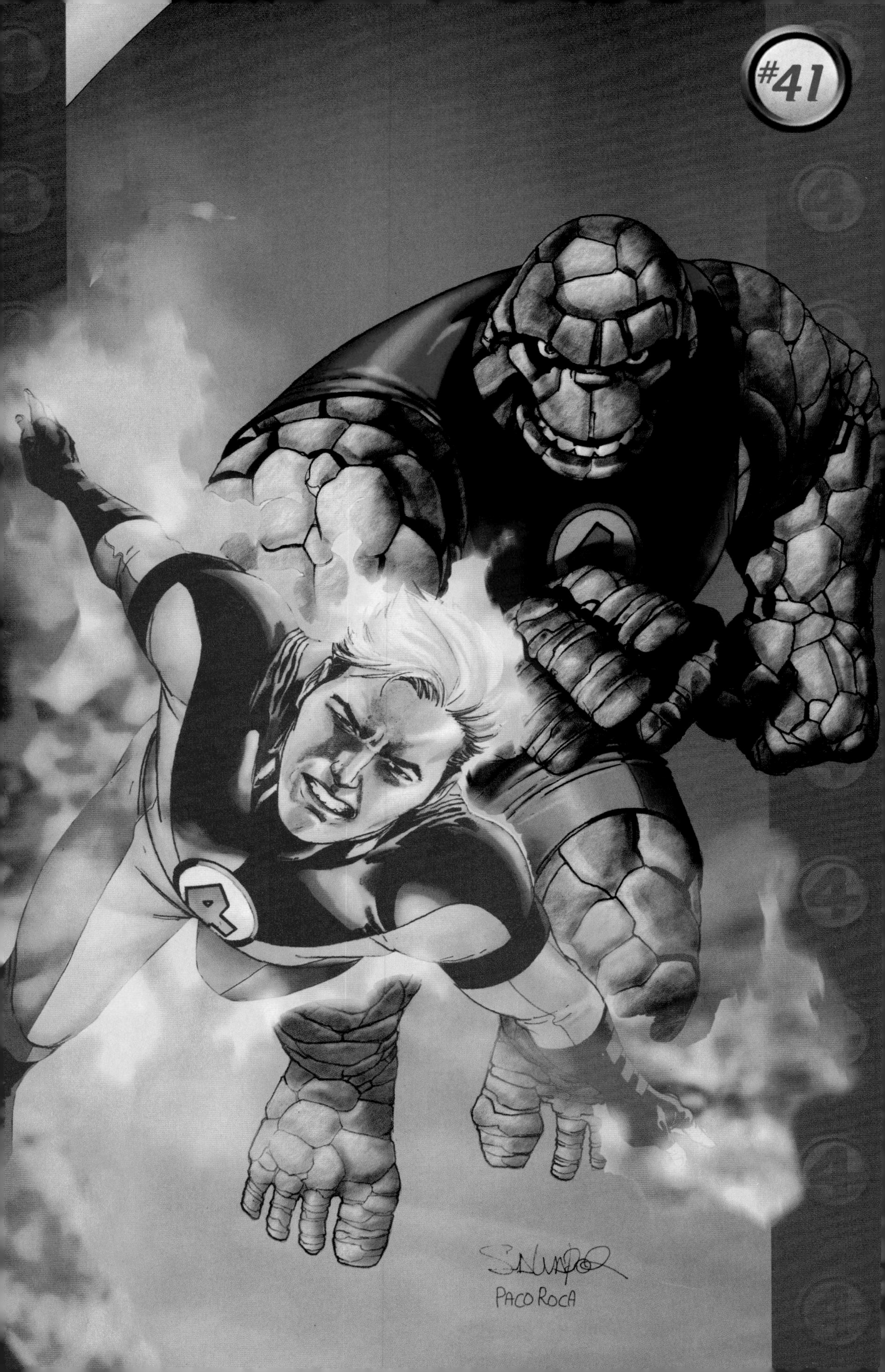
#41
PACO ROCA

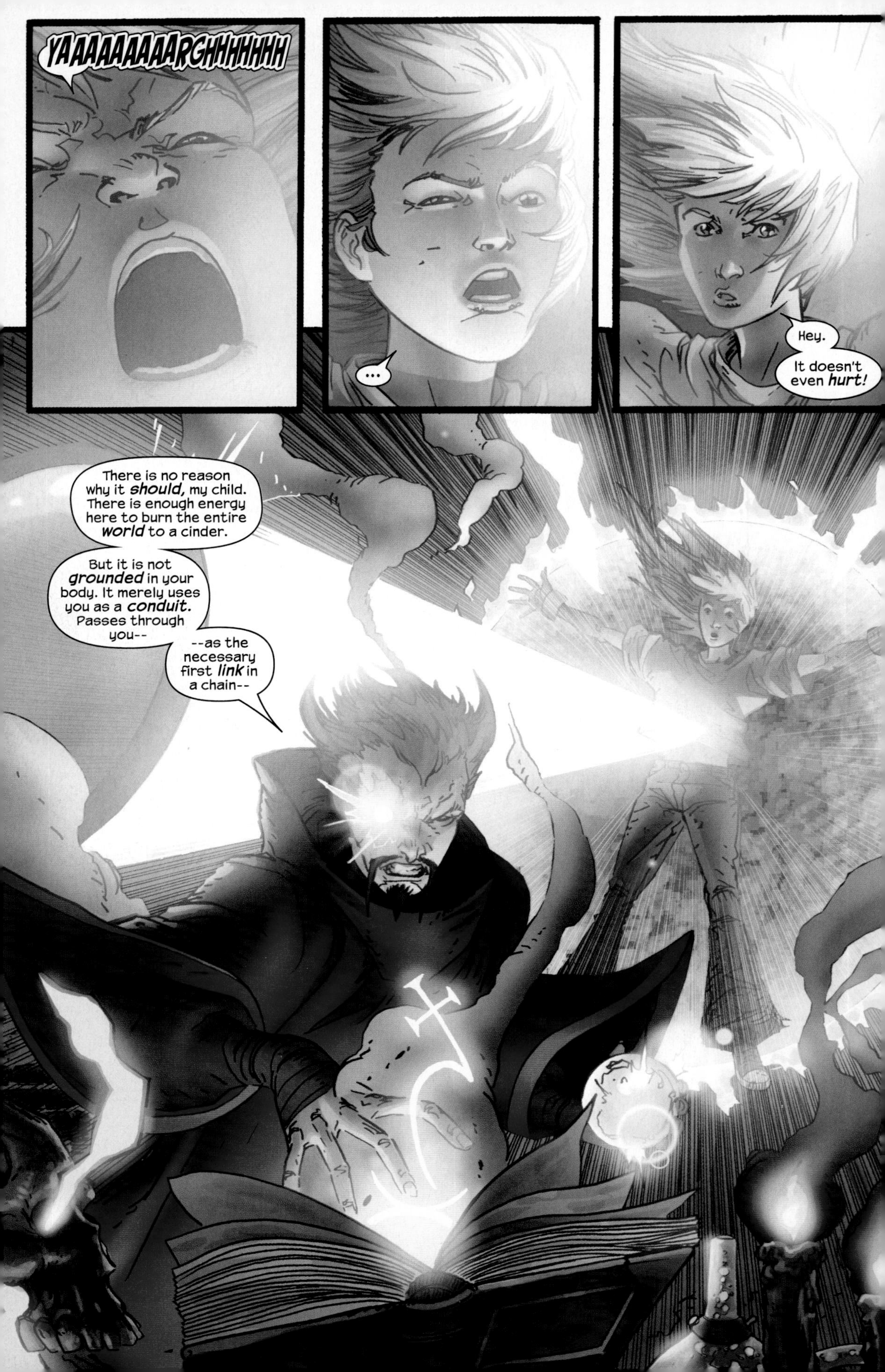
YAAAAAAAARGHHHHHH
...
Hey.
It doesn't even *hurt!*
There is no reason why it *should,* my child. There is enough energy here to burn the entire *world* to a cinder.
But it is not *grounded* in your body. It merely uses you as a *conduit.* Passes through you--
--as the necessary first *link* in a chain--

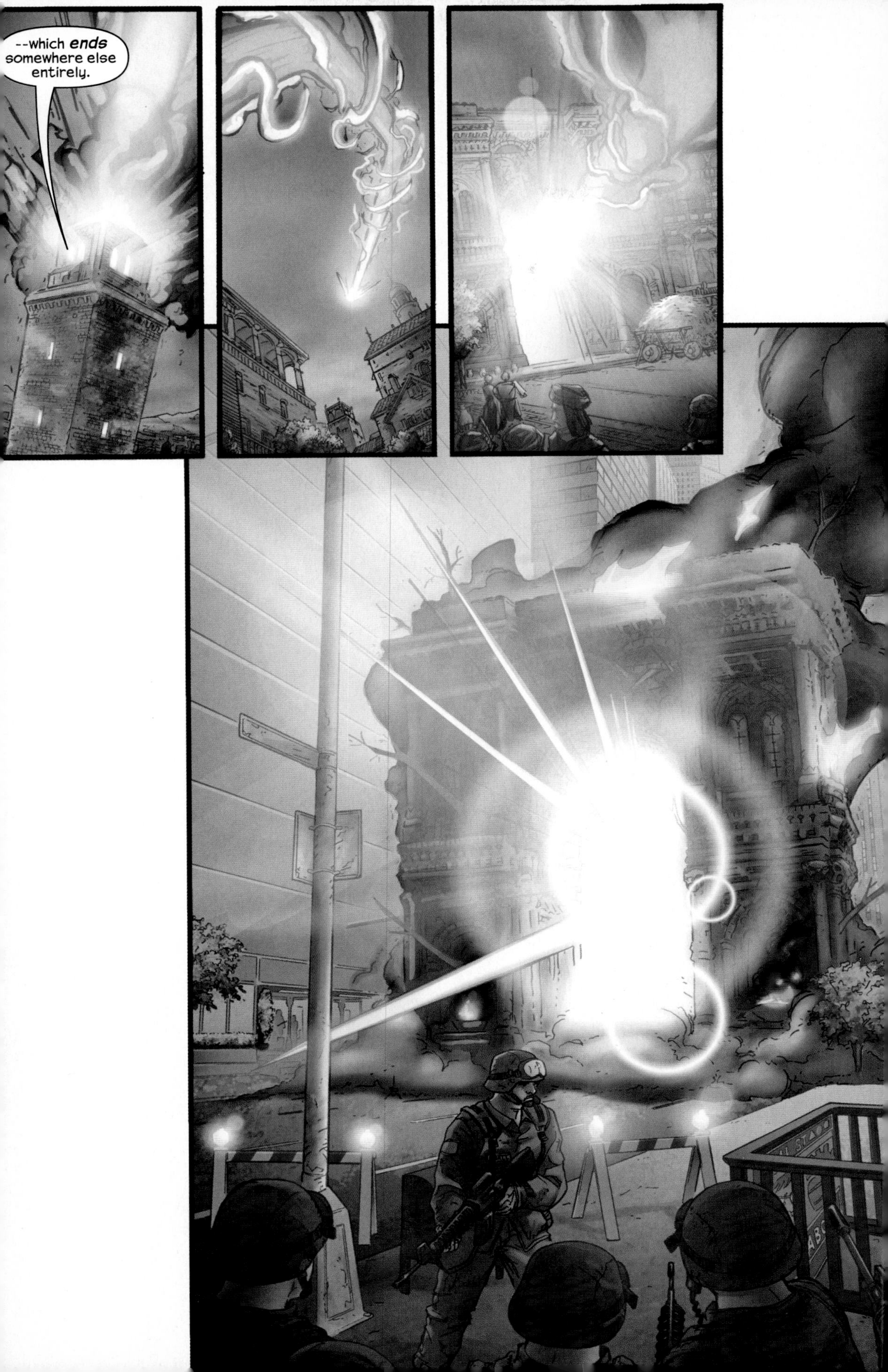
--which **ends** somewhere else entirely.

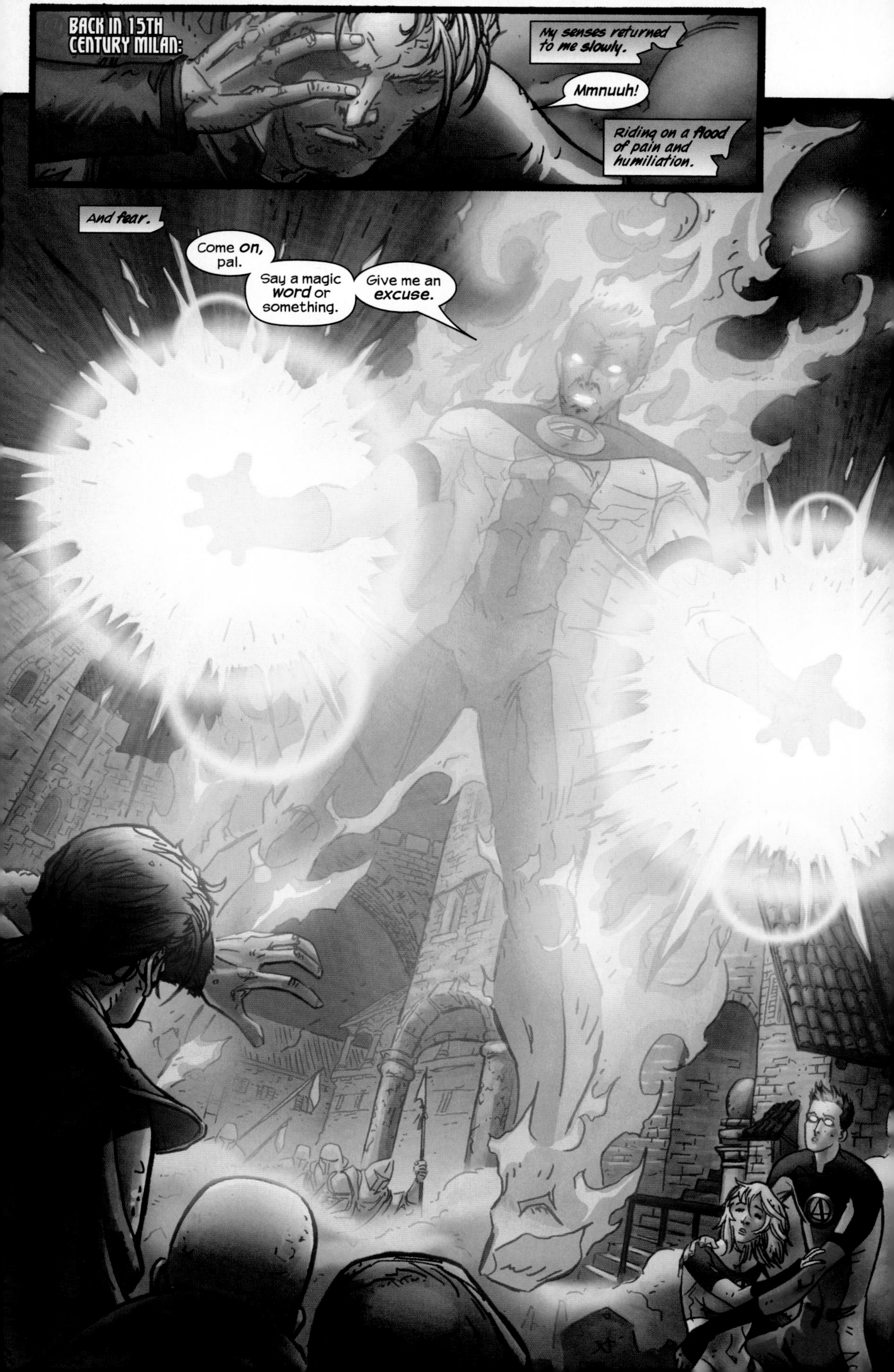
BACK IN 15TH CENTURY MILAN:
My senses returned to me slowly.
Mmnuuh!
Riding on a flood of pain and humiliation.
And fear.
Come on, pal.
Say a magic word or something.
Give me an excuse.

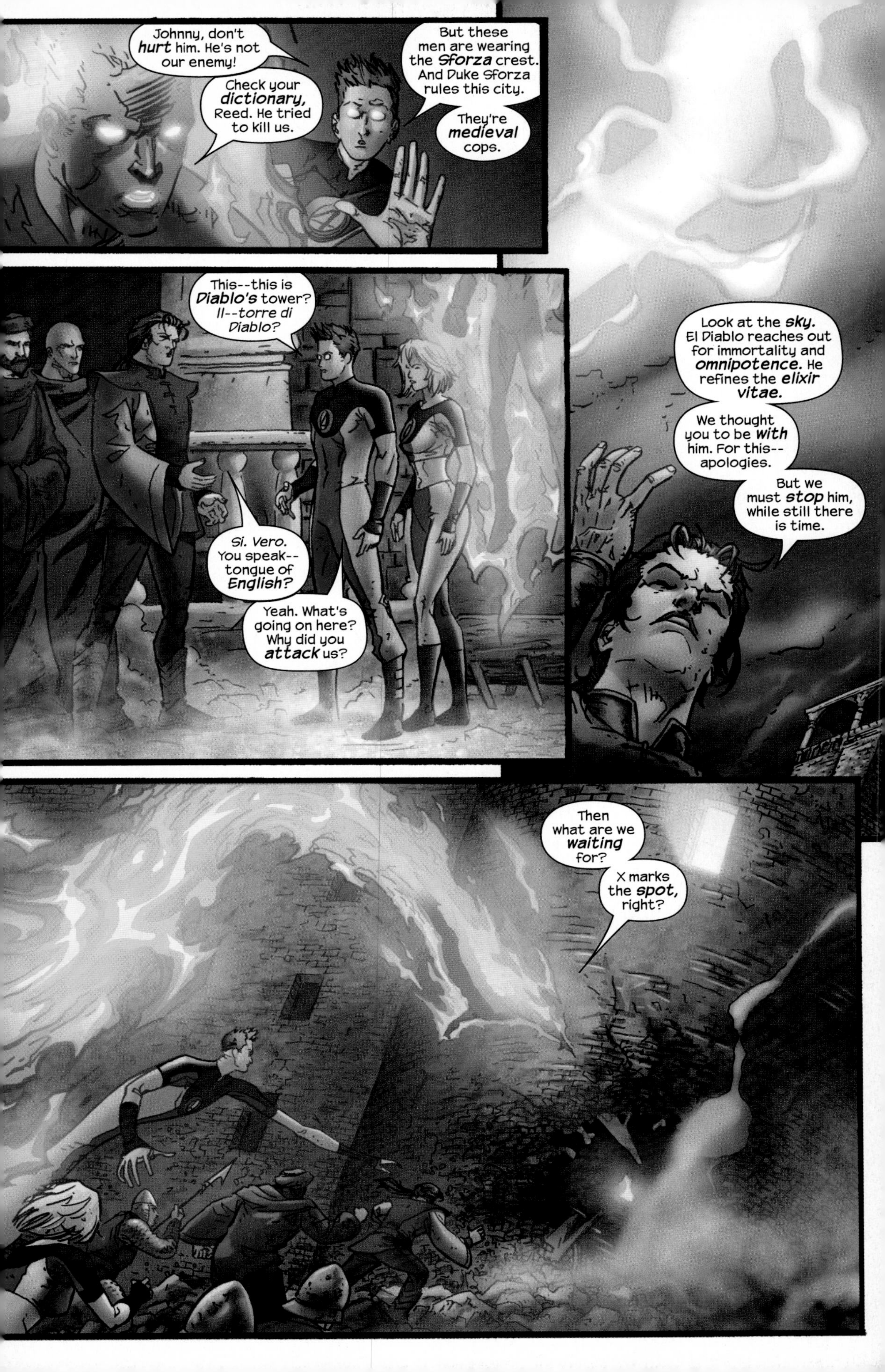
Johnny, don't hurt him. He's not our enemy!
Check your dictionary, Reed. He tried to kill us.
But these men are wearing the Sforza crest. And Duke Sforza rules this city.
They're medieval cops.
This--this is Diablo's tower? Il--torre di Diablo?
Si. Vero. You speak--tongue of English?
Yeah. What's going on here? Why did you attack us?
Look at the sky. El Diablo reaches out for immortality and omnipotence. He refines the elixir vitae.
We thought you to be with him. For this--apologies.
But we must stop him, while still there is time.
Then what are we waiting for?
X marks the spot, right?

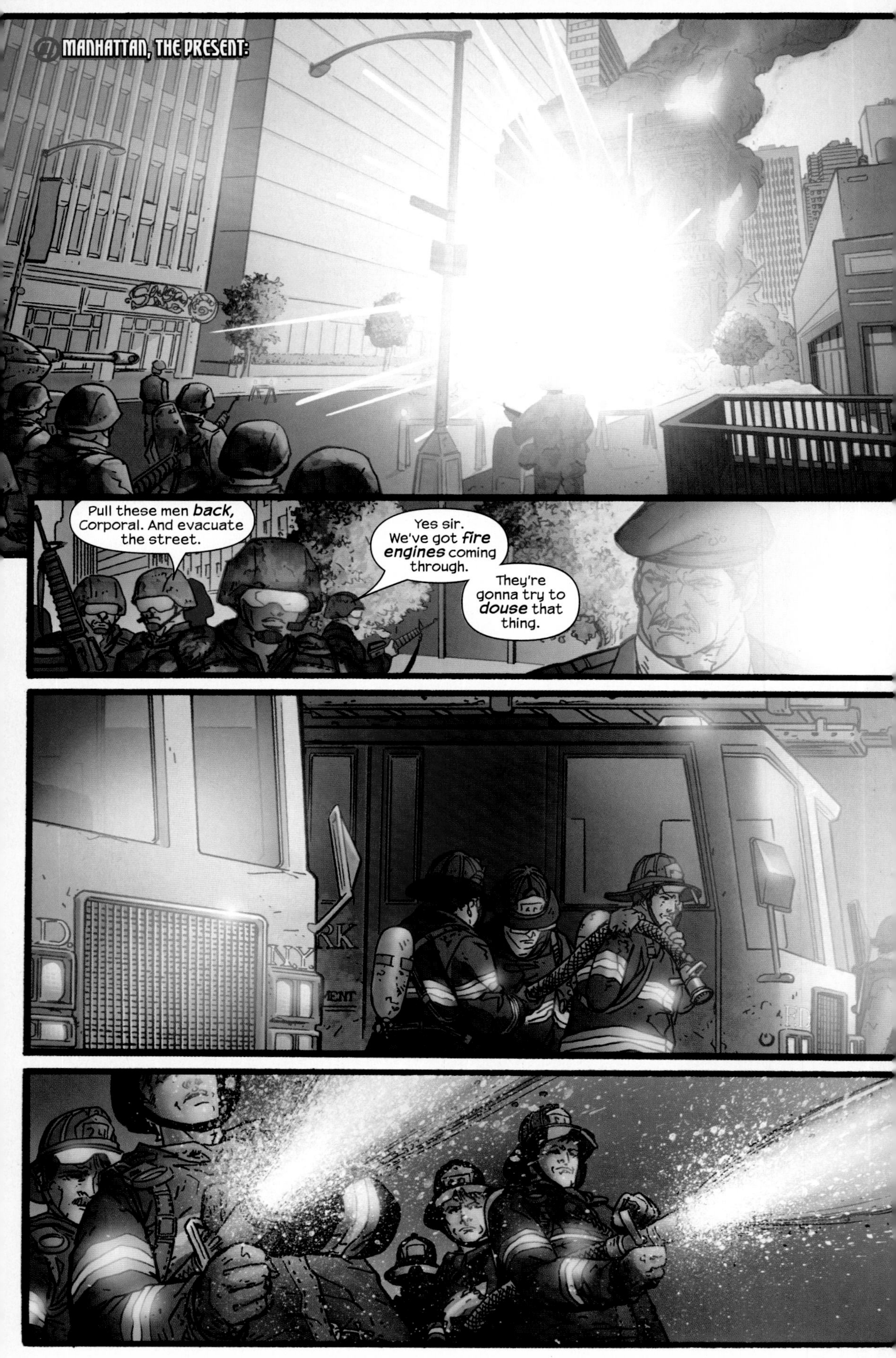
MANHATTAN, THE PRESENT:
Pull these men back, Corporal. And evacuate the street.
Yes sir. We've got fire engines coming through.
They're gonna try to douse that thing.

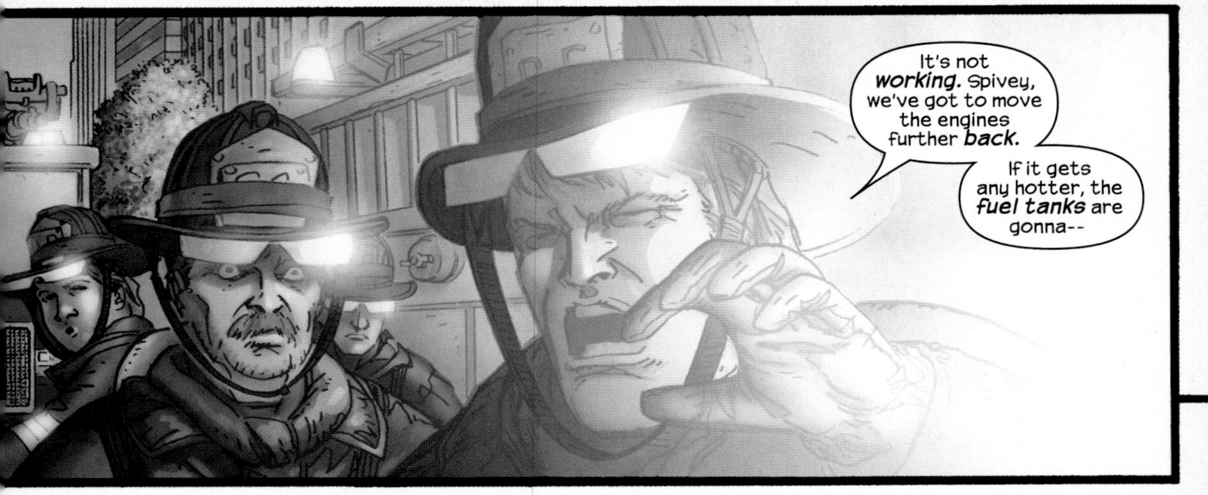
It's not **working.** Spivey, we've got to move the engines further **back.**
If it gets any hotter, the ***fuel tanks*** are gonna--

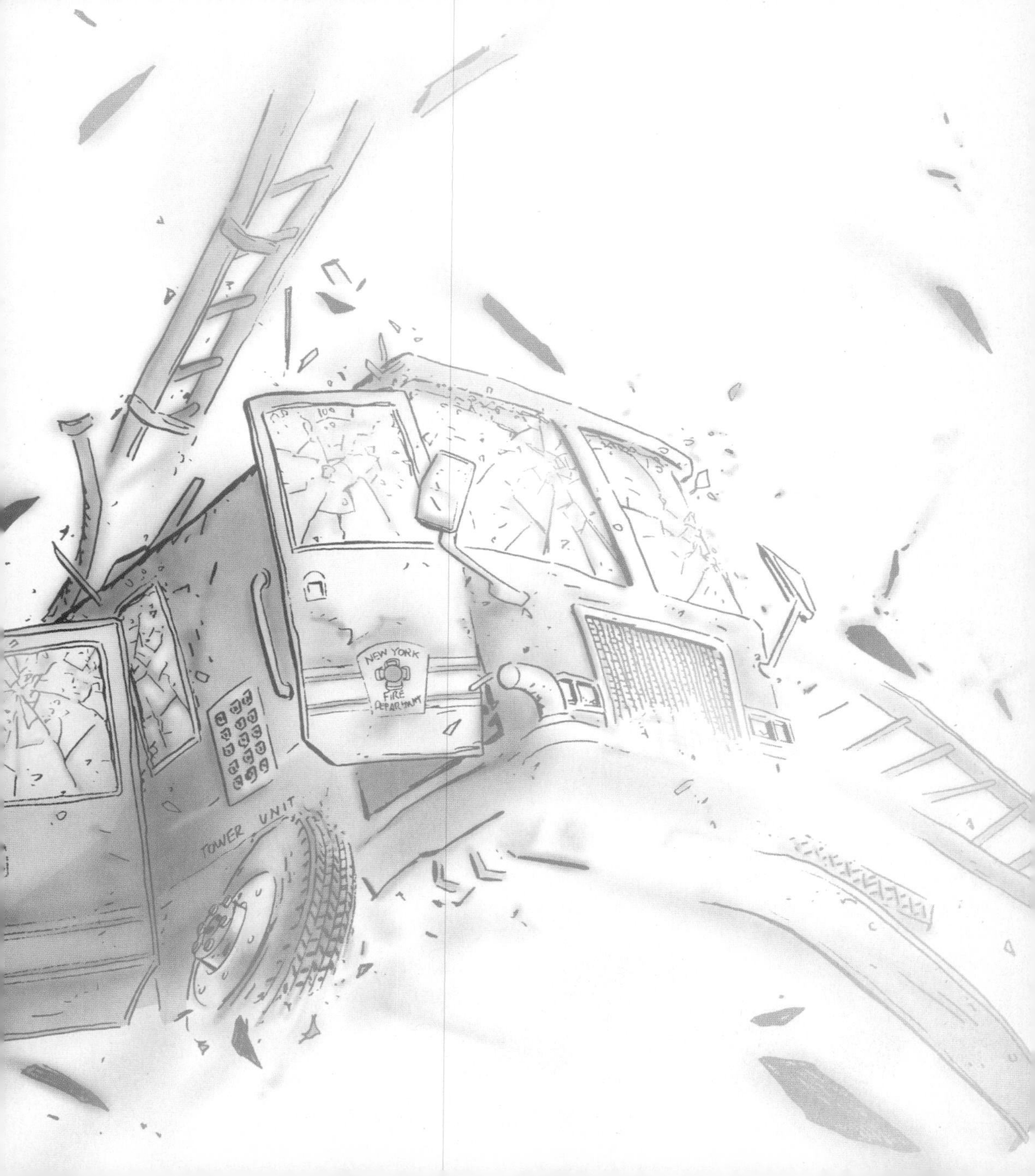
NEW YORK FIRE DEPARTMENT
TOWER UNIT

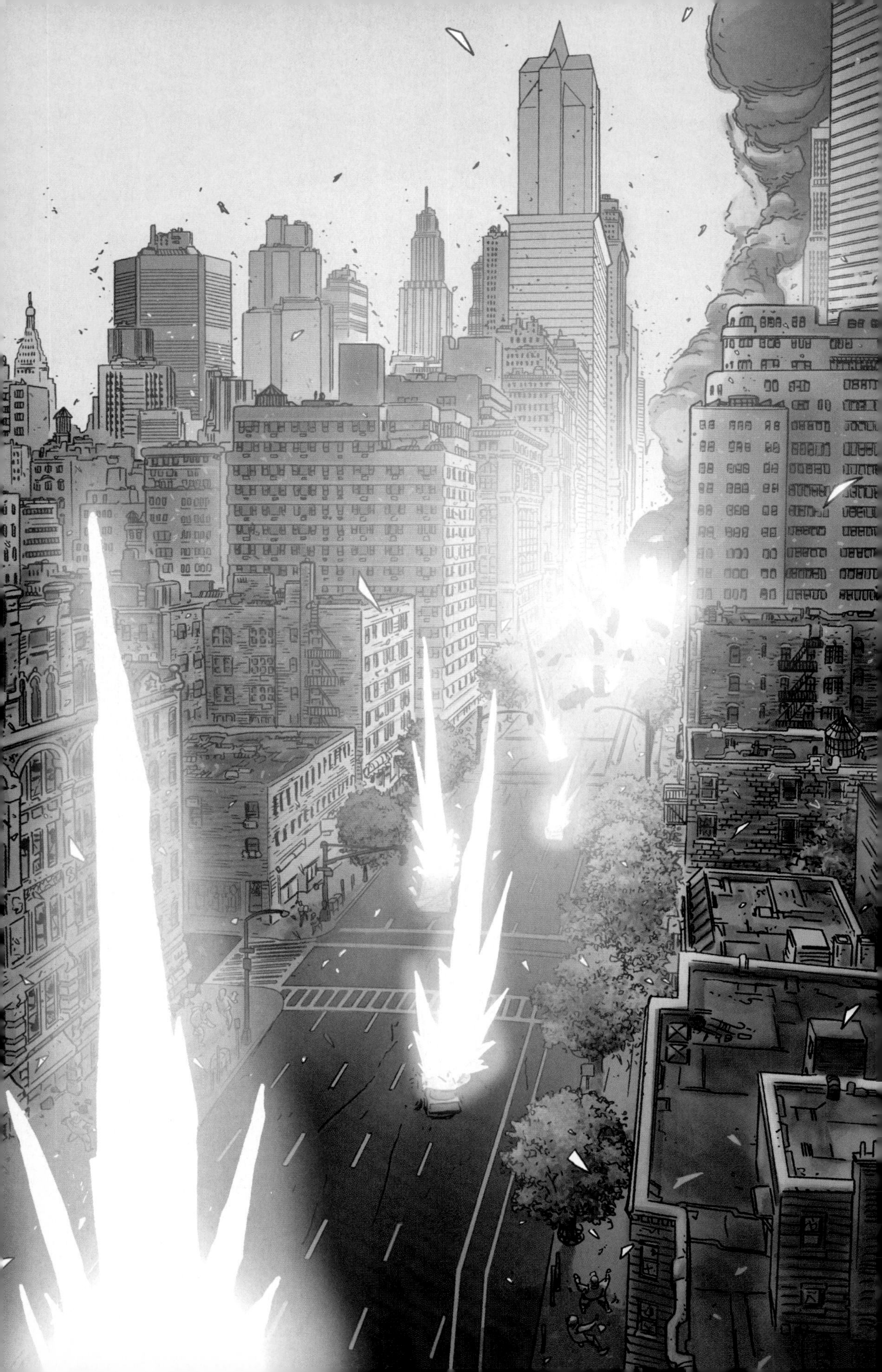

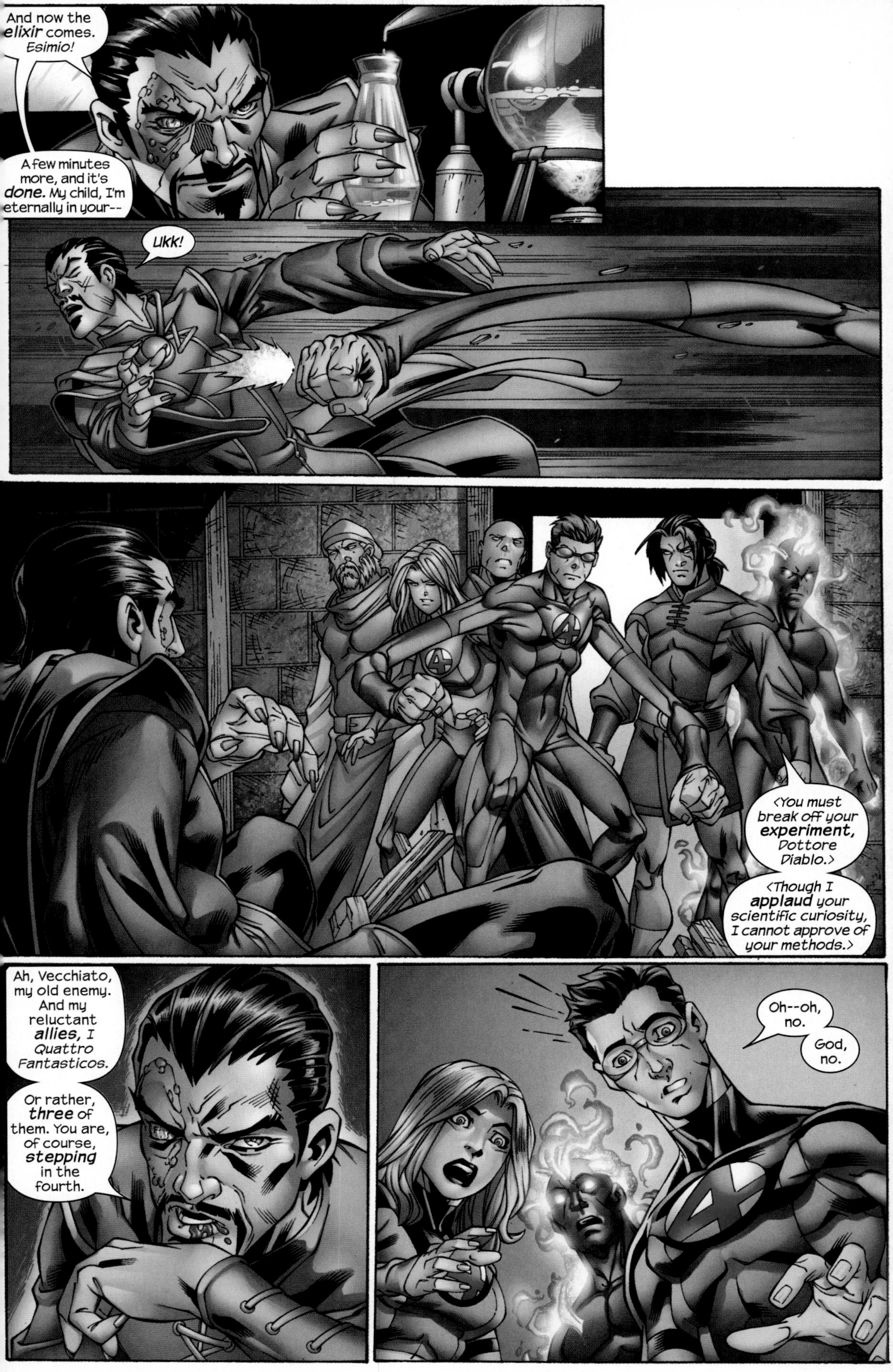

And now the *elixir* comes. *Esimio!*
A few minutes more, and it's *done.* My child, I'm eternally in your--
UKK!
<You must break off your **experiment,** *Dottore Diablo.*>
<Though I **applaud** your scientific curiosity, I cannot approve of your methods.>
Ah, Vecchiato, my old enemy. And my reluctant *allies,* I *Quattro Fantasticos.*
Or rather, *three* of them. You are, of course, *stepping* in the fourth.
Oh--oh, no.
God, no.

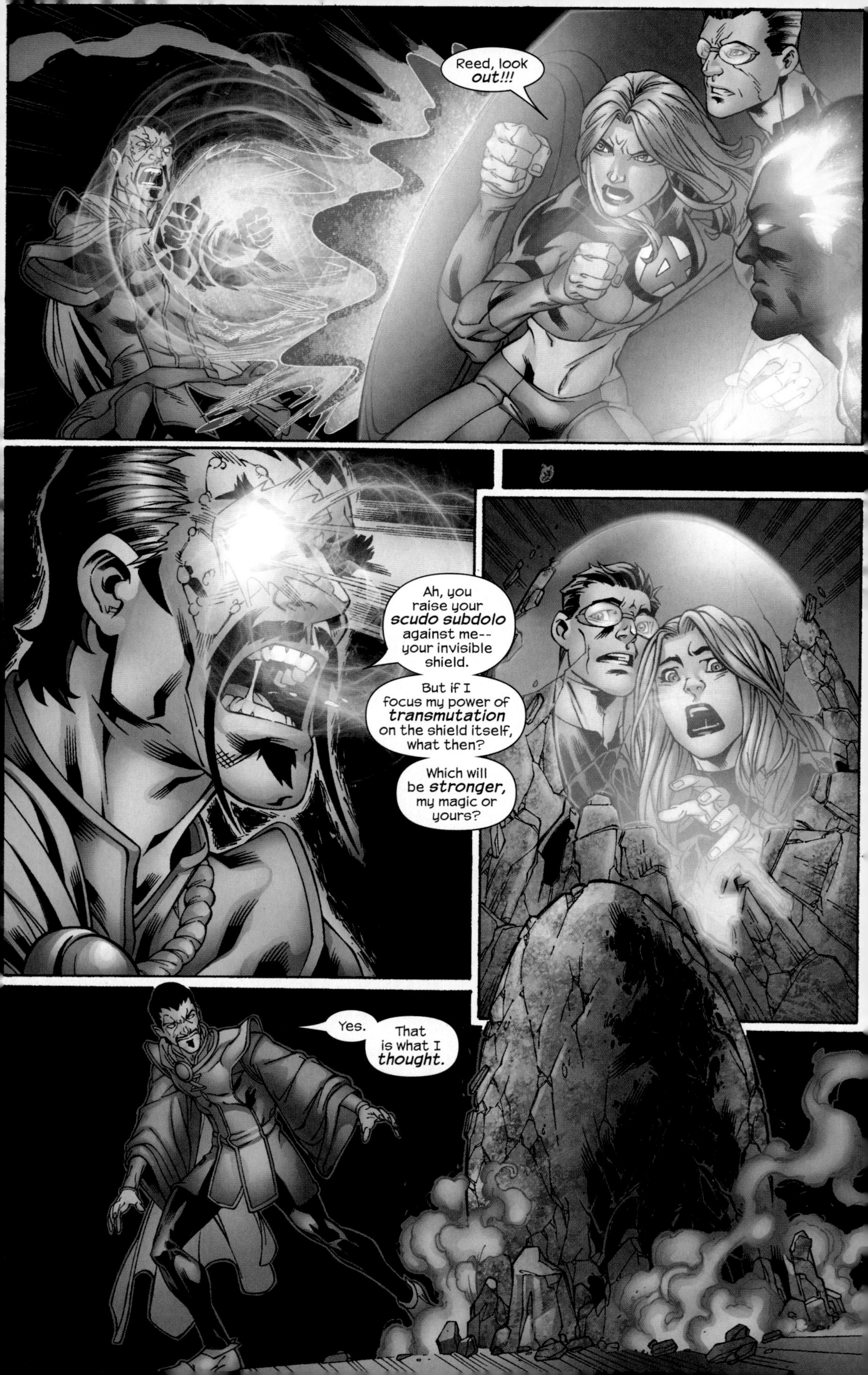
Reed, look out!!!
Ah, you raise your scudo subdolo against me-- your invisible shield.
But if I focus my power of transmutation on the shield itself, what then?
Which will be stronger, my magic or yours?
Yes.
That is what I thought.

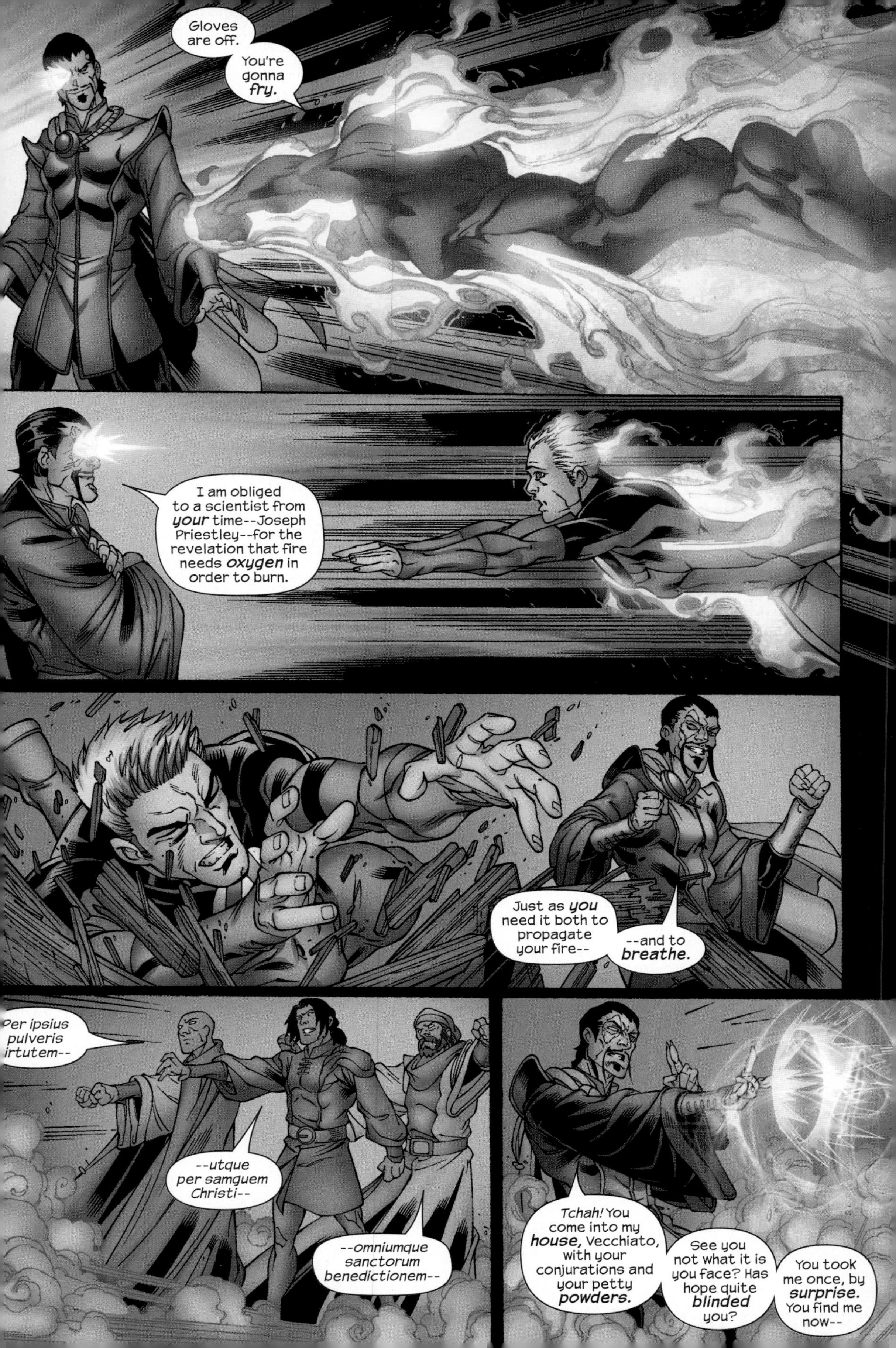
Gloves are off.
You're gonna *fry*.
I am obliged to a scientist from *your* time--Joseph Priestley--for the revelation that fire needs *oxygen* in order to burn.
Just as *you* need it both to propagate your fire--
--and to *breathe.*
Per ipsius pulveris irtutem--
--utque per samguem Christi--
--omniumque sanctorum benedictionem--
Tchah! You come into my *house,* Vecchiato, with your conjurations and your petty *powders.*
See you not what it is you face? Has hope quite *blinded* you?
You took me once, by *surprise.* You find me now--

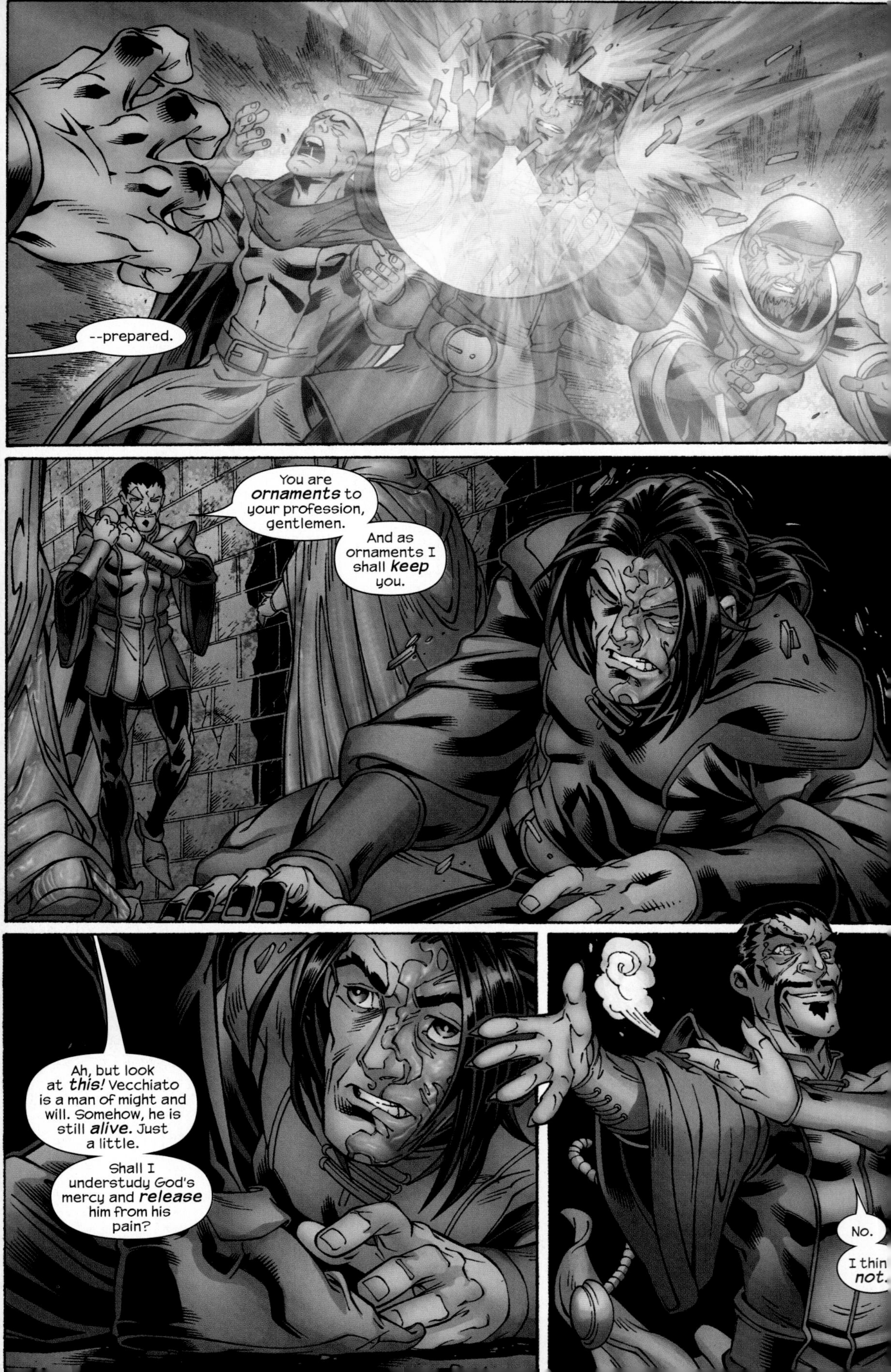
--prepared.
You are *ornaments* to your profession, gentlemen.
And as ornaments I shall *keep* you.
Ah, but look at *this!* Vecchiato is a man of might and will. Somehow, he is still *alive.* Just a little.
Shall I understudy God's mercy and *release* him from his pain?
No.
I thin *not.*

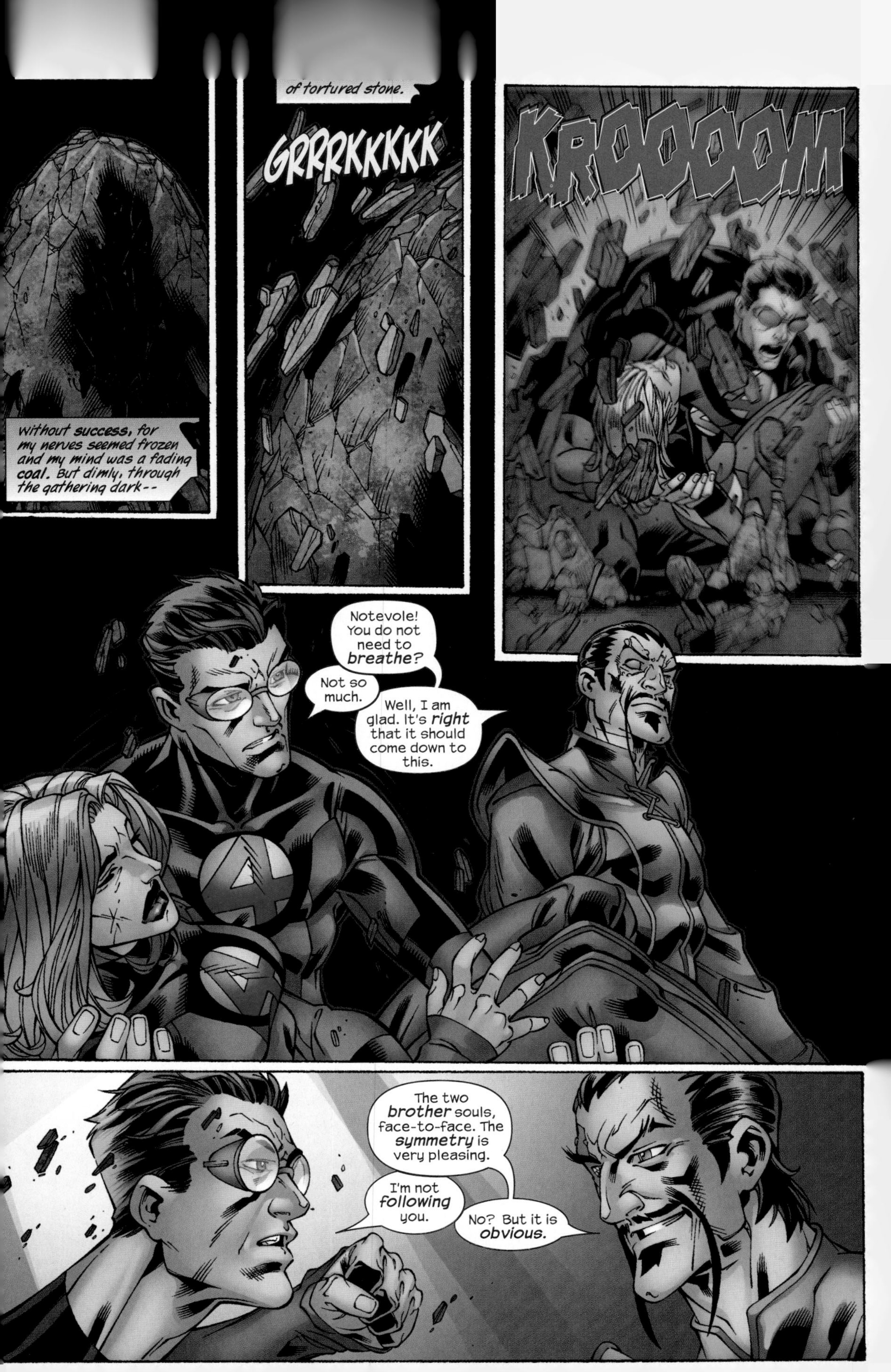
without success, for my nerves seemed frozen and my mind was a fading coal. But dimly, through the gathering dark--
of tortured stone.
GRRRKKKKK
KROOOOOM
Notevole! You do not need to breathe?
Not so much.
Well, I am glad. It's right that it should come down to this.
The two brother souls, face-to-face. The symmetry is very pleasing.
I'm not following you.
No? But it is obvious.

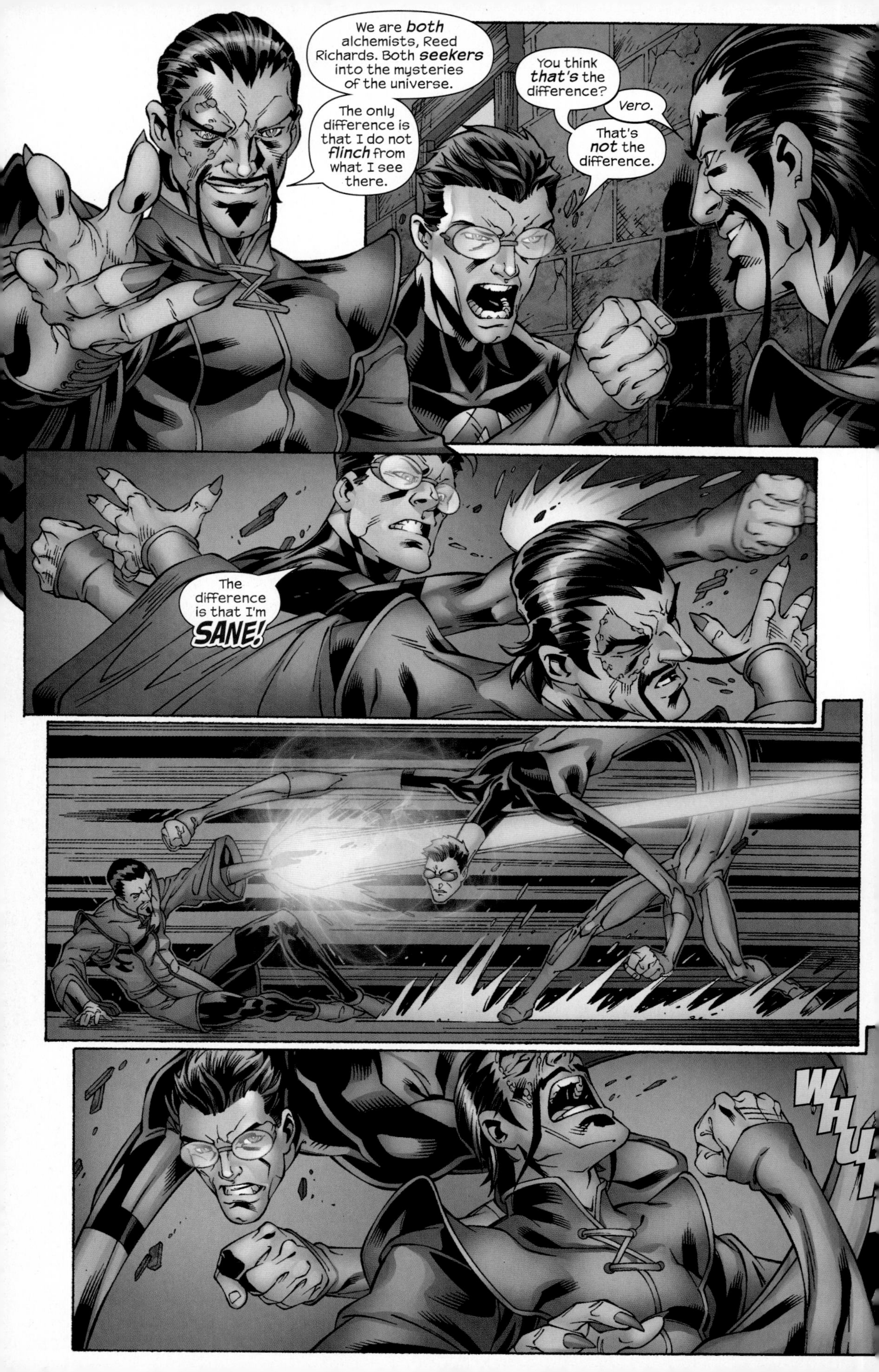

We are **both** alchemists, Reed Richards. Both **seekers** into the mysteries of the universe.
The only difference is that I do not **flinch** from what I see there.
You think **that's** the difference?
Vero.
That's **not** the difference.
The difference is that I'm **SANE!**

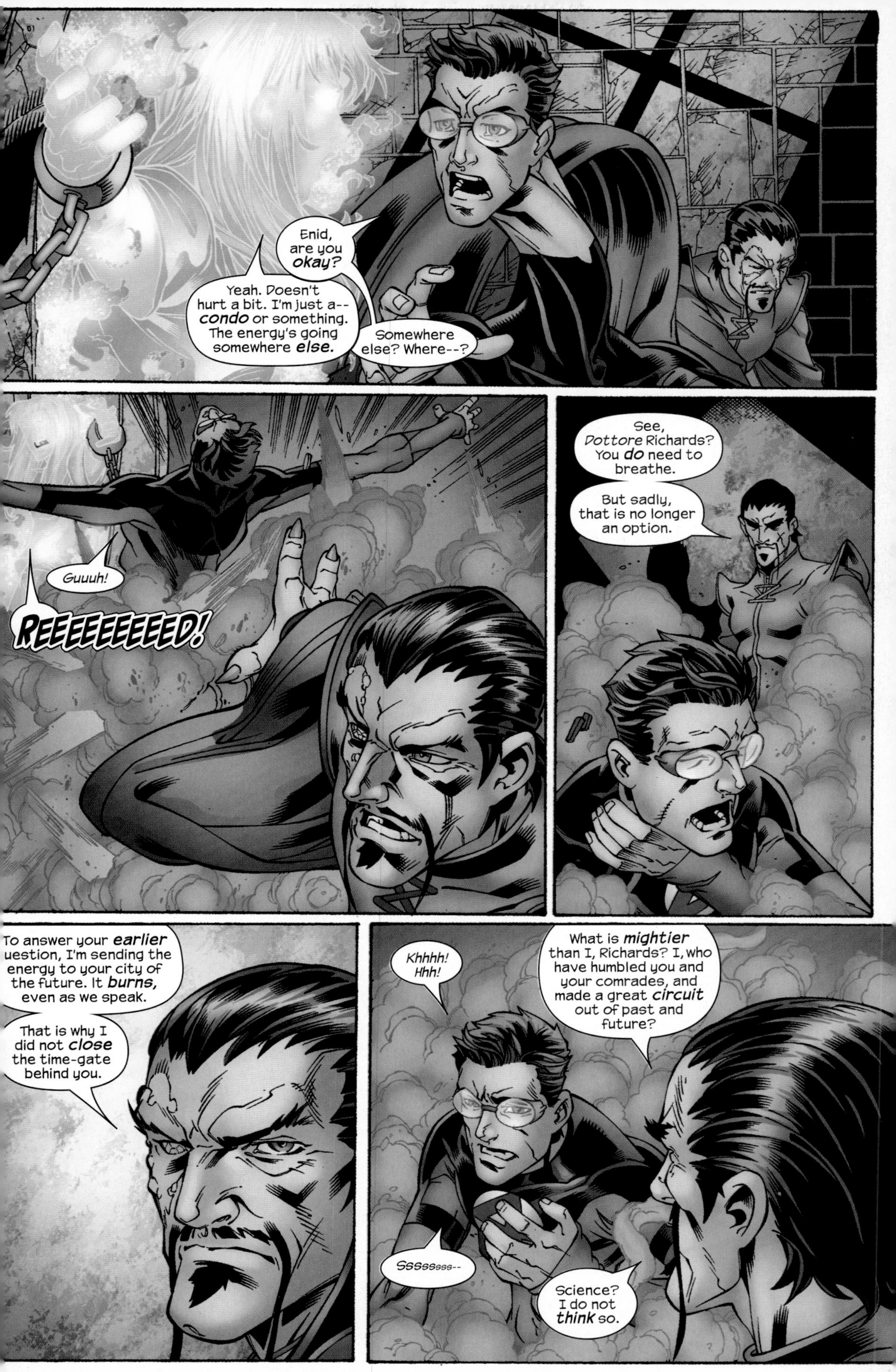
Enid, are you *okay*?
Yeah. Doesn't hurt a bit. I'm just a-- *condo* or something. The energy's going somewhere *else.*
Somewhere else? Where--?
Guuuh!
REEEEEEEEED!
See, *Dottore* Richards? You *do* need to breathe.
But sadly, that is no longer an option.
To answer your *earlier* uestion, I'm sending the energy to your city of the future. It *burns,* even as we speak.
That is why I did not *close* the time-gate behind you.
Khhhh! Hhh!
What is *mightier* than I, Richards? I, who have humbled you and your comrades, and made a great *circuit* out of past and future?
Sssssss--
Science? I do not *think* so.

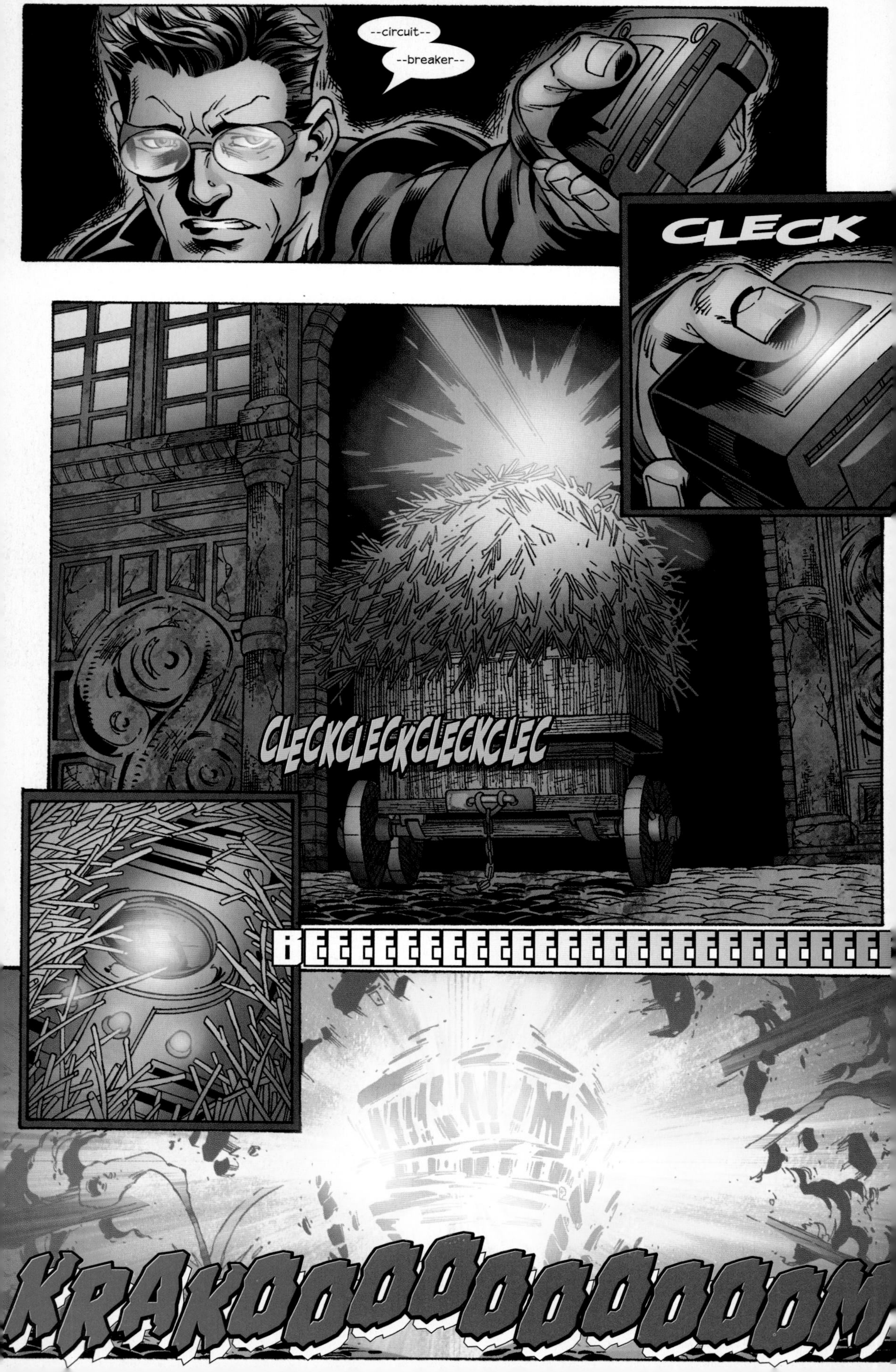
--circuit--
--breaker--
CLECK
CLECKCLECKCLECKCLEC
BEEEEEEEEEEEEEEEEEEEEEEEEEEEEEEE
KRAKOOOOOOOOOOOM

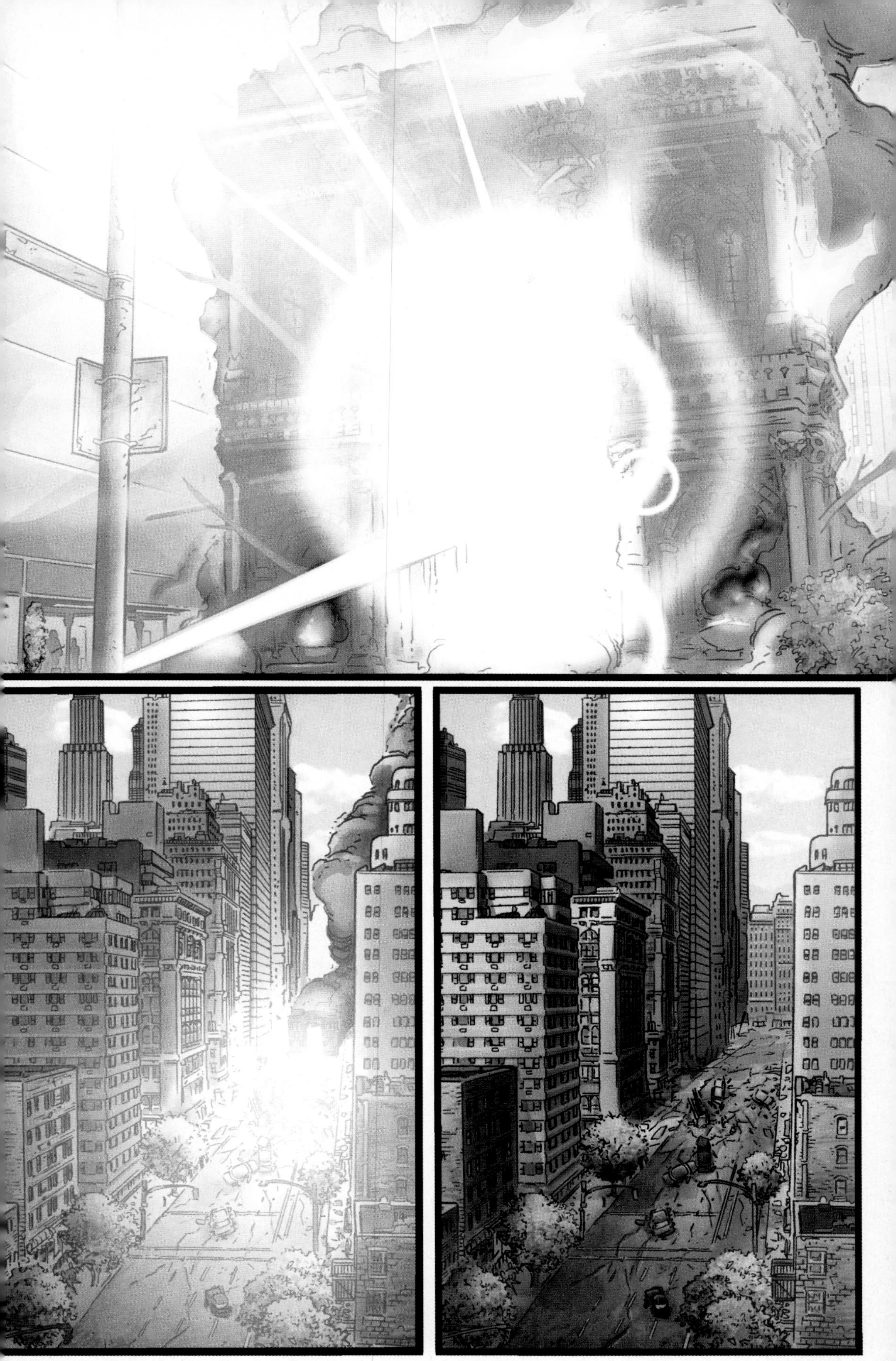

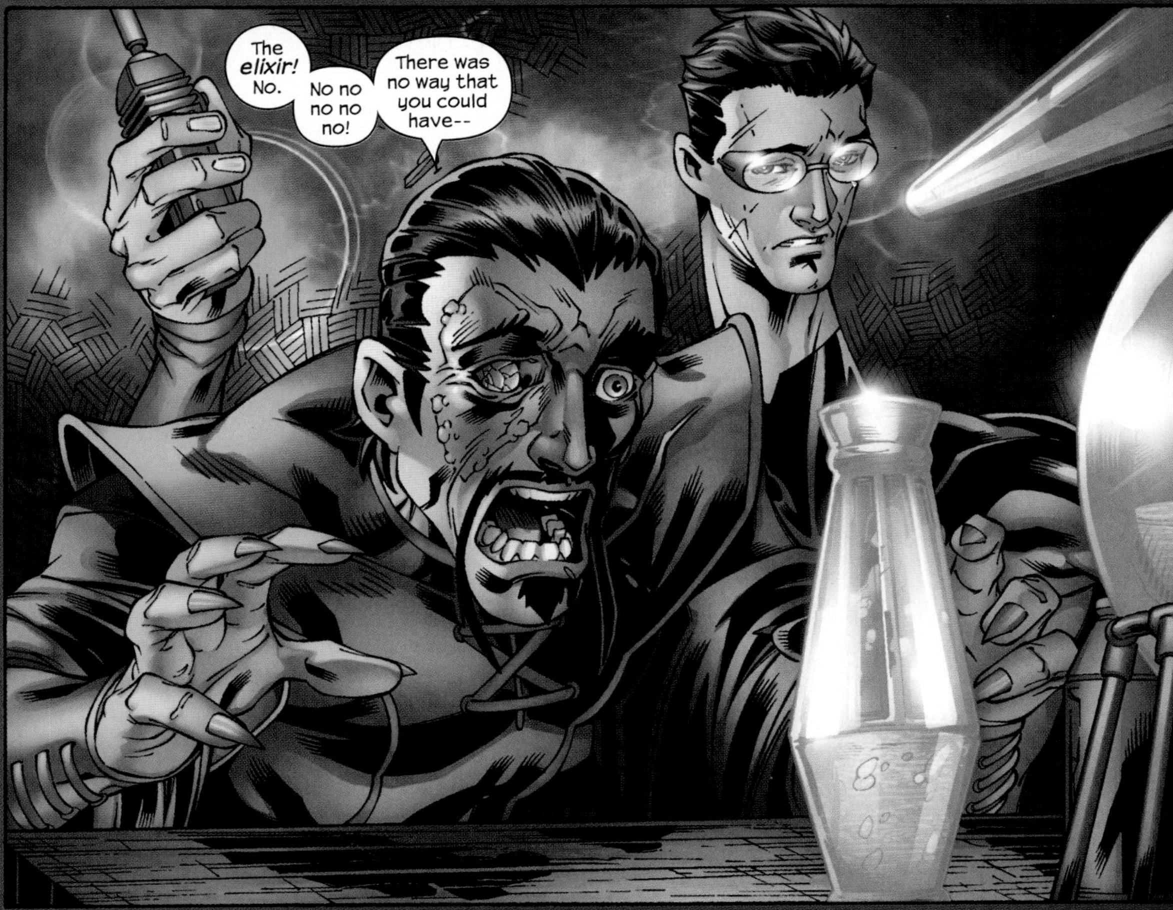
The *elixir!* No.
No no no no no!
There was no way that you could have--

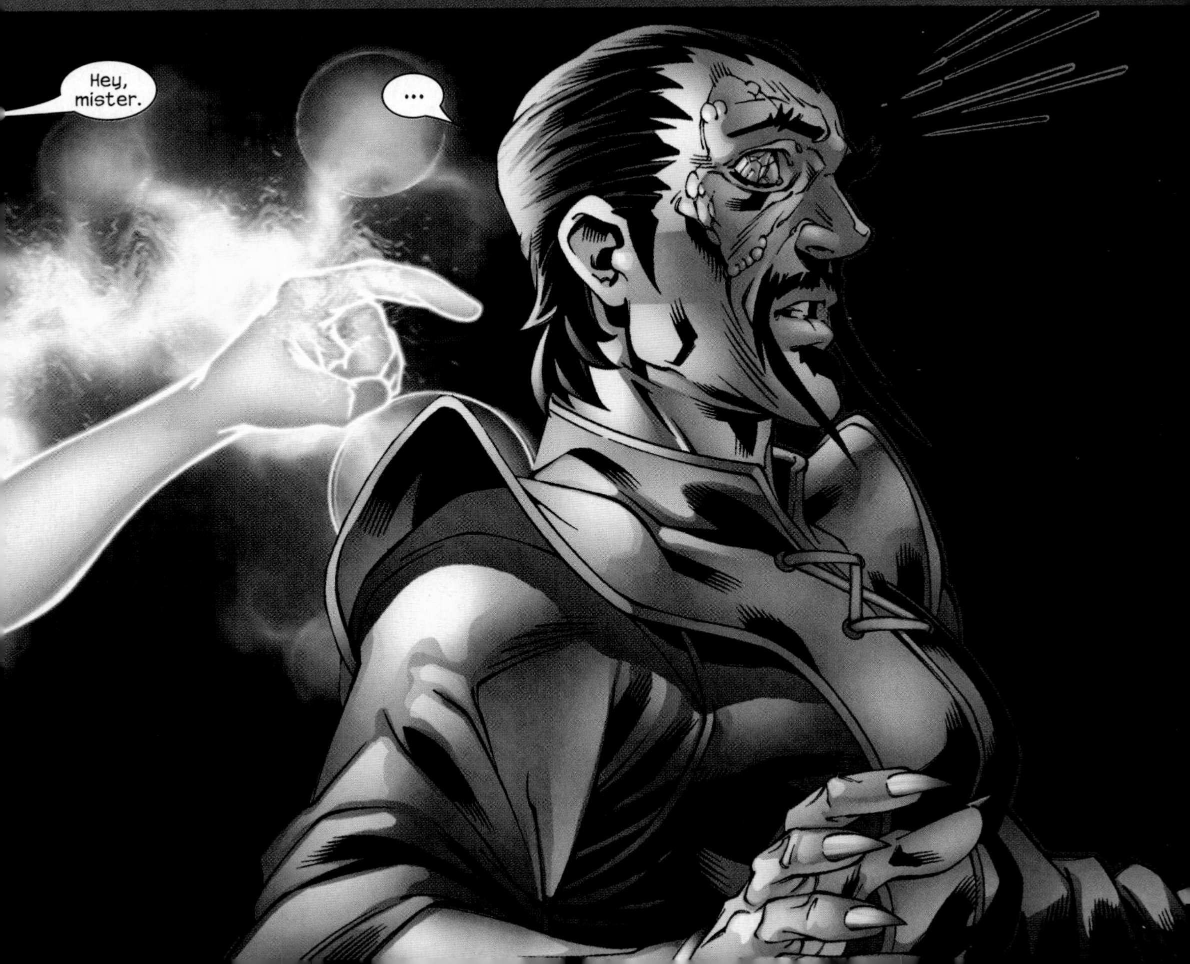
Hey, mister.
...

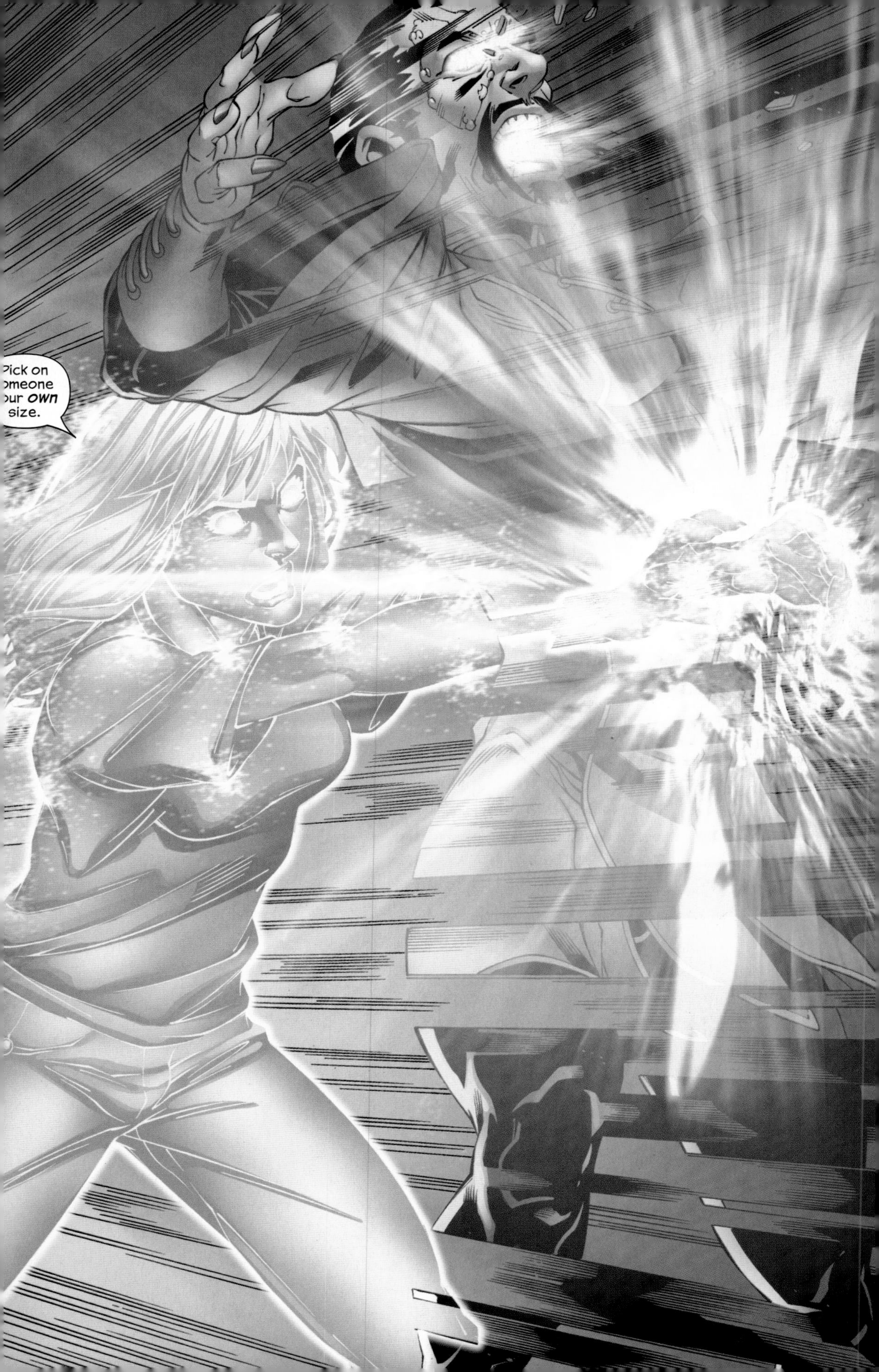
Pick on
omeone
our OWN
size.

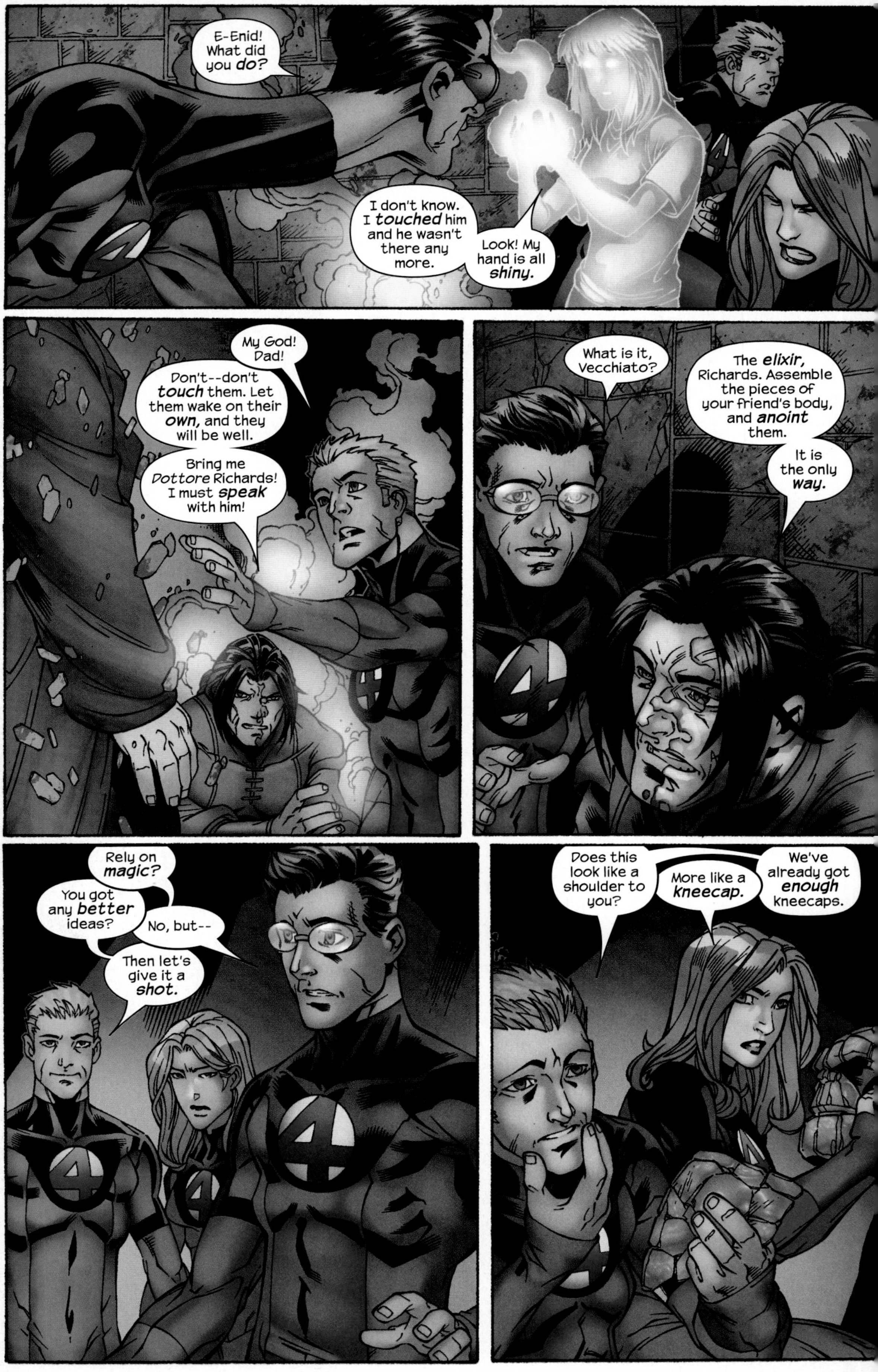
E-Enid! What did you do?
I don't know. I touched him and he wasn't there any more.
Look! My hand is all shiny.
My God! Dad!
Don't--don't touch them. Let them wake on their own, and they will be well.
Bring me Dottore Richards! I must speak with him!
What is it, Vecchiato?
The elixir, Richards. Assemble the pieces of your friend's body, and anoint them.
It is the only way.
Rely on magic?
You got any better ideas?
No, but--
Then let's give it a shot.
Does this look like a shoulder to you?
More like a kneecap.
We've already got enough kneecaps.

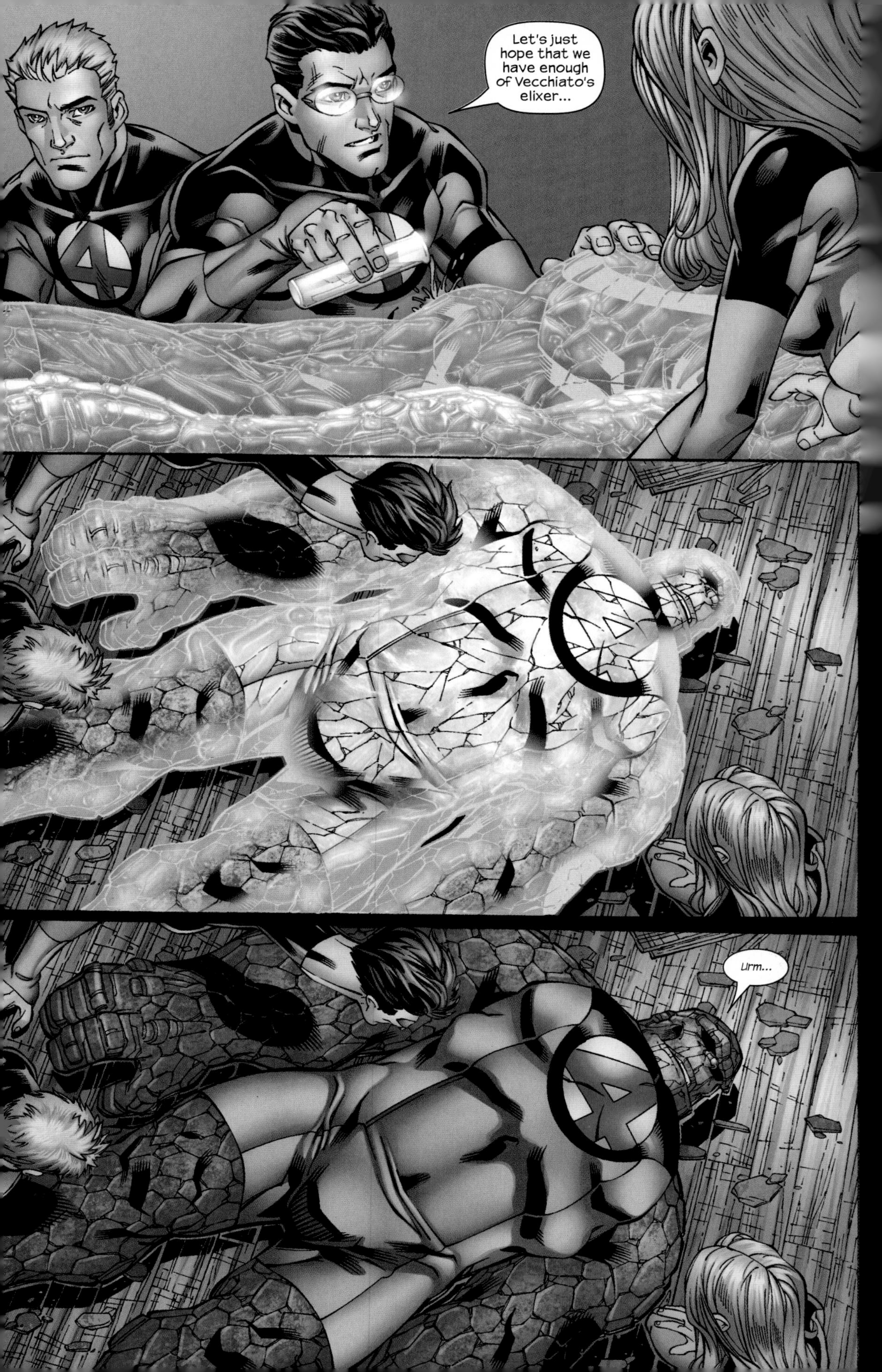
Let's just hope that we have enough of Vecchiato's elixer...
Urm...

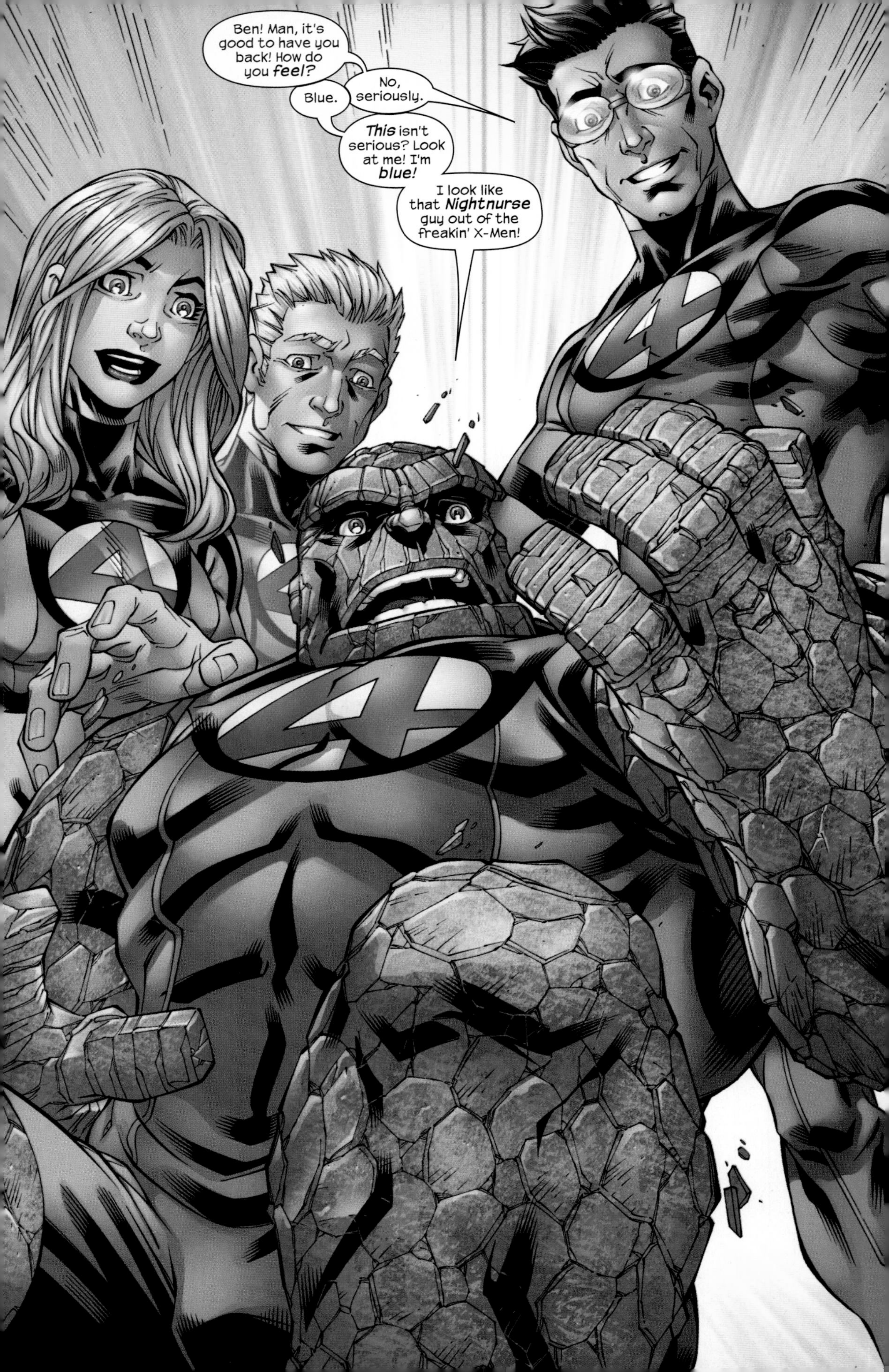
Ben! Man, it's good to have you back! How do you *feel*?
Blue.
No, seriously.
This isn't serious? Look at me! I'm *blue!*
I look like that *Nightnurse* guy out of the freakin' X-Men!

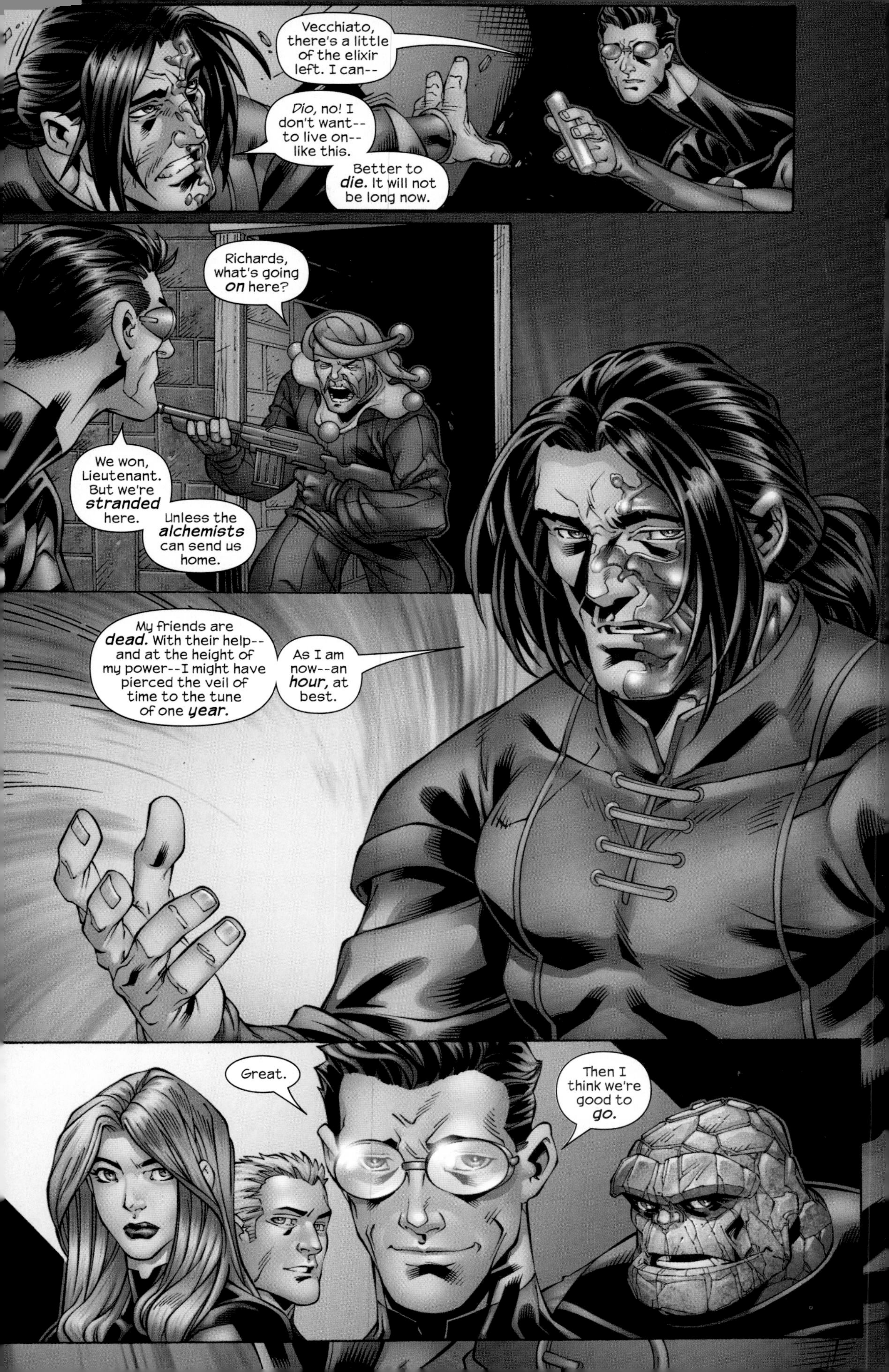
Vecchiato, there's a little of the elixir left. I can--
Dio, no! I don't want-- to live on-- like this.
Better to ***die.*** It will not be long now.
Richards, what's going ***on*** here?
We won, Lieutenant. But we're ***stranded*** here.
Unless the ***alchemists*** can send us home.
My friends are ***dead.*** With their help-- and at the height of my power--I might have pierced the veil of time to the tune of one ***year.***
As I am now--an ***hour,*** at best.
Great.
Then I think we're good to ***go.***

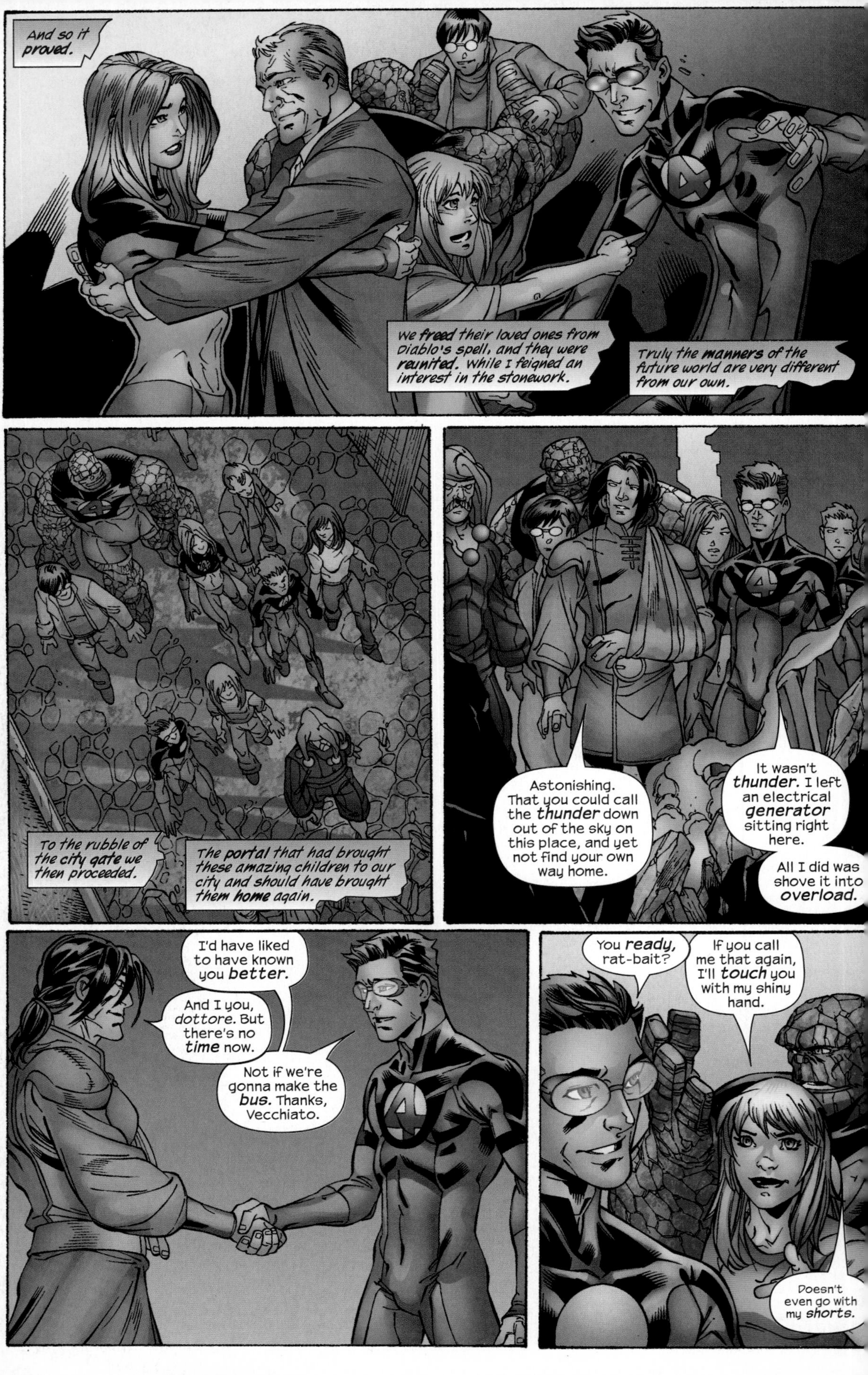

And so it proved.
We freed their loved ones from Diablo's spell, and they were reunited. While I feigned an interest in the stonework.
Truly the manners of the future world are very different from our own.
To the rubble of the city gate we then proceeded.
The portal that had brought these amazing children to our city and should have brought them home again.
Astonishing. That you could call the thunder down out of the sky on this place, and yet not find your own way home.
It wasn't thunder. I left an electrical generator sitting right here.
All I did was shove it into overload.
I'd have liked to have known you better.
And I you, dottore. But there's no time now.
Not if we're gonna make the bus. Thanks, Vecchiato.
You ready, rat-bait?
If you call me that again, I'll touch you with my shiny hand.
Doesn't even go with my shorts.

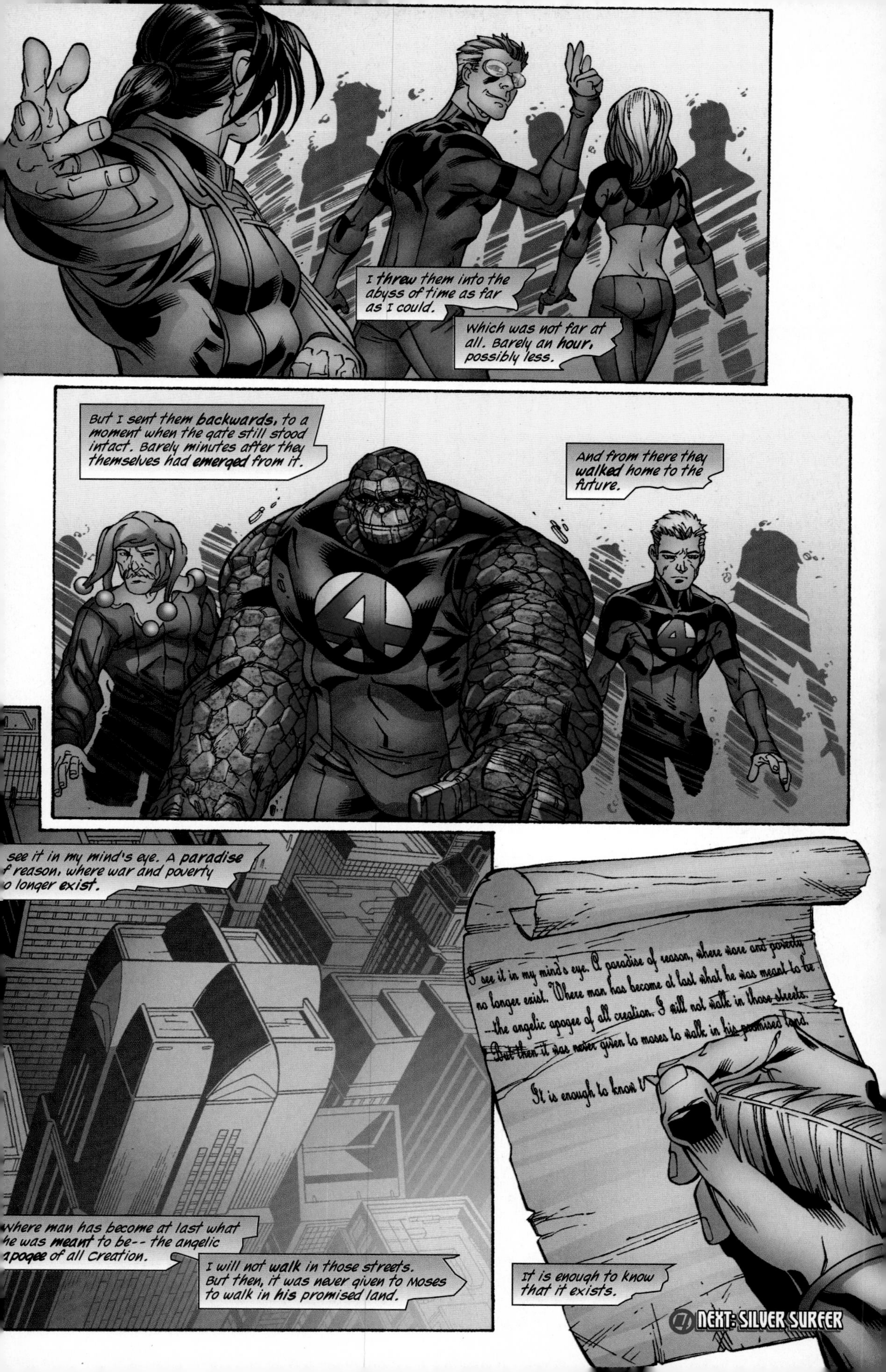
I threw them into the abyss of time as far as I could.
Which was not far at all. Barely an hour, possibly less.
But I sent them backwards, to a moment when the gate still stood intact. Barely minutes after they themselves had emerged from it.
And from there they walked home to the future.
see it in my mind's eye. A paradise
f reason, where war and poverty
o longer exist.
I see it in my mind's eye. A paradise of reason, where wars and poverty
no longer exist. Where man has become at last what he was meant to be
--the angelic apogee of all creation. I will not walk in those streets.
But then it was never given to moses to walk in his promised land.
It is enough to know t
Where man has become at last what
he was meant to be-- the angelic
apogee of all creation.
I will not walk in those streets. But then, it was never given to Moses to walk in his promised land.
It is enough to know that it exists.
NEXT: SILVER SURFER